WHAT WASHINGTON GETS WRONG

ALSO BY BENJAMIN GINSBERG

The Worth of War

The Value of Violence

WHAT WASHINGTON GETS WRONG

THE UNELECTED OFFICIALS WHO ACTUALLY RUN THE GOVERNMENT AND THEIR MISCONCEPTIONS ABOUT THE AMERICAN PEOPLE

JENNIFER BACHNER AND BENJAMIN GINSBERG

Prometheus Books

59 John Glenn Drive
Amherst, New York 14228

Published 2016 by Prometheus Books

Cover image © Media Bakery
Cover design by Liz Mills
Cover design © Prometheus Books

Inquiries should be addressed to
Prometheus Books
59 John Glenn Drive
Amherst, New York 14228
VOICE: 716–691–0133
FAX: 716–691–0137
WWW.PROMETHEUSBOOKS.COM

20 19 18 17 16   5 4 3 2 1

Library of Congress Cataloging-in-Publication Data Pending

ISBN 978-1-63388-249-2 (HC)
ISBN 978-1-63388-250-8 (EBK)

Printed in the United States of America

For Daniel and Sandra

CONTENTS

INTRODUCTION

A t a Washington dinner party, amid the political chatter and clinking of glasses, one of the authors of this book happened to mention to the woman seated to his right, an executive of Health and Human Services (HHS), the agency responsible for Americans' healthcare, that he and a colleague had undertaken a survey of Washington officials to find out what the government thought of the people. My dinner companion expressed some bewilderment and asked why we needed a survey to learn the obvious. According to this experienced public servant, "everyone knew" that Washington officialdom did not think much of the American people. After a pause she added, "Many of the people are quite stupid, aren't they?"

I have heard condescending comments like this from public officials too many times to have been surprised. Those of us who live in and around Washington, DC, often hear such remarks from federal officials of all stripes. Officials like to point to opinion surveys as well as their own occasional encounters with ordinary citizens as proof that most Americans are foolish and their views on public issues not worth much attention.

As the authors began to discuss this pattern of comments with one another, we developed the idea for this book. Many surveys have concluded that Americans know very little about their government. We thought, why not turn the tables and investigate government officials' opinions about the American people. This is an important question that, surprisingly, has never been addressed. Shouldn't public servants have an accurate picture of those whom they serve? And doesn't democracy assume that leaders possess a measure of respect for the citizenry? If public officials read the usual polls and decide that citizens are uninformed dullards, will they be willing to pay attention to popular views and interests?

Accordingly, we spent a year surveying government officials and others in the Washington policy community. What we concluded after analyzing the results was disturbing. We learned, to put the matter bluntly, that those who actually govern do not think very highly of the American people. Many civil servants expressed utter contempt for the citizens they served. Further, we found a wide gulf between the life experiences of ordinary Americans and the denizens of official Washington. We were left deeply worried about the health and future of popular government in the United States.

The phrase "popular government" as applied to contemporary America is, of course, a bit misleading. Most of America's national government today is not popular. It consists, instead, of administrative agencies staffed by unelected officials and linked to constellations of contractors, think tanks, quasi-governmental entities, and other elements of the Washington policy community that each year collectively write thousands of pages of rules and regulations possessing the force of law. This unelected government, though formally subordinate to Congress and the president, arguably does much of the actual governing of the United States, remaining in power year after year as presidents and congresses come and go. Our book focuses on this powerful unelected government—some would say the real government of the United States.

Our survey shows that official Washington lives in its own inside-the-Beltway bubble, where Washingtonians converse with one another and rarely interact on an intellectual plane with Americans at large. We found that much of official and quasi-official Washington is content to think that ordinary Americans, and the politicians whom they send to Congress, are uninformed and misguided and that policy makers generally should ignore them. This is more or less what they do. America's governmental agencies, of course, cannot completely ignore the president and Congress, but to the extent possible they pursue policy agendas of their own and expect citizens to do what they are told. Indeed, one of the ongoing discussions in official Washington concerns how best to impel citizens to obey—is it steering, compulsion, or the currently fashionable term "nudging," which means structuring alternatives to limit choices. Many officials exemplify what Aristotle called ανυπευθυνος (anupeuthunos, or civic irresponsibility).

Translated literally, ανυπευθυνος refers to rulers who think they are too good to submit to public accountability.

Interestingly, while official views and those of the general public do differ on many matters, the Washington community thinks this difference is even greater than is actually the case. Social psychologists call this sort of overestimation of difference "false uniqueness" and assert that it indicates a sense of contempt, with the members of one group believing that the other lacks intelligence and perspicacity equal to its own.

It may, to be sure, be true that many Americans know little about government and politics. But so what? Most patients know little about medicine, and most clients know little about the law. We expect, however, that doctors and lawyers will exhibit a fiduciary responsibility toward those seeking their services. The ignorance of patients and clients is a reason to listen more carefully and explain more fully, not an excuse for dismissing them as unworthy of attention. A physician or attorney who regards those dependent upon their services as fools, and undertakes actions without taking much interest in their life circumstances and without giving much consideration to their needs and preferences, is guilty of medical or legal malpractice. Similarly, public servants who have disdain for the public they serve, and show little interest in the public's needs and wishes, are guilty of civic malpractice.

No wonder many Americans have developed a sense that the government does not serve them. As Harvard law professor and quixotic presidential candidate Laurence Lessig noted, the rise of antiestablishment candidates like Donald Trump and Bernie Sanders reflects the fact that the average American sees little connection between what he or she wants and what the government actually does.

Can anything be done about the disconnect between America's unelected government and the citizenry? Or is it too late? In chapter 5, we offer some options that could make official Washington somewhat uncomfortable. Among them are our suggestions for ways Congress can curb the power of the unelected portions of the government. We also suggest real, as opposed to the current phony, "citizenship training" for Americans. Even more unpalatable might be our suggestion that a program of "rustication" for the mandarins of the nation's capital be developed, forcing them to spend time in their agencies' local offices in the fifty states where, outside the shelter of the capital Beltway, they might actually rub shoulders with their fellow Americans.

We hope that our book will serve as a vote of no-confidence in Washington and a loud wake-up call for Americans. The officials in our survey do have one thing right—Americans need to learn more about the realities of government. Perhaps when they do, they will be inspired to begin challenging the status quo, and improving their own lives in the process.

PLAN OF THE BOOK

As to the particulars, our book consists of six topics, organized into chapters. For the sake of clarity, let us outline our narrative trajectory:

1. **Unelected Government: The Folks Who Actually Run Things.** Administrative agencies have become "relatively autonomous," to borrow an idea from Marxist social theory. Though federal bureaucracies are, to some extent, overseen by Congress, the president, and the courts, America's administrative agencies exercise a good deal of discretionary authority as they promulgate rules and regulations that have the force of law. For most Americans, in realms ranging from healthcare through air travel, encounters with federal authority involve interactions with administrative agencies. Do these relatively autonomous agencies have appropriate regard or sympathy for the citizens for whom they work?

2. **The Chasm between Us and Them.** Using a statistical measure called propensity scoring, we compare citizens and officials along a number of dimensions. To summarize these comparisons, we introduce a measure we call "civic distance." This measure is derived from another useful Aristotelian notion, that of κοινον (*koinon*, or political commonality), and is designed to statistically capture the extent to which citizens and officials inhabit similar political worlds on the basis of education, income, experience, and beliefs. We discover that when it comes to politics, the two groups actually

live in rather distinct cognitive universes, viewing issues, policies, and events through disparate lenses.

3. **What Those Who Govern *Really* Think about You and Me.** Many Washington officials have little regard for the citizens they nominally serve. Inside the Beltway, ordinary Americans are seen as knowing very little about government and politics and as expressing outlandish and uninformed opinions. In truth, the attitudinal difference between officials and citizens, though significant, is less than the officials think. Officials tend to exhibit a sense of false uniqueness, thinking themselves so superior that they cannot imagine that ordinary folks share their lofty thoughts. Viewing the public as benighted, officialdom seems more concerned with how best to induce citizens to obey, than with how best to serve the public. Hence, "enforcement" is a hot topic in official Washington.

4. **What the Government Does Versus What the People Want.** Officials' lack of concern or even knowledge of the views of the general public does not leave us with much confidence that the interests of ordinary citizens will carry much weight in the process of administrative rulemaking. Using a data set drawn from the federal government's Unified Regulatory Agenda, we present an analysis of the determinants of rulemaking by federal agencies. Some scholars assert that the impetus for the thousands of rules and regulations written every year by government agencies is extrinsic—that is, determined by political and other events outside the agencies. Other scholars, though, have argued that the agencies, perhaps working with their supporting constellations of interests and stakeholders, march to and govern according to their own drummers and rhythms.[1] Our study would appear to indicate that the second group is closer to the truth. Congressional intervention into rulemaking seems to bring rules closer to public priorities. Left to themselves, though, administrators' priorities and those of the more general public seem to diverge. It is no wonder that many Americans believe the government is out of step with their views and were willing to give their support to political outsiders in the 2016 presidential election.

5. **What Should Be Done to Make the Government Listen?** Given the findings presented in chapters 1–4, can anything be done to enhance the government's "sympathy" for the people and the likelihood that policymakers will be guided by popular interests and preferences? Many institutional and procedural reforms are, of course, discussed in the policy and administrative literatures. Our focus is a bit different. We recommend changes in American civic education. Today, under the rubric of civics, American citizens are taught to be good and dutiful subjects. Fortunately, they are not taught very effectively and many quickly forget their classroom history and civics lessons. Officials, on the other hand, with one significant set of exceptions, are taught leadership skills but very little about the people whom they lead or their responsibility to those people. The one exception consists of military officers who *do* receive training in their duties to the people of the United States. Civilian officials, on the other hand, are taught little or nothing about their duties and obligations to the people. We propose that citizens be taught *realpolitik*, the German term for political realism, rather than civic mythology to prepare them to be actual citizens rather than subjects. The Athenians distinguished between citizens—individuals who had the capacity to debate in the *agora,* or marketplace—and *idiotes* who lacked that capacity. America could do with more citizens and fewer *idiotes*. We also propose measures that might remind officials of their own civic responsibilities to the citizens whom they nominally serve.

6. **What If What Should Be Done Isn't Done?** We conclude by pointing to the significance of our findings for more general issues of representative government. We also consider the relevance of our findings for understanding the major problems associated with the rise of bureaucratic governance in the United States. Bureaucrats are certain that they are more competent than ordinary citizens when it comes to matters of governance. This sense of superior competence, however, can become a dangerous delusion—damaging to both democracy and governance.

Figure I.1: Employment Distribution of Survey Respondents

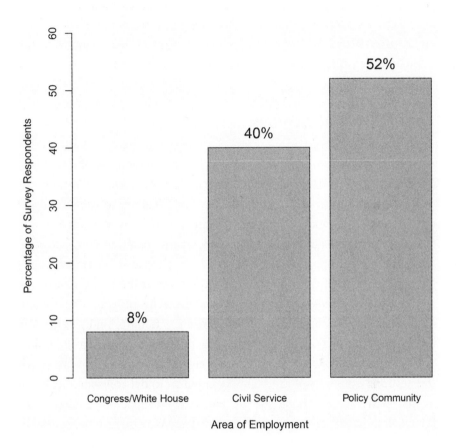

Our survey of 856 government officials and members of the policy community was conducted via an online questionnaire that included approximately three hundred questions. Although this sample size might not seem particularly large, it is appropriate for the size of our target population. Gallup, for example, uses a sample size of approximately 500 people when generalizing to a US state's population and a sample size of approximately 1,000 for a nationally representative survey.[2]

We asked respondents about their current employment, policy attitudes, and attitudes toward the American people. Their responses provide an original, rich trove of information about the perspectives of America's governing elite. We accessed our respondents through a variety of channels, including email lists, and assessed the representativeness of the sample by comparing certain responses (e.g., demographic data) against published statistics from the Office of Personnel Management.[3] The full questionnaire is presented in Appendix C.

WHO ARE THE RESPONDENTS?

As shown in figure I.1, the respondents are drawn from the three groups of unelected officials who exert significant policymaking influence: (1) staffers in Congress and the White House, (2) civil servants, and (3) members of the policy community, including those who work in think tanks, government contract firms, quasi-governmental entities, and non-profit advocacy organizations. Table I.1 lists some common job titles observed in each of the three categories. Staffers at the White House and in Congress hold positions related to either policy advising or the communication of that policy. Our civil servants generally hold positions in the realms of policy analysis and rule development. Those in the policy community largely work in policy analysis or advocacy positions. Civil servants and members of the policy community show considerable career overlap with many working side by side in Washington's "blended workforce" of civil service and contract employees. Many in the policy community, moreover, previously held civil service positions, usually employed by agencies within the same policy domains as the private or not-for-profit entities for which they currently work.

Table I.2 displays the demographic characteristics of the respondents. Overall, we see that 40 percent of the respondents in the survey are federal civil service employees working in Washington; they hold a range of responsible positions that generally involve them in the processes of rulemaking and regulation. They are relatively well-paid, well-educated, overwhelmingly white, and generally Democrats in their political orientationsa— matter to which we shall return in chapter 2.

Table I.1: Common Job Titles among Survey Respondents

Congress/White House	Civil Service	Policy Community
Chief of Staff	Economist/Senior Economist	Public Policy Analyst/ Specialist
Legislative Director	Statistician/Senior Statistician	Risk Analyst
Senior Legislative Assistant	Program Manager	Economist/Senior Economist
Senior Policy Advisor	Project Manager	Operations Researcher
Legislative Assistant	Budget Analyst	Lobbyist
Policy Advisor	Intelligence Analyst	Director of Government Affairs
Economist/Analyst	Program Analyst	Energy Analyst
Legislative Correspondent	Security Analyst	Data Analyst/Scientist
Deputy Chief of Staff	Operations Research Analyst	Consultant/Senior Consultant
Press Secretary	Transportation Specialist	Project Manager
Communications Director	Foreign Service Officer	Director of Communications
Deputy Communications Director	Foreign Affairs Specialist	Research Analyst
Counsel/Attorney	Research Analyst/ Assistant	Associate/Senior Associate
Chief Counsel	Senior Policy Advisor	Economic Analyst

Fifty-two percent of our respondents work in the larger Washington policy community. These individuals are demographically quite similar to their civil service colleagues and, as we shall see, there is a good deal of interchange between the two groups with many policy community members having previously served as civil servants and vice versa. The third and smallest group consists of congressional and White House staffers. The chief demographic difference between the staffers and the other two groups is that staffers, who are of course political appointees, are more likely to be partisan and less likely to express a moderate ideology than the others.

Table I.2: Demographic Comparisons of Officials

	Congress/ White House	Civil Service	Policy Community
Education			
Bachelor's	44.19%	28.77%	28.47%
Master's+	55.82%	71.22%	71.54%
Male	50.00%	56.13%	55.91%
White	90.00%	91.35%	89.88%
Median income	$50,000–$74,999	$75,000–$99,999	$50,000–$74,999
Political ideology			
Liberal	42.86%	32.52%	40.73%
Moderate	21.43%	49.51%	39.27%
Conservative	35.71%	17.96%	20.00%
Political party			
Democrat	59.52%	54.07%	56.68%
Independent	2.38%	17.22%	11.19%
Republican	38.10%	28.71%	32.13%

Liberals and conservatives include both strong and weak identifiers. Democrats and Republicans include both strong identifiers and those who "lean" toward the parties.

ACKNOWLEDGMENTS

During the course of writing this book we benefitted greatly from the advice of a number of colleagues whom we consulted as well as the comments we received when presenting portions of the book at professional meetings. We would, in particular, like to thank Robert Kargon, Elena Llaudet, Kenneth Meier, Daniel Naiman, Sarah O'Byrne, Alex Rosenthal, Laura Stoker, and Paul Quirk. In addition, we wish to express our gratitude to our editor Steven L. Mitchell, our agent Claire Gerus, our copyeditor Sheila Stewart, typesetter Bruce Carle, cover designer Liz Mills, production coordinator Cate Roberts-Abel, editorial assistant Hanna Etu, proofreader Jade Zora Scibilia, publicist Jake Bonar, and indexer Laura Shelley.

Chapter 1

UNELECTED GOVERNMENT: THE FOLKS WHO REALLY RUN THINGS

In the United States, as in other democracies, citizens expect their government to pay close attention to popular preferences. Most Americans, in fact, say they believe that the government listens to popular opinion most or at least some of the time.[1] To the extent, though, that they actually follow politics and governance, citizens' attention is generally drawn to the electoral and representative realm—a world in which elected officials, candidates, political parties, and so forth clamor for the public's favor. These individuals and organizations are usually avid consumers of public opinion, often employing legions of pollsters and analysts to help them discern the meaning of even the most transient shifts in the public's mood.

The focus of our attention, by contrast, will be the civil servants, quasi-governmental officials, private contractors, and advisers employed by the executive branch, as well as congressional and White House staffers. The reason for this particular focus is that these administrators and functionaries, who are not elected, cannot claim to formally represent anyone, and are barely visible to the public, play an enormous role in the governance of the nation—a role that has grown relative to that of America's formally representative institutions. Since these individuals collectively play such important roles in the governance of the United States, how they view and respond to the public has become a matter of some importance.

In the early decades of the Republic, representation and national governance were largely in the hands of the same institution, namely the Congress of the United States. Congress was the nation's principal representative body and, with the president and the judiciary playing secondary and tertiary roles, the nation's main agency of governance.[2] In contemporary America, on the other hand, representation and governance have become, at least partially, institutionally decoupled. Congress continues to function as the nation's foremost representative assembly, but in the realm of governance Congress has been eclipsed by the president and the executive branch.[3]

The president, to be sure, is an elected official, though the extent to which one person can be said to represent the people of the United States is debatable.[4] But, even putting this question aside, a good deal of the shift in power to the executive that has taken place in recent decades has involved the institutions of the executive branch more than the presidency itself. Bureaucratic agencies write rules and regulations that have the force of law. Other administrative entities of various sorts, some public, some quasi-public, and some private, develop policies and programs that have a substantial impact upon the lives of Americans. A great deal of this activity goes on without much in the way of popular, congressional, or presidential scrutiny. Even the courts, as we shall see below, give broad discretion to administrators.

Because of this ongoing shift in power, much of what is known or believed about the relationship between citizens and their government should be reexamined. A wag once averred that the term "popular government" was as much an oxymoron as jumbo shrimp, and there is more than one reason to fear this quip might embody a growing measure of truth.

THE ELECTED, THE APPOINTED, AND THE PUBLIC

Public opinion is obviously important to elected officials. These individuals must have popular backing to secure or retain their posts and have every reason to pay close attention to the popular will. There is, indeed, a good deal of empirical support for the idea that Congress and the president generally enact legislation that is consistent with popular views. Alan D. Monroe, for example, found that in a majority of cases changes in congressional policy followed shifts in popular preferences.[5] In a similar vein,

Benjamin Page and Robert Shapiro found that much of the time significant shifts in public opinion were followed by changes in congressional enactments in a direction that seemed to follow opinion.[6] Such findings are certainly affirmed by hosts of politicians who claim to be guided by the will of the people in all their undertakings and seem to poll assiduously to find out what that will is. Of course, some studies have suggested that Congress may be more likely to privilege the views of more affluent constituents.[7]

Congruence between popular opinion and the conduct of elected officials might result from a variety of factors. Voters have a regular opportunity to elect representatives who share their own views and perspectives. Some voters seek to inform themselves of candidates' positions on important issues. Others are satisfied to seek out candidates who mirror their own social, ethnic, or religious backgrounds in the not-unreasonable belief that such persons are likely to share their political sentiments as well. Elected officials, moreover, generally have some incentive to curry favor with their constituents by developing or supporting policies that respond to voters' preferences. James Madison averred that representatives' desire for reelection would induce them to develop a "habitual recollection of their dependence on the people."[8] And, in their well-known 1963 study, Warren Miller and Donald Stokes found that members of Congress seemed to vote in a manner consistent with constituency opinion, especially on the then highly salient issue of civil rights.[9]

There is, of course, a third potential source of consistency between popular sentiment and national policy. Politicians may seek to lead rather than follow opinion by proposing new programs—national health coverage is a recent example—and attempting to persuade the public to support them. Bill Clinton's pollster, Dick Morris, asserted that the president's close attention to public opinion stemmed from Clinton's efforts to lead opinion, not his desire to follow its dictates. "You don't use a poll to reshape a program," said Morris, "but to reshape your argumentation for the program so the public supports it."[10]

Whether politicians follow or lead the public, the realm of electoral politics and representative institutions is one in which public opinion matters. Few elected officials believe they can simply ignore the will of the people,

even if some behave in a manner that suggests they doubt Lincoln's assertion that it is impossible to fool all the people all the time. But however much
public opinion might matter to members of Congress and even to the president, these officials are not America's only important policymakers and the
legislation they formulate is far from the totality of American public policy.
In fact, before we turn to the substance of our empirical study, let us look in
some detail at the institutions and personnel of the government of the United
States that reside in what might be called the subterranean world of governance that operates in the offices of anonymous administrators, away from
the glare of electoral hoopla and publicity. Elected officials may have little
choice but to concern themselves with the needs and wishes of their constituents, but in the alternate universe of governance and policy the voice of the
people may be more distant and muted.[11]

WHO GOVERNS?

Civics texts tell us that the law consists of statutes enacted by Congress
and signed by the president. This idea may have been correct in the early
days of the American republic. Today, however, federal law is augmented
by hundreds of thousands of rules and regulations possessing the force of
law that are promulgated by a host of federal agencies staffed by officials
whose names and job titles are unknown to the general public.

After a statute is passed by Congress and signed into law by the
president, the various federal agencies charged with administering and
enforcing the act will usually spend months and sometimes years developing rules and regulations to implement the new law and will continue
to write rules for decades thereafter. We will examine this rulemaking
process in some detail in chapter 4. Typically, a statute will assert a set of
goals and establish some framework for achieving them but leave much to
the discretion of administrators. In some instances, members of Congress
are, themselves, uncertain of just what a law will do, and they depend upon
administrators to tell them.

In the case of the 2010 Affordable Care Act, widely known as Obamacare, for example, several legislators admitted that they did not fully understand how the act would work and were depending upon the Department of Health and Human Services (HHS), the agency with primary administrative responsibility for the act, to explain it to them. Sometimes Congress is surprised by agency rules that seem inconsistent with congressional presumptions. Thus, in 2012, the Internal Revenue Service (IRS) proposed rules to determine eligibility under the Affordable Care Act that excluded millions of working-class Americans that Congress thought would be covered by the act. Several congressional Democrats who had helped to secure the enactment of the legislation complained that the IRS interpretation would frustrate the intent of Congress.[12] The case of the Affordable Care Act is fairly typical. As administrative scholar Jerry L. Mashaw has observed, "Most public law is legislative in origin but administrative in content."[13]

The roots of bureaucratic power in the United States are complex and date to the earliest decades of the Republic.[14] Much of today's federal bureaucracy, however, can trace its origins to Franklin D. Roosevelt's New Deal. Under FDR's leadership, the federal government began to take responsibility for management of the economy, provision of social services, protection of the public's health, maintenance of employment opportunities, promotion of social equality, protection of the environment, and a host of other tasks. As the government's responsibilities and ambitions grew, Congress assigned more and more complex tasks to the agencies of the executive branch, which sometimes were only too happy to expand their own power and autonomy.[15] Executive agencies came to be tasked with the responsibility of analyzing and acting upon economic data, assessing the environmental impact of programs and projects, responding to fluctuations in the labor market, safeguarding the food supply, regulating the stock market, supervising telecommunications and air, sea, and land transport, and, in recent years, protecting the nation from terrorist plots.

When Congress writes legislation addressing these and a host of other complex issues, legislators cannot anticipate every question or problem that might arise under the law over the coming decades. Congress cannot establish detailed air quality standards, draw up rules for drug testing, or legislate the ballistic properties of artillery rounds for a new army tank.

Inevitably, as its goals become more ambitious, more complex, and broader in scope, Congress must delegate considerable discretionary authority to the agencies charged with giving effect to the law.

Just the sheer number of programs it has created in recent decades forces Congress to delegate authority. Congress can hardly administer the thousands of programs it has enacted and must delegate power to the president and to the bureaucracy to achieve its purposes. To be sure, if Congress delegates broad and discretionary authority to the executive, it risks seeing its goals subordinated to and subverted by those of the executive branch.[16] But, on the other hand, if Congress attempts to limit executive discretion by enacting very precise rules and standards to govern the conduct of the president and the executive branch, it risks writing laws that do not conform to real-world conditions and that are too rigid to be adapted to changing circumstances.[17] As the Supreme Court said in a 1989 case, "In our increasingly complex society, replete with ever changing and more technical problems, Congress simply cannot do its job absent an ability to delegate power under broad general directives."[18]

The increased scope and complexity of governmental activities promotes congressional delegation of power to the bureaucracy in another way as well. When Congress addresses broad and complex issues, it typically has less difficulty reaching agreement on broad principles than on details. For example, every member of Congress might agree that enhancing air quality is a desirable goal. However, when it comes to the particular approach to be taken to achieve this noble goal, many differences of opinion are certain to manifest themselves. Members from auto-producing states are likely to resist stiffer auto-emission standards and to insist that the real problem lies with coal-fired utilities. Members from districts that contain coal-fired utilities might argue that auto emissions are the problem. Members from districts that are economically dependent upon heavy industry would demand exemptions for their constituents. Agreement on the principle of clean air would quickly dissipate as members struggle to achieve agreement on the all-important details. Delegation of power to an executive agency, on the other hand, allows members to enact complex legislation without having to reach detailed agreement.

Congress can respond to pressure from constituents and the media to "do something" about a perceived problem, while leaving the difficult details to administrators to hammer out.[19]

As a result of these and other factors, when Congress enacts major pieces of legislation, legislators inevitably delegate considerable authority to administrators to write rules and regulations designed to articulate and implement the legislative will. Of course, in some instances, Congress attempts to set standards and guidelines designed to govern administrative conduct. For example, the 1970 Clean Air Act specified the pollutants that the Environmental Protection Agency (EPA) would be charged with eliminating from the atmosphere, as well as a number of the procedures that the EPA was obligated to undertake.[20] The act, however, left many other matters, including enforcement procedures, who should bear the burden of cleaning the air, and even how clean the air should ultimately be, to EPA administrators.

Many other statutes give administrators virtually unfettered discretion to decide how to achieve goals that are only vaguely articulated by Congress. For example, the statute establishing the Federal Trade Commission (FTC) outlaws, without expressly defining, "unfair methods of competition." Precisely what these methods might be is largely left to the agency to determine. Similarly, the statute creating the Occupational Safety and Health Administration (OSHA) calls upon the agency "to protect health to the extent feasible." What that extent might be is for the agency to determine. In its enabling act, the EPA is told to protect human health and the environment "to an adequate degree of safety."[21] As Congress continued to enact statutes setting out general objectives without specifying how the government was supposed to achieve them, the federal bureaucracy was left to fill in the ever-growing blanks.

In some instances, to be sure, Congress does write detailed standards into the law only to see these rewritten by administrators. For example, in 2006, the Securities and Exchange Commission (SEC) announced that it was issuing new rules that would significantly change key provisions of the 2002 Sarbanes-Oxley accounting reform and investor protection act. The act had been passed in the wake of the Enron scandal to reform corporate governance and prevent fraud. As enacted by Congress, Sarbanes-

Oxley contains very specific standards. However, in response to industry lobbying, the SEC announced that it would issue new standards to ease corporate obligations under section 404 of the act, which covers the financial statements issued by public corporations.[22] The agency determined that the law, as written by Congress, had forced corporations to engage in "overly conservative" practices.

Simply comparing the total volume of congressional output with the gross bureaucratic product provides a rough indication of where lawmaking now occurs in the federal government. The 106th Congress (1999–2000) was among the most active in recent years. It passed 580 pieces of legislation, 200 more than the 105th Congress and nearly twice as many as the 104th. Some, like campaign finance reform, seemed quite significant, but many pieces of legislation were minor. During the same two years, executive agencies produced 157,173 pages of new rules and regulations in the official *Federal Register*, roughly the average number for recent years.[23] OSHA, for example, introduced new regulations affecting millions of workers and thousands of businesses, the EPA drafted new air quality standards, and the SEC and Commodity Futures Trading Commission (CFTC) were announcing significant revisions of futures trading rules affecting billions of dollars in transactions.

In principle, agency rules and regulations are designed merely to implement the will of Congress as expressed in statutes. In fact, agencies are often drafting regulations based upon broad statutory authority granted years or even decades earlier, by congresses whose actual intent has become a matter of political interpretation. Congress and the president do, of course, retain a measure of power over bureaucrats and could exercise more.[24] In chapter 4 we suggest ways in which the influence of elected officials might be enhanced.

THE COURTS

The issue of delegation of power has led to a number of court decisions over the past two centuries, generally revolving around the question of the scope of the delegation. As a legal principle, the power delegated to Congress by the people through the Constitution cannot be redelegated by Congress. This "nondelegation doctrine" implies that directives from Congress to the executive should be narrowly defined and give the latter little or no discretionary power.[25] A broad delegation of congressional authority to the executive branch could be construed as an impermissible redelegation of constitutional power. A second and related question sometimes brought before the courts is whether the rules and regulations adopted by administrators are consistent with Congress's express or implied intent. This question is closely related to the first because the broader the delegation to the executive, the more difficult it is to determine whether the actions of the executive comport with the intent of Congress.

With the exception of three New Deal–era cases, the Supreme Court has consistently refused to enforce the nondelegation doctrine.[26] In the nineteenth century, for the most part, Congress itself enforced the principle of nondelegation by writing laws that contained fairly clear standards to guide executive implementation.[27] Congressional delegation tended to be either contingent or interstitial.[28] Contingent delegation meant that Congress had established a principle defining alternative courses of action. The executive was merely authorized to determine which of the contingencies defined by Congress applied to the circumstances at hand and to act accordingly. For example, the Tariff Act of 1890 authorized the president to suspend favorable tariff treatment for countries that imposed unreasonable duties on American products. In *Field v. Clark*, the court held that this delegation was permissible because it limited the president's authority to ascertain the facts of a situation. Congress had not delegated its lawmaking authority to him.[29]

The Supreme Court also accepted what might be called interstitial rulemaking by the executive. This meant filling in the details of legislation where Congress had established the major principles. In the 1825 case of *Wayman v. Southard*, Chief Justice Marshall said Congress might lawfully "give power to those who are to act under such general provisions to fill up the details."[30] In 1928, the court articulated a standard that, in effect, incorporated both these doctrines. In the case of *J. W. Hampton, Jr., & Co.*

v. United States, the court developed the "intelligible principles" standard. A delegation of power was permissible, "If Congress shall lay down by legislative act an intelligible principle to which [the executive] is directed to conform . . ."[31]

As Congress and the president worked together to expand governmental power during the New Deal era, Congress enacted legislation, often at the president's behest, that gave the executive virtually unfettered authority to address a particular concern. For example, the Emergency Price Control Act of 1942 authorized the executive to set "fair and equitable" prices without offering any indication of what these terms might mean.[32] The court's initial encounters with these new forms of delegation led to three major decisions in which the justices applied the "intelligible principles" standard to strike down delegations of power to the executive. In the 1935 *Panama* case, the court held that Congress had failed to define the standards governing the authority it had granted the president to exclude oil from interstate commerce.[33] In the *Schechter* case, also decided in 1935, the court found that the Congress failed to define the "fair competition" that the president was to promote under the National Industrial Recovery Act (NIRA). Justice Benjamin N. Cardozo called the NIRA an example of "delegation running riot."[34] In a third case, *Carter v. Carter Coal Co.*, decided in 1936, the court concluded that a delegation to the coal industry itself to establish a code of regulations was impermissibly vague.[35]

These decisions were seen as a judicial assault on the New Deal and helped spark President Roosevelt's "court packing" plan. Roosevelt threatened to seek an increase in the size of the court that might allow him to appoint several compliant justices. The court retreated from its confrontation with the president and, perhaps as a result, no congressional delegation of power to the president has been struck down as impermissibly broad in the more than six decades since *Carter*. Over the ensuing years, though, the nondelegation doctrine gradually fell into disuse, as federal judges came to accept the notion that professional administrators in the agencies were more competent than politicians in Congress to identify solutions to the nation's problems. While Congress might, via statute, identify broad policy directions, federal courts increasingly found that it was perfectly appropriate to leave the search for solutions in the hands of administrators. Thus, so long as the statute offered some vague indication of Congress's general intent, it was likely to pass muster. Indeed, the Supreme Court has said that a delegation can be valid if it "sufficiently marks the field within which the administrator is to act."[36]

Take, for example, the case of *Mistretta v. United States*.[37] This case concerned the federal sentencing guidelines promulgated by the US Sentencing Commission, established by Congress in 1984 in response to concern that some judges were too lenient when meting out sentences to convicted criminals. The commission was charged with the task of developing a set of mandatory "guidelines" that would remove judicial discretion in this realm. In creating the commission, Congress offered few guidelines of its own. The language of the statute was vague, mandating that the commission should develop sentencing rules that would guarantee such things as "certainty and fairness" in sentencing. On this basis, the commission promulgated hundreds of pages of rules and regulations specifying how sentences were to be calculated given the severity of the crime and the criminal history of the defendant. In *Mistretta*, the Supreme Court found that the statute's vague standards were entirely sufficient to guide the commission's work and upheld the congressional delegation of power to the agency. In 2005, the Supreme Court decided that the use of mandatory sentencing guidelines was prohibited by the Sixth Amendment, but did not readdress the issue of delegation.[38]

Also signaling the court's acceptance of expanded administrative exercise of legislative power is the so-called Chevron standard. This standard emerged from a 1984 case called *Chevron U.S.A., Inc. v. Natural Resources Defense Council, Inc.*[39] An environmental group had challenged an EPA regulation as contrary to the intent of the statute it was nominally written to implement. While a federal district court sided with the environmentalists against the agency, the lower court's decision was reversed by the Supreme Court. In its decision, the Supreme Court declared that so long as the executive developed rules and regulations "based upon a permissible construction" or "reasonable interpretation" of the statute, the judiciary would accept the views of the executive branch. This standard implies that considerable judicial deference should be given to the executive rather than to Congress. Indeed, the courts now look to the agencies to develop clear standards for statutory implementation rather than to Congress to develop standards for the executive branch to follow.[40] In the 2001 case of *United States v. Mead Corp.*, the court partially qualified the *Chevron* holding by ruling that agencies were entitled to Chevron deference only where they were making rules carrying the force of law and not when they were merely issuing opinion letters or undertaking other informal actions.[41] Despite this qualification, *Chevron* still applies to the most important category of administrative activity.

Generally speaking, the courts are satisfied if an agency's rulemaking process has complied with the provisions of the 1946 Administrative Procedure Act (APA). This legislation requires agencies to give public notice of proposed rules (usually by publishing them in the *Federal Register*), to invite public comment, and to hold public hearings. The APA does *not* require agencies to amend their proposals after receiving public comments. Agencies, however, like to point to positive public comments to fend off congressional critics of proposed rules. In 2015, the EPA worked with an environmental group to mount a campaign that allegedly produced hundreds of thousands of positive comments on a proposed drinking water rule. The agency then informed Congress that its proposal had widespread public support.[42]

An important recent decision that further enhanced administrative discretion came in the 2013 case of *City of Arlington, Tex. v. FCC*.[43] The case concerned a provision of the Federal Communications Act that requires state and local governments to act on zoning applications for building wireless towers and antennas "within a reasonable period of time." The Federal Communications Commission (FCC) issued a ruling defining "reasonable period of time" as 90 days for modifications of existing facilities and 150 days for new ones. This may seem a mundane ruling, but it has important implications. The plaintiff was arguing that the statute contained no provision authorizing the FCC to set rules defining "reasonable period of time." Hence, according to the plaintiff, the FCC was asserting power that Congress never intended to grant. The Supreme Court's response, consistent with the *Chevron* doctrine, was that agencies were to be afforded considerable deference even when interpreting the scope of their own power. In other words, federal agencies should be seen as the best judges of their own power.

Of course, the federal courts do not always defer to administrative agencies. Occasionally, if rarely, the courts will challenge agency rulemaking. In 2015, for example, the US Supreme Court blocked a carbon emission rule recently adopted by the EPA as part of President Obama's environmental program. The action was taken to allow lower courts to consider the many challenges to the rule that had been brought by power industry groups. Significantly, even this mild rebuke to an agency—the court only delayed implementation, it did not strike down the rule—was so unusual as to provoke a good deal of media commentary.[44]

CONGRESSIONAL OVERSIGHT OF THE BUREAUCRACY

Congress, of course, does not have to depend upon the courts to ensure that agencies will adhere to their statutory mandates. Congress possesses substantial oversight power of its own vis-à-vis the bureaucracy. Congress can hold hearings, enact new legislation, and, if it so desires, slash agency budgets. By the terms of the Congressional Review Act (CRA), moreover, agencies are required to submit proposals for significant new rules and regulations to Congress sixty days before their adoption. The act prescribes an expedited procedure through which Congress may disallow agency proposals. Bureaucratic agencies obviously cannot completely ignore Congress. In recent years, oversight hearings into such topics as failures on the part of the Federal Emergency Management Agency (FEMA) in the wake of Hurricane Katrina and the Defense Department's handling of the Abu Ghraib prison scandal in Iraq ended the careers of agency officials and forced both agencies to adopt new procedures.

In practice, Congress is better able to respond to heavily publicized abuses and crises than to engage in day-to-day supervision of the bureaucracy. This has been called the "fire alarm" form of oversight.[45] Routine oversight is often conducted by a committee that is inclined to be friendly to the agency in question or to the interest groups that support that agency.[46] Members of Congress, moreover, seldom see much political advantage to be gained from devoting time, energy, and effort to oversight, particularly if their own party is in power. As one Republican member said during the George W. Bush administration, "Our party controls the levers of government. We're not about to go out and look beneath a bunch of rocks to cause heartburn."[47] Even during the 1990s, a period of divided party government, the number of oversight hearings in both the House and Senate declined sharply as members decided that there was little political payoff to be derived from routine supervision of executive agencies.[48] Congress's chief instruments of bureaucratic control—statutory and budgetary sanctionsr— equire the approval of majorities in both houses and the signature of the president. In today's fragmented Congress, there are days on which it would be difficult to assemble a majority in favor of the proposition that the marigold is a pretty flower.

Of course, Congress exercises power informally, too, by the threat of budgetary sanction. For example, a Government Accountability Office (GAO) report criticizing an agency's contracting practices is only advisory and does not have the force of law. Agencies, however, will usually follow the GAO's recommendations, especially if these are supported by powerful committee chairmen who might be in a position to threaten the agency's budget.

BUREAUCRATIC POWER

In principle, as political scientist Theodore Lowi, legal scholar David Schoenbrod, and others have suggested, Congress could write narrowly drawn statutes that limit bureaucratic discretion. In principle, the courts could reinstitute the nondelegation doctrine and stop deferring to administrative interpretations of statutory mandates. In principle, Congress might invest more time and energy in oversight of the administrative agencies. But the reality is that the more ambitious the programs and policies that

Congress develops, the more power it must delegate to the bureaucracy. And the more power it delegates to the bureaucracy, the less able legislators will be to oversee their creations.

Once power is delegated to them, executive agencies inevitably have substantial control over its use and, in most instances, neither Congress nor the judiciary is able or willing to second-guess their actions. The result is that federal agencies write what amounts to law according to their own lights rather than those of the Congress. Indeed, whatever policy goals Congress may have had, after many years and many congresses have passed, often all that remains of a statute is its delegation of power to the executive branch.

Take, for example, the Family and Medical Leave Act of 1993 (FMLA).[49] The act requires employers to allow employees to take up to twelve weeks of unpaid leave each year to deal with childbirth, health problems, family emergencies, and other serious matters that might render employees temporarily unable to perform their duties.[50] In its report on the proposed legislation, the Senate Committee on Labor and Human Resources indicated that problems justifying leave under the law would include such matters as heart attacks, strokes, spinal injuries, recovery from childbirth, and other serious conditions that clearly justified an extended period of absence from work. Congress delegated authority to the Department of Labor to develop appropriate rules and regulations to implement the act. The record of legislative hearings attendant to the act, though, make it clear that Congress intended the legislation to cover only serious problems, not short-term conditions or minor illnesses. The Labor Department, however, had other ideas.

Each year that the department developed new rules, it expanded the scope of the act's coverage and even the number of weeks of leave to which employees were entitled. For example, under rules adopted by the department, a case of flu was considered a medical condition covered by the act. This expansion of FMLA was upheld by a federal court, which, citing the *Chevron* doctrine, deferred to the agency's interpretation of the statute.[51] Subsequently, the Labor Department ruled medical leave granted by employers under their own plans would be in addition to rather than concurrent with the leave required under FMLA.[52] This rule meant that some employees might be entitled to considerably more than the twelve weeks mandated by Congress. Perhaps the Labor Department should not be faulted for its generosity. No doubt, ill employees are more deserving of sympathy than giant corporations. Nevertheless, in this as in so many other instances, a bureaucratic agency ignored congressional intent and wrote its own laws. When Congress delegated power, it gave up control.

It is also worth mentioning another dimension of bureaucratic power— he realm of enforcement. Federal agencies make use of a variety of enforcement techniques, including warnings, fines, and criminal prosecutions. Today, virtually every federal agency—even the most seemingly mundane—employs its own armed agents to enforce rules and regulations of which Congress may have little knowledge. Several thousand armed agents are currently employed by bureaucracies such as the Bureau of Land Management, the Fish and Wildlife Service, the Environmental Protection Agency, the Labor Department, the Department of Education, and the National Oceanic and Atmospheric Administration (NOAA) Fisheries Office of Law Enforcement.[53] These are agencies not usually seen as having involvement in criminal matters but, increasingly, these regulatory and service agencies are mandated to enforce the growing number of federal criminal statutes and employ armed agents to do so.

NOAA, for example, employs 134 armed agents and has been involved in a number of recent controversies. In 2012, the agency was widely criticized for ordering 46,000 rounds of jacketed hollow-point bullets, a form of ammunition designed to cause maximum damage to the internal organs and tissue of human targets. The press wondered why weather forecasters would need this type of ammunition, generally banned under international law. A NOAA spokesperson clarified the matter, explaining that the ammunition was not intended for weather forecasters but was, instead, being issued to agents of its Fisheries Office.[54]

The NOAA Fisheries Office also made headlines in 2008 when a group of NOAA agents, armed with assault rifles, raided a Miami business suspected of having violated a NOAA regulation pertaining to trading in coral. It turned out that the coral had been properly obtained but the business owner had failed to complete some of the necessary forms. She was fined and sentenced to one year's probation.[55] Quite possibly the assault rifles had not been needed to deal with this bookkeeping dispute.

In still another case involving NOAA, Nancy Black, a well-known marine biologist and operator of whale-watching boats, saw her home and office raided by NOAA agents—also brandishing assault rifles. Black was charged with offenses relating to the allegation that one of her boat captains had whistled at a humpback whale that approached his boat. Such whistling, if proven, could constitute illegal harassment of a whale, a serious offense under NOAA regulations implementing the federal Marine Mammal Protection Act of 1972. The government lacked evidence to prove illegal whistling but claimed that Black had altered a video of the event, itself a violation. Lest anyone think that these matters are not serious, these various allegations if proven are punishable by long federal prison terms.[56] It is hard to believe that Congress intended to criminalize the practice of whistling at whales or even knew that such whistling could result in swat team raids on the homes of marine biologists. And, just in case the NOAA weather forecasters manage to borrow arms from their Fisheries colleagues, we might all be well-advised to refrain from complaining about the accuracy of their forecasts.

In 2014, the Supreme Court agreed to hear a case in which NOAA agents arrested a commercial fisherman after declaring that seventy-two of the three thousand fish in his catch were undersized. Later, when only sixty-nine undersized fish could be found, the fisherman was charged with destroying evidence. In particular, the Justice Department charged the hapless fisherman with violating the Sarbanes-Oxley Act's "anti-shredding" provision, aimed at preventing corporations from destroying records to thwart federal investigations.[57] It seems unlikely that Congress intended Sarbanes-Oxley to apply to fish. Thankfully, no assault rifles were brandished this time.

THE PRESIDENT

One elected official who exercises quite a bit of power over the bureaucracy is the president of the United States. The president is the nation's "chief executive" and controls several levers through which to influence bureaucratic behavior. Recent Republican presidents have claimed to subscribe to the theory of the "unitary executive," a constitutional interpretation that purports to show that all executive power belongs to the president, congressional and judicial claims to the contrary notwithstanding.[58]

Presidents, of course, do have a good deal of influence over agency budgets and appoint every agency's top executives. Since the Eisenhower administration introduced so-called Schedule C appointments, allowing the president to appoint high-ranking officials outside the career civil service, and the Civil Service Reform Act of 1978 expanded Schedule C to include the Senior Executive Service (SES), presidents have been able to place approximately 2,500 of their own loyalists in various slots in the executive agencies. Some presidents have used these appointments to monitor the activities of the agencies.[59]

Presidents can also influence the bureaucratic rulemaking process. Their most important instrument for this purpose is regulatory review. The regulatory review process emerged from the 1979 Paperwork Reduction Act, which created the Office of Information and Regulatory Affairs (OIRA) within the White House Office of Management and Budget (OMB). Congress was responding to complaints from business owners about the time and money they were forced to spend on the forms and records required by government regulations. Through OIRA, OMB was authorized to monitor and limit the impositions of regulatory agencies on the businesses and industries that they regulated.[60]

A month after taking office in 1981, President Ronald Reagan issued Executive Order 12291, establishing a process for centralized presidential oversight of agency rulemaking. The order required that regulatory agencies use cost-benefit analysis to justify proposed regulations. Significant new rules were not to be adopted unless the potential benefits to society outweighed the potential costs. To prove that they had complied with this mandate, agencies were now required to prepare a formal Regulatory Impact Analysis (RIA), which was to include an assessment of the costs and benefits of any proposed rule, as well as an evaluation of alternative regulations that might impose lower costs. OIRA was responsible for evaluating these regulatory impact analyses. Agencies were prohibited from publishing major proposed rules without OIRA clearance, and they were required to incorporate OIRA revisions into the rules that they eventually published. OIRA could block the publication and implementation of any rule that it disapproved.

In effect, the Reagan administration used the statutory cover of the Paperwork Reduction Act to achieve a unilateral extension of White House power. The intention was not simply to reduce red tape for regulated business firms. OIRA became an instrument through which the White House increased its control of the rulemaking process so that it could block or amend rules at will. The Reagan administration quickly used the regulatory review process to curtail the impact of federal environmental and health and safety legislation. It blocked the promulgation of new rules by the EPA and OSHA.[61]

During the eight years of the Reagan presidency, only a tiny number of proposals—an average of eighty-five per year—were returned to agencies for reconsideration or withdrawal.[62] Reagan's opponents in Congress denounced the president's intervention in the rulemaking process but were able to wrest only minor concessions from the White House.[63] Administrators in the regulatory agencies raised few obstacles to the new regime in rulemaking. Under the Civil Service Reform Act of 1978, presidents gained greater control over the assignment of senior bureaucrats to the top positions in federal agencies, and the Reaganites had taken full advantage of this opportunity to fill strategic positions with administrators sympathetic to the president's objectives.[64] The clarity of those objectives left little room for bureaucratic improvisation, especially since agency compliance was regularly monitored.[65] Given presidential control over budgets, staffing, and the general quality of agency life, most career bureaucrats found cooperation more sensible than struggle with the White House.

In 1985, President Reagan further expanded presidential control over rulemaking. By executive order, he required every regulatory agency to report annually to OIRA its objectives for the coming year. OIRA would assess each agency's regulatory agenda for consistency with the president's program and notify agencies of modifications needed to bring their plans into alignment with the views of the president. This new order went beyond Reagan's initial regulatory review program. Executive Order 12291 had authorized the White House to review rules after they were proposed. Its sequel enabled the White House to intervene before rules were drafted.[66] Reagan's order forced agencies to take account of presidential goals and not just congressional intent when formulating the rules that carried legislation into effect.

President Bill Clinton extended presidential control of regulatory agencies by directing OIRA to issue "regulatory prompts"—orders instructing agencies to adopt particular regulations. While Reagan had used regulatory review to prevent the imposition of rules to which he objected, Clinton took the further step of requiring agencies to formulate rules that he wanted.[67] Elena Kagan, a former official in the Clinton White House and now, of course, a Supreme Court justice, explains that Clinton felt hemmed in by congressional opposition during most of his presidential tenure. Determined to make his mark in domestic policy, Clinton used the bureaucratic rulemaking process to accomplish unilaterally what he was unable to achieve through Congress.[68]

In 1993, Clinton issued Executive Order 12866 to replace Reagan's two orders regarding regulatory review. Clinton preserved the essential components of Reagan's regulatory oversight system. He required agencies to submit major regulations to OIRA for review, and he extended the use of cost-benefit analysis for the evaluation of proposed rules. He also continued the annual regulatory planning process like the one created by Reagan. But Clinton added two new elements to the regulatory review process. First, he extended regulatory review to independent agencies like the Social Security Administration.[69] President Clinton did not require the independent agencies to submit proposed rules for review, but he did order them to submit their annual regulatory agendas to OIRA, which reviewed them for their consistency with the president's priorities. Though Congress had placed the independent agencies outside the orbit of presidential power, Clinton was trying to bring them under presidential control.

More important in the short run, Clinton's new order asserted that the president had full authority to direct the rulemaking activities of executive agencies—not just to block rules to which he objected, but to order the adoption of rules that advanced the administration's policy objectives. Clinton's order said only that conflicts between agencies and OIRA over proposed rules would be resolved by presidential decision, but soon after issuing the order Clinton began issuing formal orders directing executive agencies to propose for public comment rules that the president had conceived. On 107 occasions, Clinton ordered regulatory agencies to publish in the *Federal Register* rules that originated in the White House. Presidential rulemaking covered a wide variety of topics. Clinton ordered the Food and Drug Administration (FDA) to issue rules designed to restrict the marketing of tobacco products to children. The White House and the FDA then collaborated for several months on nearly one thousand pages of new regulations affecting tobacco manufacturers and vendors.[70] In other cases, the president devised rules for the Departments of Labor, Agriculture, Health and Human Services, Interior, and Treasury, governing water pollution, the inspection of imported foods, patients' rights, and assault pistols. In principle, agencies might have objected to these presidential directives and appealed to Congress for support, but Clinton did not mandate any rules that he expected the agencies to reject.[71]

Presidential involvement in agency rulemaking through regulatory review continued under George W. Bush and Barack Obama. Under the leadership of Obama's OIRA director, Cass Sunstein, who stepped down in 2012, the White House reviewed several hundred proposed rules and sent more than thirty of its own proposals to the agencies for implementation. OIRA also embarked on a "look back" at existing regulations, seeking to eliminate outdated rules.[72] Agencies suggested some five hundred rules for elimination, and OIRA secured congressional action on nearly one hundred. During that same year, it should be noted, federal agencies promulgated roughly 2,500 new rules, and even this represented a decline from the 3,500 new rules issued in 2011.[73]

These numbers tell an important story. In any conflict with the bureaucracy over rules and regulations, the president will almost certainly prevail. However, every year, agencies issue tens of thousands of rules and regulations that have the force of law. The president reviews a handful of these rules, proposes a few of his own, and secures the elimination of a few others. Presidential power in this realm is similar to the power that de Tocqueville attributed to the Roman emperor. "The emperors possessed," he said, "an immense and unchecked power," but "it was confined to some few main objects and neglected the rest; it was violent, but its range was limited."[74] In a conflict, the president is almost sure to prevail. On a day-to-day basis, far below the president's radar, the bureaucracy governs.

WHAT IS THE BUREAUCRACY?

America's federal bureaucracy consists of fifteen executive departments housing nearly five hundred agencies, authorities, and commissions. A small number of other agencies, such as the Federal Reserve and the EPA are independent of departmental authority. The oldest department is the Department of State, created in 1789, and the newest is Homeland Security, created in the wake of the 9-11 terrorist attacks in 2001. Many of these bureaucratic entities possess the power to make rules directly affecting citizens. Others, such as the Defense Department (DoD), do not have such authority, but even agencies without formal rulemaking power develop policies and manage programs that can have a substantial impact on every citizen. DoD, for example, manages the nation's military efforts, and its success and failures have what might be called existential implications for Americans.

HAS THE GOVERNMENT GONE QUASI?

In addition to these formal agencies of the federal government, America's federal bureaucracy includes a number of entities whose precise legal status is ambiguous. These are the "quasis." The quasis are hybrid organizations that exercise public power under congressional charters while remaining at least partially in private hands. These include such Government Sponsored Enterprises (GSEs) as the Corporation for Public Broadcasting, the Legal Services Corporation, and the National Passenger Railroad Corporation. One important form of quasi is the Federally Funded Research and Development Center (FFRDC), a type of private entity organized at the government's initiative to provide contract services to the government.[75] The oldest and best-known FFRDC is the Rand Corporation, created in 1948 to undertake research for the US military.

Possibly America's most important quasis are the several GSEs that play key roles in the nation's financial services industry. The best known of these GSEs are Fannie Mae (the Federal National Mortgage Corporation) and Freddie Mac (the Federal Home Loan Mortgage Corporation). The others are the Student Loan Marketing Association, known as Sallie Mae, the Farm Credit System (FCS), the Federal Home Loan Bank System (FHLBS) and the Federal Agricultural Credit Corporation (Farmer Mac). The GSEs are among the nation's largest banking institutions, collectively controlling assets of nearly $3 trillion. Fannie Mae alone is currently the nation's twenty-sixth largest business enterprise in terms of revenues and ranks third in total assets. Each of these six GSEs was originally established to overcome perceived flaws in credit markets.[76] The Farm Credit System, for example, was organized in 1916 to enhance the availability of credit in rural areas, which were then isolated from the nation's financial centers.[77] Fannie Mae was chartered in 1938 as part of an effort to create a secondary market for residential mortgages, thus encouraging financially weak, Depression-era banks to make loans available to home purchasers. Fannie Mae was a wholly owned government corporation until 1968 when it was converted into a GSE. Sallie Mae was established in 1972 to increase the supply of tuition loans to college students, a market that many commercial banks had avoided. Today, rather than compensate for perceived market failures, the GSEs operate to provide off-budget subsidies to specific groups favored by Congress.

Though there are individual variations, the financial services GSEs operate in similar ways. To begin with, GSEs raise money in the credit markets by issuing bonds and mortgage-backed securities. In principle, GSE bonds and securities, unlike Treasury and other government bonds, are not backed by the formal promise of the United States government to repay investors. Because of the GSEs' quasi-governmental standing, however, investors treat their securities as though they were backed by the full faith and credit of the US government. This perception allows the GSEs to borrow money at a rate only slightly higher than that paid by the US Treasury itself and substantially below the rate paid by commercial institutions. GSEs also benefit from exemption from state and local taxes and from a variety of other valuable privileges normally enjoyed by federal agencies. According to former Federal Reserve Board chairman Alan Greenspan, lower borrowing costs and tax exemptions are worth $6 billion per year to Fannie Mae and Freddie Mac alone.[78]

The GSEs use the funds that they borrow to make loans to private lending institutions that issue mortgages to home buyers, credit to farmers, and tuition loans to college students. These institutions borrow from the GSEs at a rate higher than the GSEs cost of funds, and the profit generated by this difference has provided a comfortable return for the GSEs and their investors. Fannie Mae, for example, produced a 25 percent return on equity in 1998, while Freddie Mac earned nearly 23 percent.[79] The GSEs also provide primary lenders with a secondary market for their loan portfolios, further encouraging them to extend credit to borrowers. By the end of 1999, Fannie Mae and Freddie Mac together owned single-family mortgage loans worth nearly $550 billion and representing 47 percent of all conventional single-family mortgages in the United States.[80]

Generally speaking, the GSEs have successfully carried out their primary missions of enhancing the availability of credit to defined classes of borrowers. But public purposes often get sidelined in private corporations, even those sponsored by government. To begin with, the GSEs are primarily responsible to their shareholders, not the government, and they regard the president, Congress, and regulatory agencies as interlopers in their affairs.[81] The president appoints a minority block of directors to each GSE's board—five of eighteen directors in the case of Fannie Mae. But the duties of these presidentially appointed directors are unclear. Though they may seem to represent the public's interests, their fiduciary responsibility is actually to the shareholders rather than to the public at large. Where public directors have sought to question a government corporation's practices, they have often been frozen out of decision-making processes and, in some instances, not even notified of board and committee meetings.[82] GSEs are less accountable to Congress than almost any other government-sponsored organizations. In general, the most effective instrument of congressional control is the power of the purse. But the GSEs have purses of their own. They finance their own activities through the profits they earn on their operations.[83] Government regulations are no more effective. Federal regulatory agencies have limited statutory power over the GSEs and often find themselves politically unable to exercise the few powers they possess. Hence, when it was discovered that the GSEs had engaged in risky practices that contributed to the nation's 2007–2008 financial crisis, federal regulators seemed surprised and mystified.

In 2014, an effort by congressional Republicans to dismantle Fannie and Freddie floundered in the face of opposition from the nation's housing industry. The industry feared a loss of liquidity in the mortgage market.

NONGOVERNMENTAL ENTITIES

Also playing an important role in governance and national policymaking are a variety of nongovernmental organizations, some for profit and some nonprofit, that offer advice, support, and contractual services to federal government agencies. The US government relies upon private firms to undertake such tasks as rating the creditworthiness of securities, including government bonds, and accrediting colleges and universities. If a school is not accredited, its students are not eligible for federally guaranteed student loans. The government relies upon private contractors to perform virtually every governmental function, and as much as $400 billion in federal spending each year flows into the coffers of government contractors. The federal workforce is often described as a "blended" workforce, with civil servants and contractors working side by side in most offices and performing overlapping tasks. Contractors prepare reports, prepare meals, provide equipment, program computers, supervise projects, and, in the case of military contractors, provide security services for government agencies. Many of the rules and regulations promulgated by government agencies are drafted by contract employees. In 2007, when the General Service Administration (GSA) sought to investigate allegations of fraud by federal contractors, the agency almost reflexively hired a contractor, CACI International, to manage the investigation.[84]

No firm numbers are available, but a number of federal agencies, including the Department of Energy and the Department of Education, employ the services of many more contractors than actual government workers.[85] And even agencies whose work is sensitive hand many tasks over to contractors. During the American occupation of Iraq, for example, the State Department allowed contract employees working for the Bear-ingPoint Corporation to take part in discussions on war strategy.[86] State also contracted with a private security firm, Blackwater, to provide armed escorts for its personnel when they traveled through the country. Charges that Blackwater troops had, without provocation, killed a number of unarmed Iraqis, forced State to terminate the contract. Soon thereafter, however, State found another military contractor to provide security forces for its diplomats. In 2013, an employee of the Booz Allen Hamilton Corporation, Edward Snowden, working under contract to the National Security Agency (NSA), leaked the details of NSA's electronic eavesdropping on American's phone calls and emails.

PUBLIC, QUASI-PUBLIC, AND CONTRACT OFFICIALS

According to some estimates, some 14 million individuals work for the federal government.[87] These include approximately 2.5 million civil servants, 1.5 million members of the armed forces, 7 million contract employees, and 3 million individuals doing government work for organizations that are not formally part of the government. Some of the employees in this blended workforce perform routine and mundane tasks, others undertake hazardous military missions, while tens of thousands of others are involved in jobs where they do research, write reports, make recommendations, and help to shape and craft agency policies, including rules and regulations that have the force of law.

Contrary to the model of government in which members of Congress and the president make the law, America's laws and policies are often developed by civil servants, contractors, the employees of the quasis, and others who have never faced the electorate, explained their actions to voters, or been forced to confront public opinion. In the contemporary world of law and policymaking, the political distance between the government and the American people may be greater than is commonly realized. Even within Congress and the White House, policy is made by several thousand unelected staffers, whose positions include such influential officials as congressional committee staff directors and the staff of the president's National Security Council. Congressional and White House staffers are oddities within the government's bureaucracy. They are not elected to office but are subject to electoral sanctions. If their bosses are not reelected, they also lose their jobs. As we shall see below, this ambiguous situation may help to explain differences in outlook between these staffers and other federal workers. Bureaucratic agencies, to be sure, are not autonomous. They operate in a political environment in which interest groups lobby them directly—sometimes through the rulemaking process—and lobby Congress and the president to bring pressure to bear upon the agencies. All this is true, but one group conspicuously absent from the politics surrounding administrative agencies is the general public.

THE STUDY: WHAT DOES THE GOVERNMENT
THINK OF THE PEOPLE?

To officials who inhabit the world of electoral politics and representative institutions, the citizenry is a more or less constant presence, to be polled and cajoled and appeased. The officials who inhabit America's large and growing alternative universe of governance and policymaking, on the other hand, have little contact with the public and, not being subject to any potential electoral sanction, may see little direct reason to defer to or, perhaps, even think about the will of the people as they play their part in governing the nation. The term "popular government" seems difficult to apply to this alternate universe of governance. The voice of the people, so loud on Capitol Hill, may be reduced to a whisper in the realm of the GSEs and FFRDCs.

Against the backdrop of these considerations, let us explore the extent to which America's unelected governors agree with, have respect for, are influenced by, or are even aware of the views of the citizenry. As we shall see, our explorations pose a number of challenges to the textbook vision of American democracy.

Chapter 2

THE CHASM BETWEEN
US AND THEM

INTRODUCTION

Hardly any American would disagree with the idea that the federal government should display some measure of competence and at least a modicum of efficiency in its handling of the nation's business. Indeed, Americans are often troubled by news accounts highlighting instances of governmental waste and mismanagement. Such reports appear with alarming frequency. Recently, for example, stories pointing to errors surrounding the launch of "Obamacare" produced an outcry over the government's apparent inability to deliver benefits that had been promised by the president. And, of course, accounts of alcohol-fueled misbehavior on the part of Secret Service agents have provided a good deal of fodder for late-night television comedians.

As the citizens of a democracy, though, Americans might reasonably believe themselves to be entitled to more from the government than competence alone. In a democracy, national leaders might also be judged by their sensitivity to the manifest interests of ordinary citizens and by their attention to the express will of the people. A regime that exhibits competence but is consistently out of touch with popular sentiment could not be said to be living up to the ideals of popular government. The framers of the Constitution seemed to endorse this view when they averred that the nation's rulers should possess a common interest and "intimate sympathy" with the ruled.[1]

How, exactly, such sympathy is to be guaranteed is one of the great questions of democratic governance. The Constitution's framers were doubtful that rulers, even "enlightened statesmen," could be fully trusted and, as is well known, incorporated numerous checks and balances in the governmental structure.[2] One important constitutional mechanism designed to produce rulers who might pay heed to the public's views is, of course, the electoral process.[3] Some of the framers were dubious about the merits of popular democracy, but most saw it as necessary and inevitable if the Constitution was to have any chance of ratification. Many also believed that, for better or worse, elected leaders would be more or less demographically and sociologically representative—drawn from "the great body of the people of the United States" without any "qualification of wealth, of birth, of religious faith, or of civil profession."[4] At the same time, elected rulers could be held accountable for their actions and might be turned out of office if they failed to meet their responsibilities. Fear of electoral rebuke would impose upon public officials "an habitual recollection of their dependence on the people."[5]

Elected bodies, to be sure, are seldom sociologically representative. Members of the US Congress differ from the population at large on the basis of such characteristics as gender, race, religion, income, and, especially, education. For example, in 2013, 74 percent of senators and 68 percent of House members boasted advanced degrees—usually law degreesa– s opposed to only 10 percent of the general American populace.[6] And, as to attitudes and opinions, fragmentary evidence going as far back as pioneering studies of public opinion conducted by the late political scientist Herbert McClosky, in the 1960s, suggests that the distribution of opinions among politicians on many policy issues is different from and frequently more polarized than attitudes on the same questions within the general public.[7] One recent study conducted at the state level indicated that state legislators conform to this same pattern.[8]

The demographically unrepresentative character of nominally representative assemblies has often been noted but does not seem especially worrisome. Members of Congress and state legislators are subject to reelection and are, as the framers' averred, "compelled to anticipate the moment when their power is to cease . . . unless a faithful discharge of their trust shall have established their title to a renewal of it."[9] In other words, whatever their own views and social perspectives, elected representatives are compelled to pay at least some attention to their constituents' opinions and interests if they wish to retain their positions. To the extent that empirical work has been conducted on this question, there appears to be support for the framers' view.[10]

Of course, some have argued that government officials should do what is best and not be swayed overmuch by public opinion. This notion is sometimes called the Burkean view of representation, in recollection of Edmund Burke, the eighteenth-century British philosopher and member of parliament, who told his constituents that he could serve them best by utilizing his judgment and experience rather than meekly acceding to their opinions. But it should be noted that elected representatives who share this perspective assume the risk of reprisal at the polls should their idea of what is best fail to comport with the interests of the public. Accordingly, even elected representatives with Burkean inclinations are under some pressure to consider their constituents' needs, if not their preferences, rather than to focus entirely upon their own. And those selfsame constituents are free to select new representatives if they are dissatisfied with the current bunch.

The same would seem less true of America's myriad appointed officials—a group that for more than a century has been insulated by law from popular displeasure. In the nineteenth century, government officials were at least indirectly subject to swings in voters' preferences. After the introduction of the "spoils system" in the early nineteenth century, most officials owed their appointments to party patronage and ran a substantial risk of being turned out of office if the political party to which they had sworn fealty went down in defeat at the polls. Patronage appointees, moreover, were fully enmeshed in the world of electoral politics. Many were associated with particular political leaders and factions and most engaged in frequent electoral work, campaigning on behalf of candidates, staffing the polls, and mobilizing voters.[11] Thus, patronage employees were almost as completely tied to elections and the electorate as the elected officials whose favor they enjoyed. Indeed, many precinct captains and other party functionaries held patronage jobs and saw government as an extension of electoral politics. The birth of the patronage system is sometimes associated with Andrew Jackson. Though Jackson did not, as is sometimes thought, actually introduce the system of party patronage, he did routinize and legitimate the practice by declaring that what he called "democratic rotation in office" would prevent the emergence of an entrenched governmental elite with little connection to ordinary Americans. In response to critics, Jackson declared, "The duties of all public officers are, or at least admit of being made, so plain and simple that men of intelligence may readily qualify themselves for their performance."[12]

The patronage system began to weaken and gradually disappear at the end of the nineteenth century as Progressive reformers, asserting that good government and partisan politics were incompatible, fought to separate the government's administrative tasks from the rough and tumble of partisan struggle.[13] As is so often the case, reformers' motives were mixed. Many Progressives were genuinely interested in enhancing the quality of America's national institutions by ensuring that only well-qualified individuals were employed by the various agencies of government. This notion was frequently repeated by the Progressive press. "It is plain to those who have studies the evils of our civil service and the methods of correcting them," declared an 1876 *New York Times* editorial, "that there can be no thorough and permanent reform until the rank and file of the civil establishment are put on an entirely non-partisan footing."[14]

At the same time, the largely upper-middle-class constituency of Progressivism saw patronage practices as the backbone of the political machines that had been organized after the Civil War by ethnic and working-class politicians. These machines were disdained by the middle classes as much for their ethnic makeup as for their corrupt practices. Civil service reform, along with other political reforms of the Progressive Era, such as the direct primary and personal registration rules, were aimed at undercutting the power of urban political machines, along with their largely Catholic and Jewish supporters, and bolstering the influence of America's old-stock upper-middle class.[15] A contemporary equivalent might be voter ID laws aimed at reducing the electoral weight of minorities and recent immigrants.[16]

A centerpiece of Progressivism, the 1883 Pendleton Act, created the US Civil Service Commission. The act went on to establish provisions under which most jobs in the federal bureaucracy would eventually be filled on the basis of merit, including competitive examinations that working-class political operatives and functionaries could seldom hope to pass, rather than political ties. The act also prohibited dismissal or demotion of federal employees for political reasons. The 1939 Hatch Act further severed the ties between federal officials and the realm of electoral politics by prohibiting civil servants from engaging in partisan activities.[17] These two pieces of legislation, justified as necessary to improve the quality of America's government, also meant that federal employees would be drawn from a substratum of the populace, would stand apart from popular politics, and would possess a measure of insulation from the vicissitudes of public opinion and the tides of electoral competition. In essence, the Pendleton Act and Hatch Act began to enlarge what we shall call below the "civic distance," or divergence in life experience and perspectives, between the American public at large and its government officials. Civil service protection generally does not apply to today's ubiquitous government contractors, consultants, and lobbyists. These worthies, however, whom we shall call the Washington "policy community," mainly work with and answer to career officials who do boast such job security, rather than to the elected officials who are still vulnerable to the judgment of the polls.

To be sure, the various hierarchies of appointed officials formally report to an elected official—the president—and their work is nominally overseen by Congress, which, among other powers, ultimately oversees administrative budgets. In recent years, indeed, presidents have made an effort to intervene in agency rulemaking, and Congress has also sought to increase its leverage over the work of the agencies. One of the newer congressional instruments of control is the incorporation of provisions known as "deadlines" and "hammers" into statutes to compel the agencies to expedite rulemaking in particular areas. Another congressional device, contained in a 1996 piece of legislation called the Small Business Regulatory Enforcement Fairness Act, is the requirement that all final rules be submitted to both houses of Congress and to the Government Accountability Office (GAO). In principle, Congress might then use an expedited procedure under the Congressional Review Act (1996) to disapprove the new rule. A congressional resolution of disapproval, however, must be approved by both houses and signed by the president. Only one rule has ever been revoked through this process.[18] As discussed in the previous chapter, administrative agencies continue to possess considerable discretion and, in many instances, the capacity to ignore or circumvent their elected supervisors.

We shall return to the relationship between elected and appointed office holders in chapter 4. For the time being, let us simply observe that the absence of an electoral sanction to bind rulers to those whom they rule inevitably challenges our confidence that officials will be attuned to the needs of the citizenry. Such confidence must then rest in some measure on the extent to which officialdom possesses sufficient similarity of background and outlook with the public, that in making decisions according to its own lights it also embraces the views of the governed even absent any obvious form of compulsion.

We should, of course, observe that an alternative source of "sympathy" might be a sufficient commitment to democratic values on the part of public officials to induce them to remain attuned to the public's preferences simply because they believe it to be the right thing to do. This idea will be considered in some detail in chapter 3. In that same chapter we shall also inquire whether officials even have sufficient knowledge of popular interests and preferences to do more than give vague lip service to the will of the people. For now, though, let us focus on the extent to which America's unelected officials seem to have enough in common with the backgrounds and views of the citizenry at large to truly sympathize with those whom they govern.

A GOVERNMENT OF THE PEOPLE?

Demographics

In our introduction, we took note of the some of the demographic and attitudinal characteristics of the government officials in our sample. In this chapter, let us explore some of the similarities and differences between officials and ordinary Americans. Let us begin with the demographics. Some might argue that citizens can be well served by government officials whose income or race is different from their own, and often this is true. Some literature, however, indicates that demographic similarity between the public and its officials increases policy responsiveness. Indeed, as we shall see below, demographic factors can be quite important.

Table 2.1 compares some demographic characteristics of government officials with those of the general public. Clearly, the officials and others in our sample do not appear randomly drawn from the public at large. The "inside-the-Beltway" crowd is more likely to be white. They are also considerably more affluent and have a substantially higher level of education than ordinary Americans. These facts are not surprising. Just on the matter of income, a recent report by the Congressional Budget Office found that on a job-to-job comparison, federal workers earned more than their private counterparts.[19]

Table 2.1: Demographic Comparison between Officials and the American People

	Congress/ White House	Civil Service	Policy Community	American People
Educational attainment				
Bachelor's Degree	44.2%	28.8%	28.5%	**17.9%**
Master's Degree +	55.8%	71.2%	71.5%	**10.6%**
Male	50.0%	56.1%	55.9%	**49.2%**
White	90.0%	91.4%	89.9%	**76.5%**
Median income range	$50,000– $74,999	$75,000– $99,999	$50,000– $74,999	**$53,046**

For the American people, data on education, gender, race, and income come from the 2012 US Census Data Profile of the United States.[20]

Indeed, across the board, federal workers earn considerably more than private sector workers. When benefits such as healthcare and pensions are included, the federal advantage over private workers is quite substantial. According to US Bureau of Economic Analysis data, in 2014, federal workers' compensation averaged $84,153, or 49 percent more than the private-sector average of $56,350. Figure 2.1 shows that average federal compensation, excluding contract employees, has grown rapidly over the last decade, outpacing the growth of private-sector wages.[21]

Figure 2.1: Growth of Federal and Private Salaries over Time

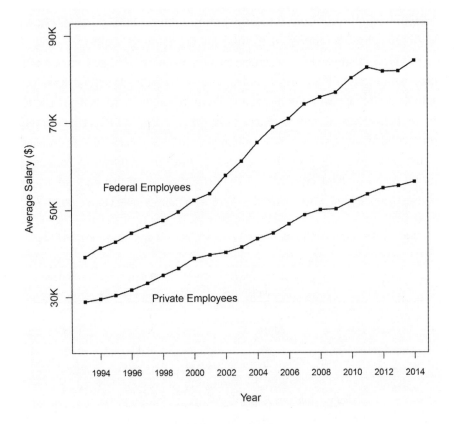

Salaries are average salaries per full-time employees (federal government civilian employees). Data come from the US Bureau of Economic Analysis.[22]

One recent study concluded that the federal workforce has become an "elite island of secure and high-paid workers, separated from the ocean of average American workers competing in the global economy."[23] This study goes on to observe that Congress has taken actions in recent years to slow the growth of federal wages but notes that federal benefits continue to grow more rapidly than those available to private-sector workers.

Given an already substantial across-the-board income disparity between federal workers and the public at large, it is hardly surprising that the federal officials in our sample earn incomes that put them in the upper ten percent of American wage earners. These officials hold positions that require skills and educational backgrounds that command high salaries. Whether or not they can be said to constitute an "elite island," they certainly comprise a rather affluent segment of the American populace. Perhaps we might go so far as to call them inhabitants of an affluent archipelago.

In a similar vein, we should not be surprised that federal workers holding responsible positions are considerably better educated than the general public. As we saw above, virtually all have earned college degrees and most hold graduate degrees in such fields as accounting, law, management, or technical specialties. It is worth noting that, with respect to education, our sample is not unique but seems to exhibit characteristics similar to those found in studies of civil servants over the past several decades. For example, as long ago as the 1970s, Kenneth Meier found pronounced differences in the educational backgrounds of senior civil servants compared with the general American public. In 1974, while only 13 percent of Americans had completed college, 96 percent of the senior civil servants in Meier's sample held college degrees.[24]

These demographic differences between the rulers and the ruled are potentially quite important. Of course, differences in income, education, and race do not necessarily mean that public officials will differ substantially from ordinary Americans in their political attitudes and perspectives. Demography is not always destiny. However, factors such as these affect individuals' life experience, capacity for mutual understanding, and perceptions of political issues and events.

Take the matter of race. In recent years, because of divergent life experiences, African Americans and whites in America have reacted very differently to such events as the acquittal of George Zimmerman, a white man accused of killing Trayvon Martin, an African American teenager, during an altercation in Florida in 2012. Nearly 90 percent of African Americans surveyed saw the case as the murder of an African American man by a white man, while nearly 60 percent of white respondents perceived the case as involving a white man defending himself against an African American assailant.[25] In this, as in other recent cases of police shootings of African Americans, police power and law enforcement are quite often perceived in very different terms by African Americans and whites.[26] This difference of perception is captured by the dispute between blacks mobilized under the "Black Lives Matter" banner and some whites who respond that "all lives matter." Members of each group often accuse the other of racism and neither can understand why the other fails to comprehend its position. Similarly, since the early empirical studies of political participation, scholars have confirmed that differences in social class background, particularly as exemplified by differences in income and education, can have important consequences for individuals' orientations to politics and society and their understandings of political realities.[27] Indeed, scholars have identified a "word gap" between the children of the wealthy and those of the poor, leaving the latter not only with smaller vocabularies but also less well able than the former to process and express ideas and concepts from a very early age onward.[28]

Political Experience and Efficacy

In addition to demographic differences, our sample of public officials differs sharply from the general public on two other dimensions that, like demographics, have implications for how individuals perceive the political world. The first of these is the dimension of political experience and efficacy. As reported by table 2.2, the three inside-the-Beltway groups pay more attention to politics, are more likely to participate in politics, and are more confident of their understanding of politics than ordinary Americans.

Table 2.2: Political Experience and Efficacy of Officials vs. American People

	Congress/ White House	Civil Service	Policy Community	American People
Reported voting in the 2012 presidential election	97.6%	89.7%	85.9%	79.9%
Believe election votes are counted fairly "very often"	61.9%	55.3%	49.3%	32.8%
Average number of days per week individual reads the news	5.6	5.1	5.1	3.6
Believe that government and politics can be understood by people like them	100%	66.1%	72.8%	29.5%

The data for the American people are taken from the 2012 American National Election Study (ANES). The survey questions are replicated from the 2012 ANES.[29]

These differences have important implications. Individuals with different levels of political experience are likely to possess divergent understandings of the political world, its symbology, and their potential role in it. For the politically sophisticated, the vocabulary of politics is likely to convey a different variety of meanings than for those without much political experience. For example, the politically experienced understand political rhetoric and political issues to include, if not serve mainly as, efforts by contending forces to mobilize supporters, stigmatize opponents, and provide a veneer of legitimacy for efforts to divert the flow of budgetary resources into the coffers of groups associated with their own political coalition.[30] The politically inexperienced individual hearing the same words and phrases might ponder the merits of competing claims about the nation's budget, healthcare system, social security system, and so forth, while Washington insiders understand that politicians employ "issues consultants" to help them conceive and articulate politically useful issues and messages.

Take, for example, the issue of "Obamacare." For the politically inexperienced, the debate was concerned largely with questions of public health and well-being. Experienced Washington insiders, on the other hand, understood that the issues raised in the debate had as much or even more to do with efforts by the Obama administration to build institutions that would provide the Democratic Party and its affiliated constellation of interests with lasting claims upon budgetary resources and voter loyalties. Washington insiders also perceived efforts by health insurance companies, pharmaceutical manufacturers, and other private entities with ties to the Democratic Party to solidify their control over healthcare markets. It was this understanding of Obamacare, not some abstract disagreement over the best way to deliver healthcare to Americans, that drove Republican leaders to oppose the president's efforts with some vehemence.[31]

Ideology and Partisanship

There is a third area in which our sample of officials, staffers, and policy community members differs from the general public, and that is the realm of political ideology and partisanship. Our officials report stronger ideological commitments than do members of the general public and, though their overt participation in partisan politics is restricted, they report stronger partisan commitments than members of the general public. In particular, the largest group consists of liberal Democrats.

To begin with, staffers, civil servants, and members of the associated constellation of contractors, think tankers, and consultants with whom they work are currently more likely to be Democratic in their partisan orientations than members of the general public. Of course, this is especially true when the president is a Democrat, but the Democrats have, of course, controlled the White House for sixteen of the past twenty-four years. Moreover, whatever the precise direction of their partisan leanings, those in our sample are, as reported by table 2.3, more likely than members of the general public to possess strong ideological commitments.

The Democratic leanings likely to be found inside the Beltway, as the conservative press likes to point out, reflect the entrenchment of the Democratic Party in the institutions of the domestic state—a phenomenon that began during the New Deal and was, ironically, strengthened by civil-service reforms nominally designed to remove politics from government. Civil-service reforms protect the agencies from partisan pressures inconsistent with the interests and inclinations of agency staff. In recent decades, several Republican presidents have sought to use their appointment powers to take control over federal agencies, only to be thwarted by agency resistance. Such resistance, indeed, led Richard Nixon to launch an ambitious but ultimately unsuccessful plan to reduce agency autonomy.[33] In the 1980s, some Republicans saw shifting control of social programs to the states as a way to reduce the power of federal social agencies they no longer hoped to capture and control.[34]

Table 2.3: Comparison of Ideology, Party ID, and Ideological Strength

	Congress/ White House	Civil Service	Policy Community	American People
Political ideology				
Liberal	43%	33%	41%	22%
Moderate	21%	50%	39%	37%
Conservative	36%	18%	20%	36%
Party identification				
Democrat	60%	54%	57%	49%
Independent	2%	17%	11%	6%
Republican	38%	29%	32%	39%
Strong Ideology	21%	9%	10%	8%

Democrats and Republicans include both strong identifiers and those who "lean" toward the parties. For the American people, data on political ideology and political party are taken from Pew.[32]

Since the 1930s, Democratic presidents and congresses have secured the enactment of a large number of social and regulatory programs, including most recently the Affordable Care Act, which greatly expanded the federal government's role in the nation's healthcare system. To administer these programs, they created or expanded such agencies as Health and Human Services (HHS), the Department of Labor (DoL), and the Department of Education (ED). These bureaucracies are linked, in turn, by government contracts and grants-in-aid to public agencies and nonprofit organizations at the state and local levels and through these to the Democratic Party's mass base.[35] This entire complex is tied to Democrats in Congress who affirm the worth of federal social and regulatory programs and defend the authority and budgets of the agencies responsible for their administration.

Individuals who work in such agencies as HHS or ED—and their counterparts in the state, local, and nonprofit sectors—are more likely to have Democratic loyalties than virtually any other segment of the populace. In our sample, more than 78 percent of those employed by domestic social agencies and their associated contractors and consultants identify themselves as Democrats.

When agencies that provide such benefits as healthcare and welfare hire employees and secure the services of consultants and contractors, they quite naturally attract individuals who by personal belief and prior training are committed to these organization's goals, and a commitment to the public sector is far more likely to be found among Democrats than Republicans. The Democrats' defense of social programs and expenditures has, over time, reproduced and reinforced the attachment of public employees to that party. Whether or not this attachment leads civil servants to pursue agendas different from those of the elected officials to whom they nominally report is a topic we shall consider in chapter 4.

In terms of our present concerns, however, the significance of ideology and partisanship is that these factors, like demographic background and political experience, function as perceptual screens through which individuals view and evaluate the issues, events, and personalities that comprise the day-to-day elements of political life. Ideology, as the late cultural anthropologist Clifford Geertz once put it, takes the "unfamiliar something" and renders it familiar and meaningful.[36] Through ideological preconceptions, individuals filter information and evaluate events. Ideology, writes Geertz, makes politics possible by "providing the authoritative concepts that render it meaningful, the suasive images by means of which it can be sensibly grasped."[37]

Any political phenomenon, be it a political issue or event or even a personality, presents numerous components and dimensions. As they encounter political objects, liberals and conservatives are likely to focus on different aspects of the phenomena on the basis of their own political predispositions and preconceptions. For example, during America's bitter budget and spending battles of 2010 through 2012, liberals focused on the threat that budget cuts might pose to America's social safety net.[38] Conservatives, on the other hand, are not altogether oblivious to the needs of the poor but, nevertheless, view increases in federal spending through a very different lens. They see such increases as expanding the size and power of the government and, in this way, representing threats to individual freedom. This conservative issue frame is exemplified by a recent online post by conservative Utah senator Mike Lee, warning that freedom itself was at stake in the budget battle.[39] Such ideological frames shape individuals' understandings of the particulars of any matter at hand and, thus, their positions on discrete issues and proposals.

Partisanship functions in much the same way.[40] As Angus Campbell, Philip E. Converse, Warren Miller, and Donald Stokes observed in their classic study, *The American Voter*, "Responses to each element of American politics are deeply affected by the individual's enduring party attachments."[41] We need look no further than a 2016 poll in which Americans were asked their reactions to the idea of Donald Trump as president. Few Americans have met Mr. Trump, but 64 percent of the Democrats surveyed were convinced he would be a terrible president, while 56 percent of Republicans thought he would be either good or great.[42]

CIVIC DISTANCE

The elements of difference we have identified between the rulers and the ruledd— emographic, experiential, partisan, and ideological disparities— give us some reason to suspect that the two groups may not perceive the political world in the same way. Taken together, these elements could well create a substantial cognitive and perceptual gulf between official and quasi-official Washington on the one hand and the American public on the othera— gulf that could interfere with the idea of a government that sympathizes with the views and interests of those it governs. Let us first examine the overall difference between officials and the American public. Then, let us see what difference the difference makes.

Figure 2.2: Density Curves for Two Random Samples of Americans

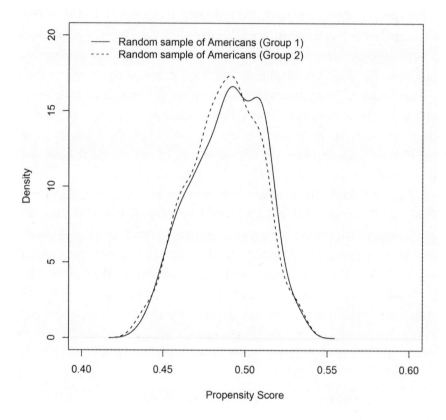

Data on the American people are taken from the 2012 ANES. In this graph, a propensity score is the probability that an individual is in Group 1 given that individual's demographic, partisan, and experiential characteristics. The graph demonstrates that the two groups are extremely similar with respect to these characteristics.

One useful method for comparing differences among the overall characteristics of two groups is propensity scoring, a method for measuring the extent to which two samples share similar attributes.[43] A propensity score is the probability that a given respondent with particular characteristics is a member of a defined group based upon the distribution of those characteristics within the group. If two groups are similar in their distributions of specified characteristics then the "densities" of the propensity scores of the members in the groups will be similar and the curves summarizing those densities will overlap. If, on the other hand, the distributions of the selected characteristics in the two groups are distinct, there will be little overlap in their density curves. Thus, for example, two random samples of Americans, compared on a variety of political and demographic characteristics, will show almost perfect overlap in their density curves of propensity scores (see figure 2.2). This overlap indicates that an individual drawn randomly from one group could equally well be a member of the other group.

Propensity Scores: Citizens vs. Officials

Now, let us assess the probability that an individual drawn randomly from the American public could, on the basis of demographic background, political experience, and political attitudes, be a government official. Recall that an individual's propensity score shows the similarity of that person to those in the government. The difference between the mean propensity scores of the two groups—the American public and government officials— summarizes the overall similarity between the two groups. We call this difference the **civic distance** between the people and their government. By comparing the mean propensity scores between the American people and our group of government officials, we can quantify the overall similarity in demographic background, political experience, and orientation to the political world between rulers and the ruled.

The notion of civic distance derives, in part, from the Aristotelian notion of κοινον (koinon), or political commonality between rulers and ruled. In his *Nicomachaen Ethics*, Aristotle famously observes that, "For where there is nothing in common between ruler and ruled, μηδεν κοινον (*meden koinon*), there can be no friendship between them either, any more than there can be justice. It is like the relation between a craftsman and his tool, or between the soul and the body, or between master and slave: all these instruments it is true are benefitted by the persons who use them, but there can be no friendship nor justice . . . for . . . they have nothing in common."[44]

In other words, where rulers have little in common with the ruled, those in power are unlikely to exhibit sympathy, as the Constitution's framers might have put it, for their subjects. Rulers are likely, instead, to view their subjects instrumentally much, says Aristotle, as they might see their tools, horses, oxen, or slaves, and deal with them in an unjust manner. Aristotle thought this problem was most likely to manifest itself in tyrannical states where rulers and ruled formed distinct strata, and least likely to develop in democracies where, says Aristotle, rulers and ruled "have many things in common."

Aristotle's understanding of democratic government was, of course, shaped by his experience of direct democracy, in which citizens and rulers were, to an extent, one and the same. What we conceive as democracy today is a mainly representative system, in which popularly elected assemblies coexist with large and quasi-permanent administrative establishments. In this form of democracy, rulers are not identical with the ruled and the idea that the two have "much in common" is not self-evident.

Our measure of civic distance is composed of four variables that capture individuals' demographic background, political experience, and partisanship. These variables include household income, news consumption, perceived complexity of the political system, and strength of partisan identification. Table 2.4 displays summary statistics for these variables among the three groups of government officials under analysis, as well as the American people.

The variables displayed in table 2.4 are used to generate a propensity score for each individual. The propensity score tells us how similar that individual is to our group of government officials (congressional/White House staffers, civil servants, and members of the policy community).[45] Figure 2.3 presents the density curves of these propensity scores. Each graph compares the density of propensity scores for the American public and a particular group of government officials (Congressional/White House staffers or civil service; we return to the policy community shortly). Each density curve visualizes the distribution of members in that group. If two groups are very similar, their density curves will overlap substantially. The less similar two groups are to each other, the less their density curves will overlap. The graphs in figure 2.3 demonstrate that, for most Americans, there is little overlap and considerable civic distance between themselves and Washington officials. Based upon the combination of demographics, experience, and partisan strength, Washington officialdom is quite distinct from the citizenry it governs. This is true for both those who work for congressional and White House staffs as well as for civil servants.

Table 2.4: Summary Statistics of Variables That Compose Civic Distance

	Congress/ White House	Civil Service	Policy Community	American People
Household income				
= 1 if annual household income is above the national median, 0 otherwise.	0.64 (0.49)	0.92 (0.28)	0.82 (0.38)	0.47 (0.48)
News consumption				
Number of days per week the individual reads the news (online or in print).	5.55 (1.85)	5.10 (2.21)	5.10 (2.14)	3.64 (2.63)
Perceived complexity of the political system				
Scale (1–5) where 1 is an individual who strongly agrees that the political system is too complex to understand and 5 is an individual who strongly disagrees with this statement.	4.52 (0.51)	3.73 (1.26)	3.93 (1.20)	2.71 (1.27)
Strength of partisan identification				
Scale (1–4) where 1 is an independent and 4 is a strong partisan.	3.23 (0.97)	2.44 (2.60)	2.60 (1.02)	2.88 (1.07)

The mean values of the variables for each group are displayed with the standard deviations in parentheses. The standard deviation quantifies the amount of dispersion in a variable. A high standard deviation indicates that the values of the variables are very spread out, whereas a low standard deviation indicates that the values of the variables are clustered around the mean value. Data for the American people come from the 2012 ANES.

Figure 2.3: Civic Distance between
Government Officials and the American People

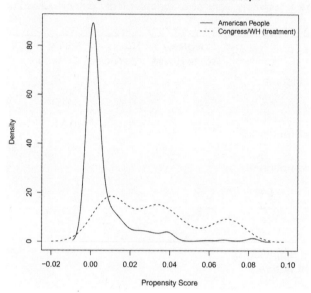

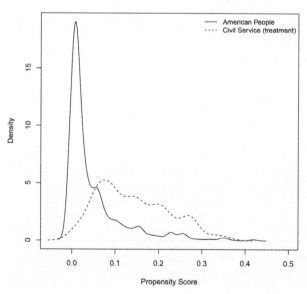

A comparison of means further highlights and quantifies the civic distance between the American people and their government. Table 2.5 displays the mean propensity score of each distribution, the absolute differences between the means, and the statistical significance of this difference. In both cases, the difference between the means is statistically significant at the 1 percent level, which tells us that we can have confidence that the difference is real and did not result from chance alone. These findings indicate that the American people are quite different from government officials on the basis of demographics, political experience, and partisanship. Using our vocabulary, there is considerable civic distance separating ordinary Americans and the nation's officials.

This comparison of mean propensity scores also reveals, however, that ordinary Americans and congressional/White House staffers are much more similar to one another than members of the public are to other government officials. While the difference in the mean propensity score between the congressional/White House staffers and American people is .02, the difference between the civil servants and the American people is .10 (five times larger). This shows that while congressional staffers are a bit different from ordinary Americans, the difference pales by comparison with the differences between citizens and government officials.

Table 2.5: Mean Comparisons of Propensity Score Distributions

	Congress/WH vs. American People	Civil Service vs. American People
Mean of Government Distribution	0.03	0.14
Mean of American People	0.01	0.04
Difference in Means	0.02**	0.10**

** Statistically significant at the 1 percent level (p < .01). This means that there is only a very small chance the difference resulted from chance alone.

Based upon the propensity scores, a randomly selected American magically transported to the offices of a Washington administrative agency might think he or she had arrived on a different planet and was listening to conversations among extraterrestrials. What, for example, would an average citizen make of a discussion of regulations governing banks' ability to trade asset-backed securities, or how fair health insurance premiums are to be calculated, or whether the newly adopted cranes and derricks standard should apply to underground construction work? Each of these questions can become the basis for heated discussions among government officials but would have little meaning to the average American.

The same American, however, might have better luck in a conversation with congressional or White House staffers who seem, at least, capable of speaking the same language as ordinary Americans. The difference in mean propensity score between the American people and congressional/ White House staffers is significant but much smaller than the difference between the people and those in the civil service. The main reason for this is partisanship. Congressional/White House staffers and the American people have stronger partisan ties than both members of the civil service and the policy community (see table 2.4). The partisanship of staffers is closer to that of ordinary Americans—reflecting election outcomes. This puts them on a closer cognitive plane with the general public. This is reinforced by contact and electoral activity.

Privatization of Government

An important pattern of findings also emerges if we compare the demographics, experiences, and beliefs of members of the general public to those of the consultants, upper-level government contractors, and employees of think tanks and nonprofit entities in today's Washington policy community who generally work closely with public officials.

Most federal civilian and military programs are run by what political scientist Donald Kettl and others have called "government by network."[46] Governance networks consist of federal agencies, private firms, nonprofit agencies, and even international organizations working together to resolve a policy problem or manage a federal program. Such networking may entail the Park Service turning to a nonprofit group to help it raise money for environmental cleanups, the Internal Revenue Service (IRS) working with tax preparation firms to develop better electronic filing methods, or the US military turning to private firms to manage its training, logistics, and transport. One military contractor said, "You could fight without us, but it would be difficult. Because we're so involved, it's difficult to extricate us from the process."[47]

In many federal offices it is, in fact, difficult to distinguish the upper-level contract employees from the federal civil servants nominally charged with administering governmental functions.[48] Administrators refer to this phenomenon as the "blended workforce." Working alongside actual federal employees, contractors provide management and administrative services and oversee governmental programs. In a number of agencies, such as the Department of Energy, the Department of Education, and NASA, a small number of civil servants work in close collaboration with a much larger number of contract employees to manage the agencies and perform their tasks. Even within the Defense Department, according to one report, "contractors shape and influence many decisions made by the federal government . . . including those . . . once characterized as inherently governmental."[49]

The employees of nonprofits and think tanks, and even lobbyists, are also important members of the policy community. They advise, interact with, and not infrequently interchange jobs with civil servants and commercial contractors to form a tight-knit source of policy leadership in the nation's capital. In our sample, approximately 80 percent of those employed in these professions previously held a civil service job. At the same time, nonprofits and think tanks depend for their incomes upon government grants and contracts to administer public programs and, in turn, undertake policy research for future programs they hope to administer. Most Americans regard nonprofits as charitable organizations that raise money from public donations. Most Washington nonprofits, though, depend for their funding mainly upon government contracts or upon sponsoring litigation under numerous federal statutes containing "citizen suit" provisions, which reward plaintiffs for bringing to light possible violations of the law in environmental, consumer, and other areas.[50]

Recent government shutdowns help to reveal the extent to which the federal government and nonprofit sectors are intertwined. Not only were government agencies closed but, absent the flow of federal dollars, a large segment of the nation's nonprofit community was also forced to limit its operations.[51] Contractors are involved in every aspect of public management, sometimes helping to write rules and regulations, in effect making the law.[52] In the nation's capital today, it is increasingly difficult to say where government stops and the private sector begins. For convenience, we have referred to quasi-governmental employees as members of the "policy community," but in Washington they are sometimes known as "quasis." One Washington wag once commented that there were so many of them that the government could be said to have gone quasi.

Using density curves, we can learn two things about the "quasis." First, taken as a group, the policy community is virtually indistinguishable from the civil service. Figure 2.4 displays three propensity score distribution comparisons: (1) employees of the Congress/White House vs. the policy community, (2) employees of the Congress/White House vs. the civil service, and (3) the policy community vs. the civil service. The graphs demonstrate that those in the policy community are hardly likely to stand out from their civil service fellows in any government office.

Further, figure 2.4 demonstrates that there is a nontrivial amount of civic distance between congressional/White House staffers and both the civil service and policy community. In the first graph, approximately 60 percent of the density overlaps, and in the second 55 percent of the density overlaps. In third graph, however, which compares members of the civil service and policy community to each other, 86 percent of the density overlaps. Members of the civil service and policy community are far less distant from each other, in terms of our civic distance measure, than they are from congressional/White House staffers.

Second, we can use density curves to examine the relationship between the policy community and the general public (see figure 2.5). The pattern we find is similar to the one we found when looking at the civil service. The is little overlap in the constellation of demographics, political experience, and partisan strength used to construct the propensity scores between ordinary Americans and the inside-the-Beltway crowd of contractors, policy advocates, and consultants. Or, to use the terminology suggested above, the civic distance between the two groups is substantial.

Figure 2.4: Civic Distance between the Congress/White House, the Civil Service, and the Policy Community

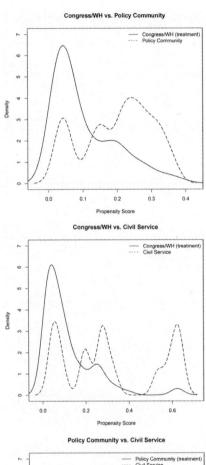

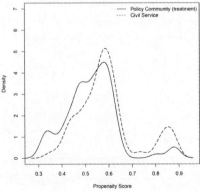

Figure 2.5: Civic Distance between the
Policy Community and American People

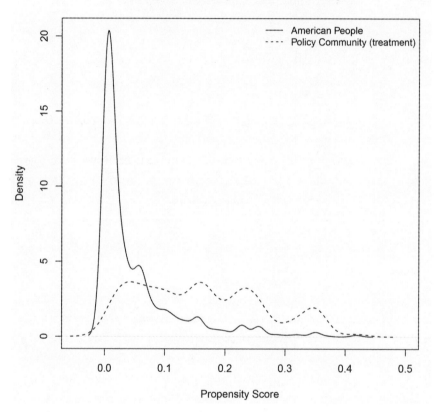

Policy Community vs. American People

The average American, transported to lunch at Washington's Palm Restaurant for a nice meal with consultants, policy advocates, and contractors would feel as out of place as he or she might at a meeting with HHS officials.

Contributions of the Components of Civic Distance

All four of the components of civic distance contribute to the differences displayed in the propensity score graphs. One way to see this numerically is to calculate the change in similarity between ordinary Americans and government officials when each of these components changes. For statistically minded readers, these calculations, and a table of results, are shown in Appendix B. We find, for example, that when an individual's household income increases from below to above the national median, that individual's similarity to government officials increases by 13 percentage points. When an individual changes from strongly agreeing that the political system is too complex to understand to strongly *disagreeing* with this this statement, their similarity to government officials likewise increases by 13 percentage points. When an individual changes from not following the news to reading the news every day of the week, that person's similarity to government officials increases by seven percentage points. Overall, to become more similar to government officials, average Americans would need to have household incomes above the national median, read the news every day of the week, believe that they can easily understand how the political system functions. and weaken their partisan ties a bit.

Civic Distance between Officials and the Well-Educated

Of course, the world of public officials is not, nor could it be, completely divorced from those of ordinary Americans. Officials are not extraterrestrials but are drawn from the American public. However, they are drawn from a very small segment of the public: the educated, upper-middle-class segment. Further, officials tend to be drawn from a somewhat ideologically distinct fragment of that segment and have different life experiences even from their fellow members of that elite group. Taken together, even though they are linked by education, there is still considerable civic distance between our officials and the educated Americans from which they are drawn.

This idea is illustrated if we recalculate propensity scores (i.e., recompute the civic distance), this time comparing officials with Americans whose levels of education are similar to their own. In figure 2.6, we find considerably more, albeit imperfect, overlap of density curves of propensity scores, indicating that educated Americans are somewhat more similar to government officials in terms of general political orientation. Unlike their benighted fellow Americans, the educated might hold their own at a

Figure 2.6: Civic Distance between the Well-Educated Americans and Government

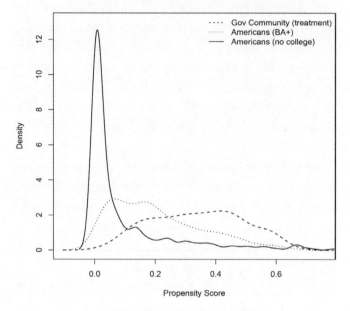

Entire Government Community vs. American People

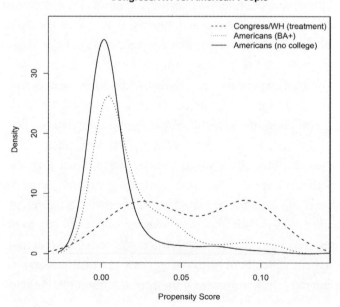

Congress/WH vs. American People

Civil Service vs. American People

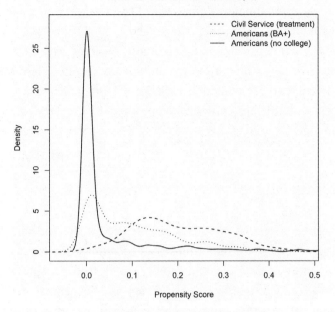

Policy Community vs. American People

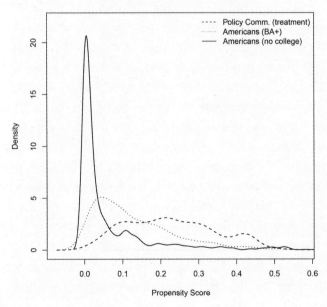

Washington lunch, though even they might be challenged at times. Turning to the graphs, approximately 66 percent of the density overlaps in a comparison of educated Americans (those who hold a bachelor's degree or higher) to the entire government community, whereas only 24 percent of the density overlaps when this community is compared to less well-educated Americans (those without a bachelor's degree). Thus, to the extent that government officials represent anyone, they represent the nation's cosmopolitan elite—a finding that would have pleased the Progressives.

POLICY ISSUES

What difference does the civic distance between rulers and ruled make? One area in which civic distance makes a difference is the realm of policy issues. On quite a number of contemporary issues, there are substantial differences between the American public's view and the general view of official Washington. Figure 2.7 displays differences in preferences for federal spending across six policy areas: crime, defense, public schools, science, social security, and welfare. We can see, for example, that while the average American believes federal spending on social security should be increased, the average government official believes this spending level should remain at the status quo. Conversely, the average American believes that federal spending on welfare programs should be decreased, while government officials tend to believe that this spending should also be kept the same.

Overall, in four of the six policy areas, there is a statistically significant difference in the mean preference between the American people and the civil service and policy community. The preferences of congressional and White House staffers, however, are better aligned with the governed. In this comparison, the differences in mean preference are only significant for two of the six policy areas: defense and social security.

One reason for these differences in policy preferences is perceptual. Policy preference differences are not random but are highly correlated with the civic distance between government officials and ordinary citizens.

Figure 2.7: Policy Differences between the Government and American People

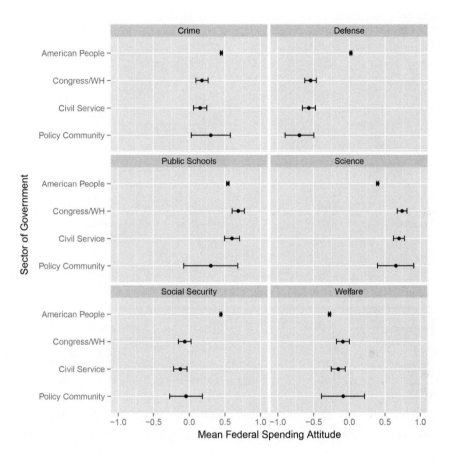

This graph displays the mean federal spending attitude (decrease = -1, keep the same = 0, increase = 1) for each sector of government and the American people across six policy areas. The 90 percent confidence intervals are also shown as horizontal lines through the point estimates.

Table 2.6: The Effect of Civic Distance on Policy Preferences

	Social Sec.	Schools	Science	Crime	Welfare	Defense
All Gov. Comm.						
Propensity score	-1.11**	-0.37**	0.89**	-0.87**	-0.23**	-0.82**
	(0.11)	(0.12)	(0.11)	(0.11)	(0.10)	(0.11)
Partisan ID	-0.06**	-0.13**	-0.08**	-0.03**	-0.15**	0.08**
	(0.01)	(0.01)	(0.01)	(0.01)	(0.01)	(0.01)
Constant	0.63**	0.98**	0.57**	0.53**	0.24**	-0.29**
	(0.03)	(0.02)	(0.03)	(0.03)	(0.03)	(0.03)
Congress/WH						
Propensity score	-5.36**	-6.40**	2.59**	-6.39**	-0.63	-2.13**
	(0.06)	(1.08)	(1.03)	(1.03)	(0.78)	(0.85)
Partisan ID	-0.06**	-0.13**	-0.07**	-0.03**	-0.14**	0.08**
	(0.01)	(0.01	(0.01)	(0.01)	(0.01)	(0.01)
Constant	0.61**	0.96**	0.59**	0.53**	0.19**	-0.28**
	(0.03)	(0.03)	(0.03)	(0.03)	(0.03)	(0.03)
Civil Service						
Propensity score	-1.71**	-0.61**	1.26**	-1.38**	-0.89**	-1.11**
	(0.21)	(0.24)	(0.22)	(0.22)	(0.20)	(0.21)
Partisan ID	-0.05**	-0.13**	-0.08**	-0.03**	-0.14**	0.08**
	(0.01)	(0.01)	(0.01)	(0.01)	(0.01)	(0.01)
Constant	0.61**	0.95**	0.58**	0.53**	0.23**	0.28**
	(0.03)	(0.03)	(0.03)	(0.03)	(0.03)	(0.03)
Policy Comm.						
Propensity score	-1.41**	-0.90**	1.20**	-1.29**	-0.41**	-0.92**
	(0.17)	(0.20)	(0.19)	(0.19)	(0.17)	(0.18)
Partisan ID	-0.06**	-0.13**	-0.08**	-0.03**	-0.15**	0.08**
	(0.01)	(0.01)	(0.01)	(0.01)	(0.01)	(0.01)
Constant	0.63**	0.97**	0.57**	0.53**	0.22**	0.29**
	(0.03)	(0.03)	(0.03)	(0.03)	(0.03)	(0.03)

Cells display OLS coefficients with robust standard errors in parentheses. ** $p < .05$. The six dependent variables measure respondents' federal spending preference in each policy area (-1 = decrease, 0 = keep the same, 1 = increase). The six models were run for each government-American people comparison.

Table 2.6 displays the relationship between civic distance and policy preferences. For each area of government, as well as the government community as a whole, we can examine the relationship between an individual's propensity score and his or her federal spending preference for social security, public schools, science, crime, welfare, and defense. The results demonstrate that an individual's similarity with government officials is a strong predictor of that person's policy preferences, even after controlling for partisanship. Notice that all of the coefficients on the propensity score variables, which capture the civic distance between the American people and government officials, are statistically significant. This means that the civic distance that separates the American people from government officials is highly predictive of policy preferences, even after accounting for partisan preferences.

Further, the magnitude of the relationship between civic distance and policy preferences is quite substantial. We can use the regression estimates in table 2.6 to calculate expected changes in policy preferences that are associated with a change in one's propensity score. For example, if an individual goes from having a 30 percent probability of being a member of the government group to a 70 percent probability, that individual is likely to move .44 points (on a scale of -1 to 1) closer to preferring that the federal government decrease spending on social security. This same increase in the probability of being a member of the government group is associated with a .35 point move closer to preferring that the federal government increase spending on science and technology.

These results suggest that officials and ordinary people think about the major policy issues of the day quite differently; they inhabit different politico-cognitive universes. Issue differences between the rulers and ruled are highly correlated with differences in propensity scores. In other words, the civic distance between the two groups is strongly associated with the divergence in policy positions.

This finding is brought into particularly sharp focus if we examine issue divisions within official Washington. As one might expect, there are sharp differences between Democratic and Republican officials across the policy spectrum. It is clear that Democrats and Republicans in government disagree with each other on policy matters, just as Democrats and Republicans in the American public disagree. Democratic and Republican officials, however, are equally likely to be civically distant from their partisan constituents (see table 2.7). Partisan officials have propensity scores that are similar to each other but quite different from the American people. Notice, for example, that the mean propensity score among Republican civil servants is .13 and the mean propensity score among Democratic civil servants is .12—quite similar. This indicates that while Washingtonians differ sharply on policy issues, they speak the same political language and live in the same cognitive world; Washingtonians are civically close to one another despite their stark partisan (and accompanying policy) divide.

Table 2.7: The Effect of Partisan Identification on Civic Distance

	Congress/WH vs. American People	Civil Service vs. American People	Policy Comm. vs. American People
Republicans			
Mean Propensity Score of Gov. Distribution	0.04	0.13	0.16
Mean Propensity Score of American People	0.01	0.04	0.06
Democrats			
Mean Propensity Score of Gov. Distribution	0.03	0.12	0.15
Mean Propensity Score of American People	0.01	0.03	0.04

THINKING INSIDE THE BELTWAY

One way to understand these findings is that membership in the inside-the-Beltway world of officials, staffers, contractors, quasis, and so forth, imposes a certain commonality of outlook that goes beyond differences and separates members of this world from their partisan counterparts in the general public. All in all, officials, staffers, and members of the policy community seem more like one another than like members of the public.

That is, while they may disagree on particular issues and policies, they share a commonality of outlook and a common political vocabulary that they do not share with the general public.

The differences between Washingtonians and ordinary folks goes further than simple issues. Their civic difference gives officials and ordinary folks somewhat distinct worldviews. They see the world differently on policies, priorities, how the government works, and its ultimate purpose. One way to summarize and visualize this is to plot the civic distance against policy preferences. The first graph in figure 2.8 displays this plot for those policy areas in which (on average) the government community is less supportive of spending, and the second graph displays this plot for those policy areas in which the government community is more supportive of spending.[53] Civic distance is plotted along the y-axis and spending preferences are plotted along the x-axis. Notice that members of the government are clustered in one space while the American people can be found elsewhere. It is clear that employees of the Congress/White House, civil service, and policy community inhabit a similar preferential and cognitive space in the political world—a space that is quite distant from the one inhabited by those they govern.

The upshot is that there is an inside-the-Beltway culture that links congressional/White House staffers, civil servants, and members of the policy community in a common language and set of ideas. Culture is important and is often studied at the level of individual federal agencies. Long-established bureaucratic agencies usually evolve priorities and procedures that advance both the internal and external goals of their leadership cadres. That is, agency executives will identify a mission and set of practices that justify their own agency's budgetary claims and power vis-à-vis other institutions, while simultaneously reinforcing the established structure of power within the agency itself. Over time, this mission and these associated practices can become so deeply ingrained in the minds of agency executives and staffers that adherence to it becomes a matter of habit and reflex. Students of bureaucracy refer to this set of established pattern of practices and beliefs about the organization's role and purpose as the agency's institutional "culture."[54]

Figure 2.8: Civic Distance and Policy Distance between the Government and the People

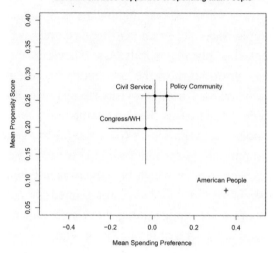

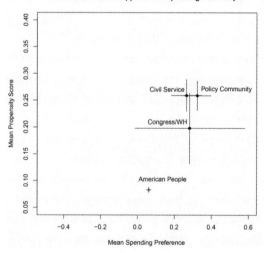

Federal spending preferences are coded as follows: -1 = decrease, 0 = keep the same, 1 = increase. The government is, on average, less supportive of spending in the areas of crime, defense, schools, and social security. The government is, on average, more supportive of spending in the areas of science and welfare. The lines indicate 95 percent confidence intervals.

James Q. Wilson has observed, "Every organization has a culture . . . a persistent, patterned way of thinking about the central tasks of and human relationships within an organization. Culture is to an organization what personality is to an individual . . . it is passed from one generation to the next. It changes slowly, if at all."[55] Agency cultures are sometimes born with agencies' original missions, the personalities of their early leaders, and the character of their earliest supporters. Once established, agency cultures can be remarkably resistant to change as agencies recruit employees and executives thought to be sympathetic to the agency's values and, for good measure, subject them to a lengthy process of training and indoctrination.

Military indoctrination, including the curricula of the service academies and the training practices of the "boot camps" endured by new recruits, has become the stuff of folklore and the topic of many popular films. The new recruit, whether officer or enlisted person, is subjected to an intense period of indoctrination aimed, in large measure, at imbuing him or her with the culture and traditions of the service in question. Marine recruits are subjected to a week of "disorientation" designed to sever their ties to civilian life and then are taught the values of the Corps. According to one authority, "To be in the Corps is to be in a state of mind that dictates ones relationship to the rest of the world."[56] While civilian bureaucracies do not run boot camps, most conduct orientation programs, and some, most notably the US Forest Service, approach military methods in their efforts to ensure the loyalty of new personnel.[57]

What is true at the agency level is also true at a larger level, namely the inside-the-Beltway world that has been described by journalists, which imposes its own conformities and habits of mind on those who wish to "fit in."

The emergence of a "Washington community" even in the early decades of the Republic was described by James Young.[58] Despite a variety of cleavages and conflicts, members of the executive establishment during the early nineteenth century were expected to interact professionally and socially in order to develop a certain commonality of experience and outlook that would facilitate their ability to govern. Constant social interaction among senior officials was deemed to be an important part of this undertaking. "For executives," writes Young, "the end of the workday signaled the commencement of a busy round of 'at home,' teas, card parties, receptions, dinners and balls. Suggesting the importance of such socializing in the life of the executive community, roughly as much time appears to have been allotted to it as was reserved each day for the conduct of public business, the daily routine for Secretaries being six hours at the office and the remainder of the day, often until midnight, consumed in entertaining. Sociability was officially decreed, indeed, by a presidential document promulgated for the specific purpose of 'bringing the members of society together.'"[59]

What is now known as the inside-the-Beltway culture is very pronounced today. Perhaps its foremost chronicler is Mark Leibovich, chief national correspondent for the *New York Times Magazine*. Leibovich's description of the 2008 memorial service for the late television newscaster Tim Russert reveals a city in which various sorts of cleavages—partisan, ethnic, factional, and so forth—are important. Yet the insiders are part of a common culture and share more with one another than with their nominal copartisans or coreligionists outside the capital. "Guests at the funeral," writes Leibovich, "are here to pay respects like heads of Mafia families when a rival godfather falls. . . . Bill and Hillary walking a few feet away from Newt and Callista Gingrich. . . . Bill and Hill . . . [find seats] . . . next to Madeline Albright, the former secretary of state and Condoleeza Rice, the current one."[60] Also present are NBC correspondent Andrea Mitchell and Washington power broker Ken Duberstein. Mitchell and Duberstein, both Jews, once spent *erev* Yom Kippur, the holiest night on the Jewish calendar, with Dick and Lynne Cheney and other Washington luminaries, at a social function hosted by Prince Bandar bin Sultan, the Saudi ambassador to the United States. It was an important social function for Washington insiders and interacting with the right people inside the Beltway was more important than outside-the-Beltway religious issues. "We both decided that the Lord and our parents would somehow understand," said Mitchell.[61]

The inside-the-Beltway world is separate from the world of ordinary Americans, even educated Americans. There is overlap and points of connection, but it is not representative. It is not a nomenklatura, as the top and untouchable layer of Soviet officialdom was called, but is not in any way a representative group. There is an inside-the-Beltway culture, a popular culture, and a good deal of civic distance between the two.

CONCLUSION

Our findings about the world of Washington officialdom are not, by themselves, cause for alarm. We want well-educated and competent officials, and perhaps the average American does not have the ability to run a government agency. But, as the citizens of a democracy, Americans do have the right to expect public officials to be "sympathetic" to the people when they make decisions. We certainly would like officials to be aware of popular interests and sensitive to popular preferences. Let us see in the next chapter if official Washington is able to overcome its civic distance from ordinary Americans and achieve some measure of what we will call "civic responsibility."

Chapter 3

WHAT THOSE WHO GOVERN *REALLY* THINK ABOUT YOU AND ME

In a democracy, the actions of the government are ostensibly guided by the will of the people. Abraham Lincoln famously described democratic rule as government "of the people, by the people and for the people." Lincoln's characterization implies that, in a democracy, both rulers and ruled have particular roles to play. The phrases "of the people" and "by the people" suggest that leaders should be drawn from the citizenry and that democratic citizens should take part in their own governance. The phrase "for the people" indicates an expectation that democratic rulers should pay attention to the interests and wishes of those they govern.

Does Lincoln's aphorism accurately describe America's government today? We wonder. Take the idea of government for the people. In recent years, we have learned that America's veterans do not receive adequate care from the Veterans Affairs (VA) healthcare system. VA bureaucrats attribute problems to lack of funding. Lack of funding, however, did not prevent the VA Palo Alto Health Care System in California from spending "at least $6.3 million on art and consulting services," according to Congressman Jeff Miller, the Chairman of the House Veterans' Affairs Committee.[1] This included $482,960 spent on a giant rock and $807,310 for "site preparation." The rock, "cut into cubes with a laser and pieced together," is meant to evoke "a sense of transformation, rebuilding, and self-investigation," according to the designers. No wonder there was no money left to care for veterans; VA bureaucrats had spent what might have been healthcare dollars on pet rocks.

Lincoln seemed to imply that democratic rulers and ruled had reciprocal obligations, imposing particular burdens on each. Government of and by the people would seem to require democratic citizens to become sufficiently aware and active to engage in politics, understand political issues, and make judicious choices at the polls. For its part, the idea of government for the people might lead us to expect democratic rulers to be cognizant of popular interests and preferences, and respectful of citizens' views.

If we consider citizens' capacities to fulfill their democratic responsibilities, the picture is not altogether promising. Americans' general level of political knowledge and awareness has frequently been discussed in the academic literature, and the extent to which citizens actually live up to what might be called democratic expectations has been closely scrutinized and seriously questioned. Studies almost invariably seem to suggest that many Americans know little about their nation's history, political institutions, leaders, or current political or policy debates.[2]

In a recent survey, 43 percent of Americans could not correctly identify the Electoral College, with many describing it as a training school for politicians. Forty percent thought the Constitution assigned the power to declare war to the president—perhaps a forgivable error given the history of the past half century.[3] In 2013, despite the enormous media coverage over the Affordable Care Act (Obamacare), most Americans had no idea how the law might affect them, and quite a few knew nothing at all about the new law.[4] But, before we criticize ordinary Americans about this particular lapse, we might recall that many members of Congress also expressed confusion about the act.[5]

In truth, some Americans' knowledge of contemporary political issues is limited to half-remembered facts or claims viewed in ads or heard on newscasts. And, once they acquire a piece of information, many individuals will retain it long after it ceases to have any relevance. In a 2005 Harris poll, for example, more than a third of the respondents believed that Iraq possessed weapons of mass destruction at the time of the American invasion—this despite the fact that even President Bush had long since acknowledged that no such weapons had existed. Apparently these respondents hadn't been paying attention. It seems that neither had 2014 Iowa Republican Senate hopeful (later elected to the Senate) Joni Ernst, who declared in a May 2014 debate that she had reason to believe that Saddam Hussein had, indeed, possessed such weapons.[6]

The unfortunate fact of the matter is that a fair number of Americans lack sufficient understanding of basic political and social realities to understand or to adequately evaluate competing political claims and proposals. Certainly, a minority of individuals—perhaps one-fourth of the public, according to some estimates—are knowledgeable about public issues and possess the intellectual tools to evaluate and act upon them.[7] A somewhat larger group knows something about government and politics without commanding much detail. Unfortunately, in their political involvements, the remainder, perhaps 25 percent, are what economists call "noise traders," that is, individuals whose actions are based upon faulty information and questionable reasoning. Some scholars have asserted that, in the aggregate, the public can possess wisdom even though many individuals may be foolish. This "wisdom of crowds" argument, though, is based upon rather dubious statistical and logical assumptions.[8]

While the shortcomings of America's citizenry has been the topic of much scholarly commentary, the extent to which democratic rulers fulfill their own duty to govern "for the people" has received far less scrutiny. The imperfections of the citizenry hardly absolve officials of their own democratic responsibilities. We might observe that where *agents* (in this case officials) have a fiduciary responsibility to *principals* (in this case citizens), we normally expect these agents to make an effort to understand and act in accordance with the goals, desires, and interests of their principals, even if the latter are sometimes a bit confused and inarticulate. Physicians, attorneys, and accountants, for example, are expected to pay heed to their patients or clients, even though those who engage their services are unlikely to possess more than a superficial understanding of, say, physiology, criminal procedure, or the tax code. Fiduciaries are expected, nevertheless, to listen to their patients or clients, identify their wants and needs, and offer them the best alternative (if alternatives are possible) approaches to achieve their goals.

In the political realm, we might refer to rulers' fiduciary duties as their "civic responsibility." The idea that officials have fiduciary responsibilities to the citizenry is recognized in such federal statutes as the 1988 Federal Mail and Wire Fraud law, which outlaws "honest services fraud." This statute essentially defines corrupt conduct by public officers as a breach of fiduciary responsibility.

One might argue that because citizens lack political sophistication, this justifies efforts by officials to do what they think is best while paying scant attention to popular wishes. Bureaucratic officials, in fact, often make this argument. One thinks here of the Confucian bureaucracy that ruled imperial China for many centuries, asserting a legitimacy based upon its capacity to provide benevolent and virtuous governance. Some contemporary scholars believe that this Confucian model is appropriate not only for China but for other nations today.[9]

The problem with this idea, though, is that officials who hold such Confucian views may too easily begin to see the world through the lenses of their own interests rather than those of the citizenry. Over time, indeed, the Confucian bureaucracy became quite corrupt. Aristotle might have described such officials as guilty of ανυπευθυνος (anupeuthunos), or civic irresponsibility—literally regarding themselves as exempt from the regular audit and discussion in the ἐκκλησία (ecclesia), or popular assembly, to which public officials were customarily subject.

CIVIC RESPONSIBILITY

Whatever the failings of the citizenry, fulfillment of their own civic responsibilities imposes at least three requirements upon public officials in a democracy. First, rulers should know something about the citizenry and its wants and needs. Rulers divorced from the populace and ignorant of its character and desires, as Aristotle observed, seem unlikely candidates to pay heed to the will and interests of the people. We might recall that the phrase, "if they have no bread, let them eat cake," commonly if incorrectly attributed to Queen Marie Antoinette of France, stands as much for a ruler's ignorance about the ruled as her indifference toward them. Law professor Peter Shuck has recently argued that even when they have good intentions, federal agencies are not very good at collecting information about the public or the problems it faces. This difficulty is, of course, exacerbated when officials think they possess information they actually lack or do not care enough to make an effort to ascertain the public's wants and needs.[10]

Second, we might expect rulers in a democracy to have some modicum of respect for citizens' views and beliefs. Many citizens may, to be sure, be uninformed and inarticulate. It seems, nevertheless, no more appropriate for officials to assume a dismissive posture toward the public than it would be for a physician to dismiss a patient's poorly expressed concerns. An assumption that the people are ignorant can distort rulers' perceptions and lead them to develop a more contemptuous view of public beliefs than is warranted by the facts. Moreover, rulers who view the people as inept and foolish seem likely to seek ways to ignore, manipulate, or circumvent, or even treat their subjects instrumentally, rather than listen to the will of the people, even if they give lip service to some abstract duty to govern "for the people."

Would anyone consider, say, the officials of the Bureau of Land Management (BLM) to possess a sense of fiduciary responsibility? Consider the Supreme Court's 2007 decision in the case of *Wilkie v. Robbins*. The case involved an effort, over a period of several years, by officials of the BLM to force Wyoming land owner Frank Robbins to give the BLM an easement through his property. In retaliation for what BLM saw as Robbins's intransigence, BLM agents repeatedly harassed and sought to intimidate Robbins, videotaped guests at his ranch, broke into his guesthouse, pressured other government agencies to impound Robbins's cattle, and filed trumped-up charges against him without probable cause.[11] While recognizing that these actions constituted what the Court called "death by a thousand cuts," and conceding that some may have violated Robbins's constitutional rights, the Court refused to provide a remedy for Robbins, saying that to provide relief would open a potential flood of litigation from others asserting that a government agency had acted to retaliate against them—a rather telling admission of a pattern and practice of government wrongdoing.

Finally, it seems reasonable to hope that rulers in a democracy would accept the idea that the government should seek to ascertain and listen to the will of the people, especially as expressed through representative institutions. Officials who are unconvinced that the government should listen are likely to seek ways of sidestepping popular and even congressional preferences when these conflict with their own.

This other side of the democratic coin has received little scholarly scrutiny and then only in the case of elected officials who *do* seem interested in learning what they can about the public they serve. Empirical studies suggest that elected officials want to know what the public thinks and will adapt their conduct in office to accord more fully with constituents' preferences if they believe their information about these preferences to be reliable.[12] Of course, members of Congress and the state legislatures are compelled to campaign for reelection on an almost constant basis. They rub shoulders with their constituents at town meetings, shopping centers, American Legion halls, houses of worship, and so forth. Elected representatives cannot help but learn something about the electorate and some, perhaps, even develop a capacity to articulate constituents' often inchoate positions and preferences. But what of appointed officials? These individuals exercise a good deal of power but, according to our findings in chapter 2, may also show considerable civic distance from average Americans on the basis of demographic backgrounds, political experience, and political views. Can such officials be trusted to govern *for* the people?

Against the backdrop of these considerations, let us assess the extent to which the civil servants, members of the Washington policy community, and staffers in our sample are familiar with the preferences, needs, and even basic life circumstances of the 325 million Americans whom they help to govern. We shall go on to examine officials' perceptions of the competence of ordinary citizens. We will, moreover, consider whether the various groups in our sample believe they have a responsibility to pay attention to popular interests and preferences.

Of course, according to the government's organization charts, our appointed officials and their advisors all report to an elected official—the president—and are overseen by a body of elected officials—the Congress of the United States. Perhaps appointed officials should not make their own assessments of the public's needs and preferences but should merely follow the guidance of their elected overseers. We shall consider this idea in more detail below and in chapter 4. For the present, however, it is worth recalling that many of the decisions made by bureaucrats and their associates are made without much in the way of external scrutiny. Rules and regulations are written for statutes enacted and signed into law by Congresses and presidents long gone from public life. Indeed, even current Congresses and presidents exercise only spotty supervision over the activities of their bureaucratic subordinates. Thus, since they are not always subject to direct oversight, it is worth asking whether appointed officials and other members of the Washington policy community have sufficient respect for the elected leaders, who formally represent the public's views, to follow their guidance nonetheless. If, however, America's unelected officials believe they should be ανυπευθυνος, or "unauditable," perhaps they resent congressional oversight as much as the idea of public scrutiny. In a recent congressional hearing, for example, Consumer Financial Protection Bureau Director Richard Cordray told Rep. Ann Wagner (R-MO) that she, and presumably the American people, had no business asking how much money his agency spent on its new headquarters—estimates are $125 million. Cordray's exact words were, "Why does that matter to you?"[13] Let us see if our survey can help us assess officials' sense of civic responsibility.

OFFICIALS' KNOWLEDGE OF THE CIRCUMSTANCES AND OPINIONS OF AVERAGE AMERICANS

We saw in chapter 2 that public officials and ordinary citizens have rather different conceptions of the political world, but this "civic distance" does not preclude the possibility that officials possess a measure of knowledge about the life circumstances and opinions of the citizens they govern. Conceptual proximity is not an absolute prerequisite for knowledge. Through careful and patient study, cultural anthropologists, for example, can learn a good deal about groups whose backgrounds are quite dissimilar from their own. By the same token, public officials might commit themselves to developing some understanding of the many Americans whose backgrounds and viewpoints may be quite different from those encountered inside the capital Beltway.

Let us, then, begin with a quiz. Citizens are often quizzed to ascertain what they know about the government and castigated for their lack of knowledge. We shall turn the tables and see what the government, or at least one part of it, knows about the people. The Pew Research Center frequently conducts polls to determine what the American people know about their government and current events. We asked officials and members of the Washington policy community a number of questions, modeled after the Pew news quiz, that were designed to test their factual knowledge of the life circumstances of average Americans—knowledge of Americans' incomes, educations, ethnicity, and so forth.[14] Figure 3.1 displays the distribution of answers for questions from this quiz.

As is evident in figure 3.1, government officials, generally speaking, have a rather imprecise picture of the American public—a picture only slightly more accurate than the American public's view of the government. There is, however, significant variation across the questions. With respect to the unemployment rate and poverty rate, government officials appear quite knowledgeable; 89 percent correctly identified the unemployment rate and 76 percent correctly identified the poverty rate. Average Americans, in contrast, are far less familiar with these basic economic indicators. In a Pew survey administered during a similar time period as our own, 58 percent and 46 percent of the American public correctly identified these numbers, respectively.[15]

Officials seem to have somewhat less knowledge when we turn to the questions that ask about Americans' racial composition and socioeconomic status. With respect to race, it is evident that government officials perceive the American public as more racially diverse than it is in reality. Approximately 42 percent of government officials overestimated the percentage of African Americans in the US population and 79 percent underestimated the percentage of white Americans.

Among government officials, there is also a sense that Americans are older and less well-off than they are in reality. Approximately 80 percent of respondents overestimated the percentage of citizens 65 years old or older. We also find that 64 percent of respondents underestimated Americans' median income, 80 percent underestimated the homeownership rate, and 64 percent underestimated the number of Americans with high school diplomas. Apparently, there is a widespread inclination among government officials to underestimate the socioeconomic status of average Americans. Taken together, the results reported by figure 3.1 show that, as a group, public officials exhibit substantial gaps in their knowledge of the citizens whom they govern.

Figure 3.1: Knowledge of the Circumstances of Average Americans

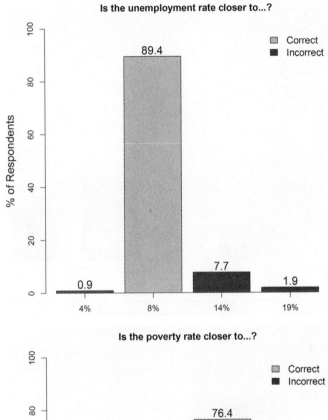

Is the unemployment rate closer to...?

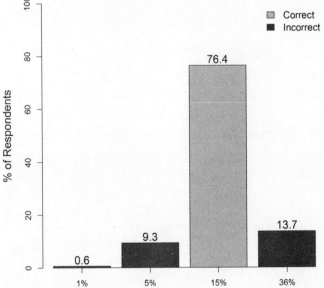

Is the poverty rate closer to...?

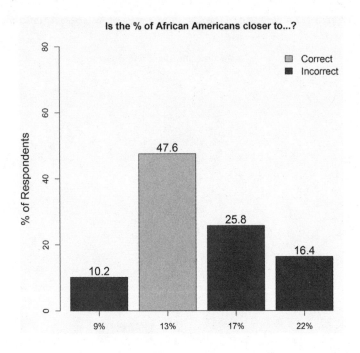

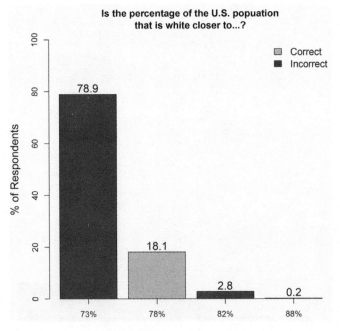

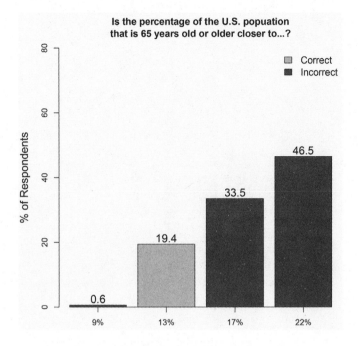

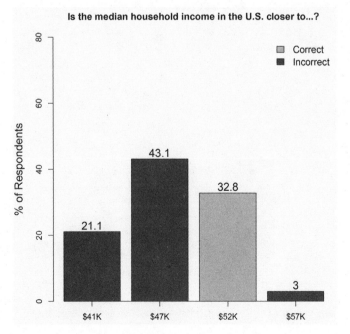

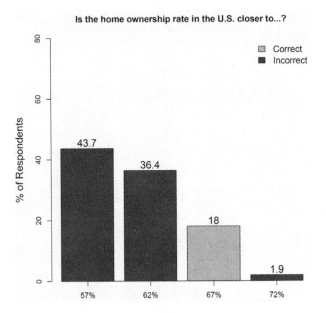

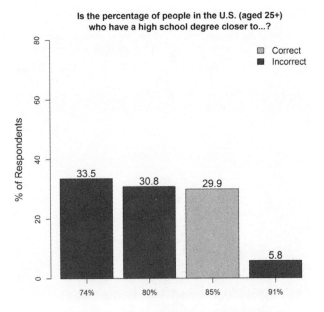

Respondents were given multiple choice questions (with four answer choices each) about the circumstances of average Americans.

KNOWLEDGE OF THE POLICY PREFERENCES
OF AVERAGE AMERICANS

Of course, even if their knowledge about Americans' life circumstances is imperfect, public officials might still be committed to familiarizing themselves with citizens' opinions and preferences. At least in principle, a government might be attentive to public opinion despite lacking detailed economic and demographic knowledge about the public.

To explore this possibility, we asked our respondents what they thought the average American's opinions were with respect to federal spending in various policy areas.[16] Democratic governments claim they are bound by or at least interested in the will of the people. Our officials, though, do not seem to have a very good idea of what that will might be. On question after question, a substantial percentage of respondents gave incorrect answers when asked what they thought the public believed. The results indicate that government officials overestimate, by an average of eight percentage points, the proportion of Americans who support increasing spending in the areas of public schools, crime prevention, welfare, and childcare. The largest "misses" are with respect to support for maintaining the status quo. In all nine policy areas under analysis, government officials underestimate the public's support for maintaining current levels of federal spending; the average gap is a striking eleven percentage points. All told, official Washington seems to have an inaccurate view of popular preferences.

FALSE UNIQUENESS

There are many possible reasons why officials and members of the policy community might err in their understanding of public opinion. They might be uninterested in or indifferent to public opinion, or they might be projecting their own views upon the general public. This sort of projection is a common psychological phenomenon sometimes called "false consensus," where individuals assume that others hold views similar to their own. When we explored the reasons that officials tended to err in their understanding of public opinion, however, another explanation presented itself. Rather than indications of false consensus, what we found instead was "false uniqueness." Most denizens of official Washington believed that their own views were quite different from those of ordinary Americans on most public issues (see figure 3.2).

Figure 3.2: Government Officials Who Think the Average American Holds a Different Opinion

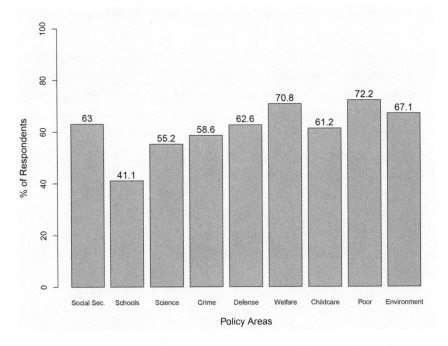

On all but one policy issue, a majority of officials believe that most Americans hold views different from their own. And, significantly, officials tend to substantially overestimate the actual amount of difference between their own views and those of ordinary citizens.

Figure 3.3 is based on the questions in which government officials were asked about their (1) preferences for federal spending on various policy areas (answer choices: increase, keep the same, decrease) and (2) perceived federal spending preferences of the American people. For each policy area (social security, science and technology, schools, welfare, aid to the poor, crime, environment, childcare) we determined whether government officials actually agreed with the average American and whether they perceived a disagreement.[17] Then, for each government official, we calculated the total number of policy areas in which he/she (1) actually agreed and (2) perceived disagreement.

Figure 3.3: Overestimation of Policy Differences by Government Officials

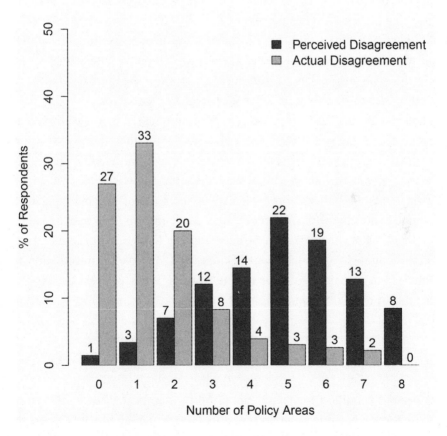

The graph displays the frequency distributions of these two variables. For example, the graph shows that 27 percent of government officials actually differ on zero policy areas (meaning they agree on all policy areas), but only 1 percent of them believe that they differ on zero policy areas. On the other side of the graph, we see that only 2 percent of government officials actually differ on seven policy areas, whereas 13 percent believe they differ on seven policy areas. The distributions are nearly inverses of each other. On average, government officials believe they differ on 4.9 policy areas but they actually differ on only 1.6 policy areas. The graph thus shows that government officials substantially overestimate their amount of policy disagreement with the average American.

This sort of overestimation of differences is a phenomenon social psychologists call *false uniqueness*. False uniqueness describes a situation in which individuals perceive a greater difference between their own attitudes or abilities and those of others than is actually true. Generally, false uniqueness tends to reflect a sense of cultural or intellectual superiority, with respondents assuming they possess greater knowledge or ability than those to whom they are comparing themselves. As social psychologist Ronald Ostman observes, false uniqueness is a way in which members of one group view themselves as "better than thou" in relation to another group.[18] As we shall see below, public officials and policy community members, indeed tend to view the citizenry with some disdain, or even contempt. Perhaps this explains why members of the governing elite tend to overestimate the differences between their own ideas and the views of those whom they govern. Officials and policy community members simply cannot imagine that average citizens would have the information or intellectual capacity needed to see the world as it is seen from the exalted heights of official Washington.

RESPECT FOR THE OPINIONS OF THE AMERICAN PEOPLE

A second condition for civic responsibility is respect. Rulers who view those whom they rule as ignorant and foolish seem more likely to ignore or manipulate the citizenry than to do its bidding. Unfortunately, our findings are consistent with the idea suggested above, that America's rulers regard members of the public as generally incompetent and uninformed on most policy questions. Table 3.1 displays government officials' perceptions of Americans' knowledge about various policy areas. In eight of the nine policy areas, a plurality of respondents think that Americans know "very little" about that area. The percentage of respondents who think Americans know "a great deal" about a policy area does not exceed 6 percent across all the areas. Respondents think Americans know the most about public education (39 percent think the average American knows at least "some" about this topic) and the least about aid to the poor (72.1 percent think the average American knows "very little" or "none").

**Table 3.1: Government Officials' Perspective on
Americans' Knowledge of Policy Areas**

	A great deal	Quite a bit	Some	Very Little	None
Social Security	5.6	17.1	37.4	**38.5**	1.5
Public Schools	4.4	19.1	**39.3**	36.4	0.9
Science & Technology	0.6	3.2	25.1	**59.9**	11.2
Crime	1.2	8.5	37.8	**50.7**	1.8
Defense	5.3	17.6	30.2	**43.1**	3.8
Welfare	2.6	7.0	32.3	**55.1**	2.9
Childcare	1.2	7.0	31.4	**56.6**	3.8
Aid to the Poor	0.3	2.1	25.5	**69.5**	2.6
Environment	1.2	5.0	30.5	**58.9**	4.4

Cell entries are the percentage of respondents. Bolded entries are the largest for each row.

The same pattern emerges if we examine officials' perspective on the knowledge of average Americans with respect to specific policy proposals (see table A1 in appendix A). For example, 66 percent of government officials think the average American knows very little or none about the proposal for the government to pay the cost of prescription drugs for seniors on low incomes, and 54 percent of government officials think the average American knows very little or none about a proposal that would grant illegal immigrants a path to citizenship. Officials likewise do not think Americans know very much about tax-related policy proposals or proposals related to the protection of citizen privacy. In sum, it is fair to say that government officials do not think the governed know very much about even the most salient policy issues. This scornful view of the public's understanding of policy seems quite clear, as we might have anticipated from officials' sense of false uniqueness described above. Generally, this attitude is hidden behind official Washington's public claims of respect for the American people, but occasionally officials or members of the policy community slip and publicly voice their true sentiments. Thus, in November 2014, news accounts revealed that Jonathan Gruber, a key consultant in the development of the Affordable Care Act, described average Americans as "stupid." Gruber apologized for his comments but did not seek to retract them.[19] Anyone who has lived in Washington knows that Gruber's views are the norm, not the exception in the nation's capital.

In point of fact, while Americans do not know as much about government and politics as we might hope, they know more than officials think. In response to a recent Pew quiz testing Americans' knowledge of public affairs, 42 percent of all respondents, on average, answered each question correctly.[20] Similarly, in response to a recent Annenberg public affairs survey, most questions were answered correctly by 40 percent or more of the respondents.[21] Civil servants who wish to cluck their tongues at these scores might do well to remember that their own knowledge about the people was hardly more accurate.

Indeed, a bit of disdain for the public is not limited to any particular segment of the nation's unelected leadership. America's governing elites are divided among themselves on many issues, but they seem fully agreed on this one matter—they share the view that Americans do not know very much. To depict this visually, we created a measure that combines officials' convictions that ordinary Americans know very little about federal spending and a number of other policy areas, such as income taxes, prescription drugs, and illegal immigration. This measure thus combines eighteen variables with each variable ranging from 1 (the average American knows a great deal) to 5 (the average American knows nothing).[22] The final measure ranges from 18 to 90, where a higher number indicates a higher level of conviction that Americans know very little about policy questions.

Figure 3.4 displays the distributions of misgivings about the people on the part of various groups within official Washington. These distributions reveal that mistrust of the people does not vary across the common dimensions of attitudinal difference within official Washington. On many issues, policymakers might be divided by partisanship, gender, and ideology. When it comes to doubts about the competence of average Americans, however, these normally divisive factors do not interfere with the general inside-the-Beltway view of an American public lacking basic knowledge of key policy issues and proposals. In all four of the graphs in figure 3.4, the distributions overlap to a large degree. In sharp contrast to the usual picture of strife and disagreement in official Washington, when it comes to disdain for the perspicacity of average Americans, consensus and harmony prevail. Who says that America's leaders can never agree on anything?

Figure 3.4: Similarity in Official Contempt for the
American People across Party, Ideological, and Gender Lines

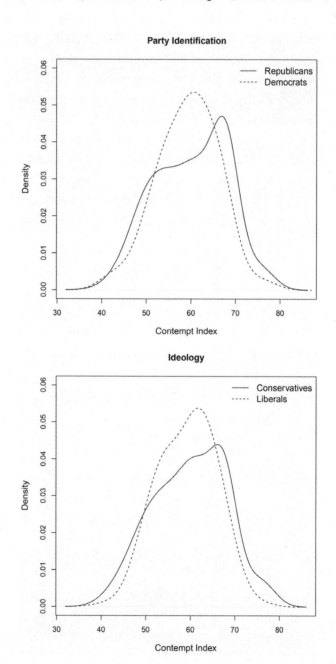

Gender

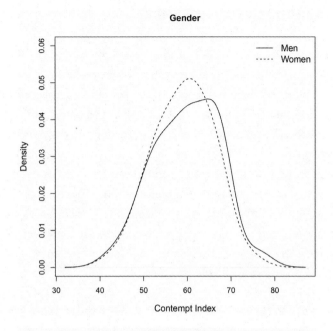

Partisan Strength

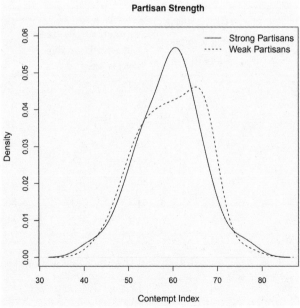

ACCOUNTABILITY TO THE PEOPLE

A third element of civic responsibility, noted above, is accountability to the people. Rulers in a democracy might be expected to accept the idea that they should pay heed to the will of the people as expressed directly or through representative institutions. As we observed above, officials unconvinced that the government should listen to the citizenry seem likely to sidestep popular and even congressional views when these clash with their own. The fact that many officials seem unfamiliar with or even contemptuous of public opinion may already lead us to doubt their commitment to heeding the will of the people. And, indeed, the overwhelming majority of America's unelected officials and policy community members responding to our survey say that it is more important to do what they think is right than to listen to the voice of the people.

Table 3.2: Government Officials' Perspective on Heeding Public Opinion

	Always/Mostly Follow Public Opinion	Give Equal Consideration to Public Opinion and What It Thinks Is Best	Always/Mostly Do What It Thinks Is Best
Social Security	17.7	**43.7**	38.6
Public Schools	21.2	**43.1**	35.7
Science & Technology	9.8	37.6	**52.6**
Crime	14.7	40.2	**45.1**
Defense	9.1	39.2	**51.7**
Welfare	12.9	**45.4**	41.7
Childcare	17.7	**47.1**	35.2
Aid to the Poor	12.3	**46.1**	41.7
Environment	12.0	41.7	**46.3**

Cell entries are the percentage of respondents. Bolded entries are the largest for each row.

Table 3.2 displays the percentage of government officials who think they should always/mostly follow public opinion on policy issues, give equal consideration to public opinion and what they think is best, or always/mostly do what they think is best. Across all nine issues, the distributions are negatively skewed. There is not one issue where a plurality thinks that that the government should always or mostly follow public opinion. With respect to science and technology and defense, a majority of officials think the government should always or mostly do what it thinks is best. Overall, officials believe their own judgments should be weighted equally or more in the policymaking calculus.

In the parlance of the social sciences, table 3.2 indicates that most respondents characterize themselves as "trustees" rather than "delegates." We can also examine this issue directly with a question that asked respondents to place themselves on a delegate-trustee scale (1–7). Figure 3.5 shows the distribution of responses for congressional/White House staffers, civil servants, and members of the policy community. With the exception of the staffers who work directly for delegates, our respondents characterized their role as doing what was best for the people of the United States. They held their offices "in trust" for the people.

Unfortunately, many of the individuals who describe themselves as "trustees" for the public actually know very little about the public for whom they claim to be working. While nearly all of the officials in our survey demonstrated a lack of knowledge about the circumstances of average Americans, those who describe themselves as trustees know, on average, even less than those who self-classify as delegates. On a 0–8 knowledge scale, the self-described delegates scored an average 3.7, whereas the self-described trustees scored an average of 3.4. It is difficult to put aside the thought that for at least some so-called trustees the term is a euphemism for authority to govern in a manner that serves their own interests.

RESPONSIVENESS TO REPRESENTATIVE INSTITUTIONS

To some extent, of course, unelected officials are ultimately responsible to elected officials—members of the Congress and the president. These elected officials can exercise considerable power over bureaucrats and members of the policy community, perhaps forcing them to obey the will of the people as expressed through representative institutions whether they like it or not.

Figure 3.5: A Government of Trustees

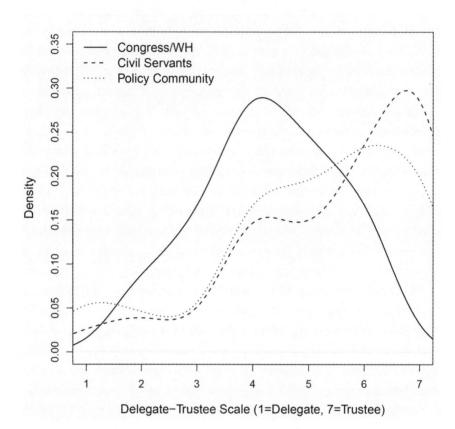

Delegate–Trustee Scale (1=Delegate, 7=Trustee)

The survey question read, "As you think about your job, where would you place yourself on a scale of delegate to trustee, where delegate represents a policymaker who acts strictly on the preferences of voters and trustee represents a policymaker who uses his or her own best judgment to decide issues?"

As we observed, however, unelected officials have a good deal of discretion and many opportunities to make policy when the president and Congress are looking elsewhere. Even when not subject to direct presidential or congressional scrutiny, unelected officials might still make it their business to identify congressional and White House priorities and develop agendas based upon those priorities. We shall return to this topic in chapter 4, where we will offer direct comparisons of legislative and bureaucratic agendas in the United States. In the meantime, though, it may be useful to observe that where bureaucrats are not compelled to follow the dictates of elected officials, the likelihood that they will endeavor to ascertain and implement congressional priorities is likely to be related to the respect that unelected officials and policy community members have for representative institutions. If bureaucrats believe, for example, that Congress, as America's national legislature, is worthy of their trust and respect, it seems reasonable to think that they would be inclined to seek and follow congressional leadership. In this way, America's unelected government might be indirectly responsive to the people. If, on the other hand, unelected officials harbor the sort of contempt for elected officials that they do for the citizenry, this avenue of responsiveness seems likely to be closed. Unfortunately, America's unelected officials manifest a considerable measure of contempt for the nation's elected leaders.

Figure 3.6 displays the extent to which government officials perceive government institutions to be trustworthy and competent. Neither Congress nor the president is viewed in a particularly positive light. Congressional and White House staffers exhibit the most faith in these institutions, though even these government officials, on average, place the House of Representatives at 2.2 on a 1–10 scale of trustworthiness, the Senate at 4.9, and the presidency at 5.5. Civil servants and members of the policy community have even less trust in these institutions. A similar pattern emerges when officials were asked to evaluate the competence of Congress and the presidency.

While the president seems to fare relatively well on this chart, this seems to be mainly an artifact of partisanship. We should recall that at the time of our survey, the White House was occupied by a Democrat. If we separate out Democratic respondents, the president's score on trustworthiness and competence falls sharply (see figure 3.7).

Given their rather jaundiced view of representative institutions, it seems unlikely that officials would voluntarily make much of an effort to carry out the will of these institutions when not compelled to do so.

Figure 3.6: Contempt for Congress and the President

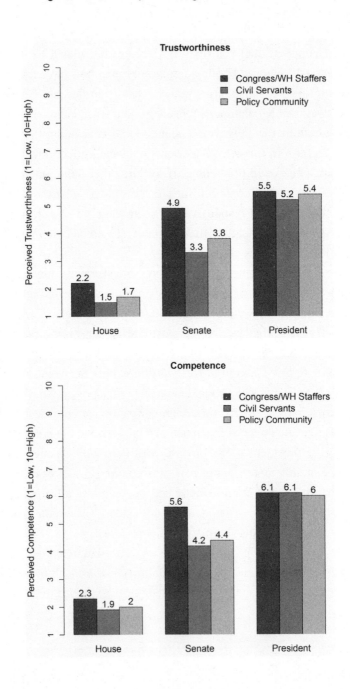

**Figure 3.7: Contempt for Congress and the President by
Partisan Identification (Government Officials Lumped Together)**

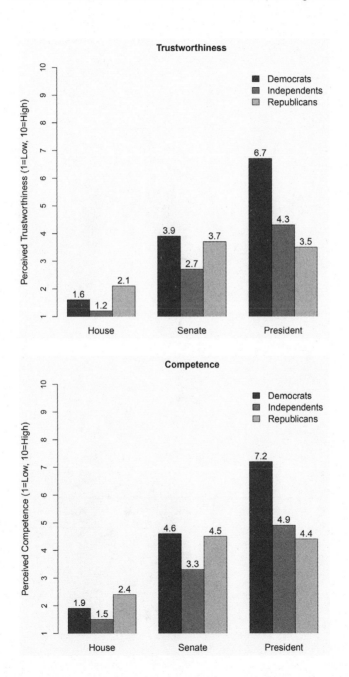

Figure 3.8: Reciprocal Confidence in Congressional Staffers, Government Agencies, and the Policy Community

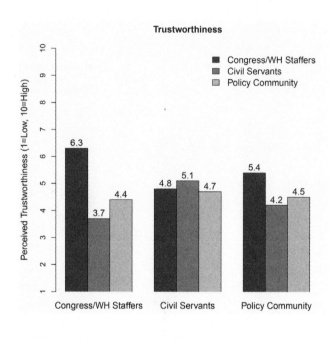

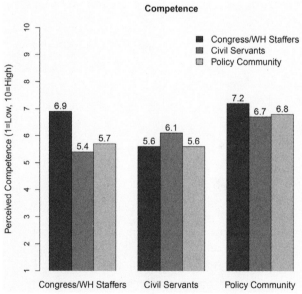

WHOM DO YOU TRUST?

Standing in sharp contrast to their lack of confidence in the citizenry and its elected representatives, public officials and members of the Washington policy community have a comparatively high degree of trust for one set of governmental actors—one another. Civil servants, staffers, and policy community members give one another far higher marks for trustworthiness and competence—nearly twice the overall average—than they assign members of Congress or the president (see figure 3.8).

Together with our earlier findings pointing to the general contempt that civil servants and policy community members exhibit toward the citizenry, these findings hardly seem consistent with our hope that the officials of a democracy will possess a conviction that it is their duty to govern for the people. If, indeed, as we have suggested, government for the people requires that officials know something about the people, possess a modicum of respect for the people, and show a measure of commitment to responsiveness to the needs and wishes of the people, America's civil servants and policy community members seem to fall short on every dimension.

CIVIC (IR)RESPONSIBILITY

Instead, taken together, officials' spotty information about the citizenry, low regard for the public, and lack of commitment to the idea of responsive government seem very consistent with Aristotle's idea of ανυπευθυνος (anupeuthunos), or civic irresponsibility. Aristotle equated irresponsible rulers with tyranny, but civically irresponsible leaders need not be harsh and malevolent. We might say they favor a form of rule closer to the Confucian model, in which scholar-officials govern according to their own lights. In their view, ordinary people should respect authority and obey. What explains this irresponsibility? First, we find that civic distance is a strong determinant of an official's perspective on the extent to which government should follow public opinion.[23] As table 3.3 shows, officials who are more civically distant from the governed are more likely to believe that the government should simply do what it thinks is best when making policy decisions.[24] The dependent variable, government responsiveness, combines responses to the variable summarized in table 3.2—the scale ranges from 9 (the government should follow public opinion in all nine policy areas) to 45 (the government should do what thinks is best in all nine policy areas). Recall that the civic distance measure (based on propensity scores) tells us the probability that an individual is a member of our group of government officials. Using the estimates presented in the table, we can determine that as this probability increases—for example, from 5 percent to about 20 percent (from the 20th percentile to the 80th percentile)—that individual moves up the scale of government nonresponsiveness 1.7 points. When this probability increases from 1 percent to 35 percent (from the 5th percentile to the 95th percentile), the individual is expected to move up the scale of government nonresponsiveness 3.2 points. It is thus clear that as one's similarity to government officials increases, one is more likely to believe that government officials should act according to their own best judgments, rather than follow public opinion, when engaging in policy making.

While civic distance is supremely important in explaining government responsiveness, it is not the only determining factor. The mentality of a government official is composed of a constellation of factors, including a trustee mentality, false uniqueness, and contempt for the American people (see figure 3.9).

Table 3.4 examines the effect of each of these factors above and beyond the effect of civic distance. The trustee mentality variable captures the extent to which a government official believes policymakers should make decisions based on their own judgments (1–7 scale). The false uniqueness variable captures the number of federal spending areas on which officials perceive a preference disagreement with the average American (1–8 scale, see figure 3.3). And finally, the contempt variable indicates the amount of knowledge officials believe the average American has about various policy areas (9–45 scale, see table 3.1). Together, the models show that each of these factors matters, even after controlling for the others. Further, the effects are statistically and substantively significant.

Table 3.3 The Effect of Civic Distance on Government Nonresponsiveness

	Government Nonresponsiveness
Civic Distance	9.50*
	(5.06)
Republican	-0.61
	(1.63)
Independent	-2.85**
	(1.20)
Conservative	3.15
	(2.01)
Moderate	-0.069
	(1.07)
Age	-0.77
	(0.57)
Constant	32.7***
	(2.27)

Increases in Civic Distance Measure

20th percentile → 80th percentile	1.71*
	(0.91)
5th percentile → 95th percentile	3.23*
	(1.72)

OLS coefficients with robust standard errors in parentheses.

*** $p < 0.01$, ** $p < 0.05$, * $p < 0.1$

Figure 3.9: Predicting Nonresponsiveness

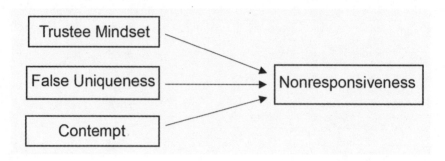

For example, the results in table 3.4 show that as a government official's contempt for the American people increases by ten points, that official's moves up the nonresponsiveness scale 2.6 points (model 1). When an official's false uniqueness increases ten points, the official moves up the nonresponsiveness scale 6.5 points (model 2). And when an official's trustee mentality increases 10 points, that official moves up the nonresponsiveness scale 11.2 points.

IRRESPONSIBLE GOVERNANCE

Perhaps for these reasons, official Washington has little interest in its nominal duty to govern for the people. To the extent that it considers the views of the people, official Washington is concerned with two concepts: "steering" and "enforcement." Steering, the topic of much discussion among scholars of governance, refers to the government's capacity to shape public opinion to serve its needs.[25] Enforcement, of course, refers to the rather delicate matter of compelling citizens to obey rules promulgated by regulatory institutions even though average Americans might find these rules difficult to understand. Take the case of a family in Virginia, fined $535 in 2011 after their young daughter, Skylar, rescued an injured woodpecker.[26] The US Fish and Wildlife Service deemed Skylar's effort to save the bird an example of the illegal transportation of a member of an endangered species in violation of rules and regulations promulgated by the agency under the Federal Migratory Bird Act. After a media outcry, the fine was rescinded, but the agency did not apologize for an enforcement effort that most Americans found ludicrous. Let us consider the questions of steering and enforcement.

Table 3.4: Additional Determinants of Government Nonresponsiveness

	Model 1	Model 2	Model 3
Trustee mentality			1.12***
			(0.31)
False uniqueness		0.65**	0.68**
		(0.31)	(0.32)
Contempt	0.26**	0.25**	0.25**
	(0.12)	(0.12)	(0.12)
Civic Distance	11.0**	10.1**	8.78*
	(4.73)	(4.81)	(5.03)
Knowledge of public opinion	0.11	0.52	0.22
	(0.37)	(0.39)	(0.41)
Knowledge of circumstances	-0.13	-0.036	-0.096
	(0.29)	(0.29)	(0.31)
Republican	-2.97**	-3.14**	-3.49**
	(1.50)	(1.48)	(1.73)
Independent	-2.64**	-2.74**	-2.30*
	(1.28)	(1.27)	(1.38)
Conservative	5.31**	5.01**	5.64**
	(2.07)	(2.05)	(2.28)
Moderate	-0.28	-0.27	-1.21
	(1.06)	(1.04)	(1.08)
Age	-0.69	-0.54	-0.72
	(0.59)	(0.60)	(0.59)
Constant	24.0***	-41.3	-46.9
	(5.33)	(31.7)	(32.2)
R-squared	0.108	0.138	0.217

OLS coefficients with robust standard errors in parentheses. *** $p < 0.01$, ** $p < 0.05$, * $p < 0.1$. The dependent variables in all three models is the extent to which officials believe the government should do what it thinks is best (rather than follow public opinion) on scale of 9–45.

Steering the Public

Despite laws prohibiting propaganda, many government agencies spend time convincing the people to think what the government believes they should think. In recent decades, government agencies have propagandized incessantly via press releases, publicity stunts, and hidden advertising to persuade the public of their conception of the public interest. One federal agency that has become notorious for staging particularly expensive and dangerous publicity stunts is the National Aeronautics and Space Administration (NASA), the government entity charged with administering America's space program. NASA is an agency whose culture was formed during the heady days when America raced against the Soviet Union to launch men into space and President John Kennedy dedicated America's resources to putting a man on the moon. That era reached its climax in 1969 with the Apollo 11 lunar landing. Since that time, political leaders have not seen space exploration as a top priority, and public interest in space has waned. Working closely with major defense contractors, NASA was able to secure funding for the construction of a small number of space shuttles, but the agency found its budgets constantly under attack and its efforts to promote interest in more ambitious exploratory programs generally thwarted. Indeed, most space scientists have urged NASA to scale back its endeavors, arguing that most of the cost and risk of NASA's program involves the difficulty of keeping human beings alive in space, while virtually all the scientific payoff could be achieved with much cheaper unmanned flights. For NASA executives, though, manned spaceflight is the agency's *raison d'etre* and issues of cost and scientific value are secondary.[27]

To stimulate support for its ongoing commitment to manned spaceflight, NASA has resorted to publicity stunts, sometimes with disastrous consequences. In 1985, the agency invited America's school teachers to compete for a spot in the space shuttle program. Agency executives reasoned that conducting a contest to send a teacher into space would generate enormous interest in the space program, particularly among millions of school children and their parents. Indeed, on the day that Christa McAuliffe, the winning teacher, was launched into space on the *Challenger* shuttle, televisions in classrooms throughout the country were tuned to the event. NASA executives were thrilled. Unfortunately, NASA's publicity stunt turned into a major public relations disaster and human tragedy when the *Challenger* exploded, killing six astronauts as well as the unfortunate teacher.

Undeterred, the agency has continued to seek ways of dramatizing its manned spaceflight program. In 1998, for example, NASA sent the aging Senator John Glenn into orbit on the *Discovery* space shuttle. Three decades earlier, Glenn had been the first American to orbit the earth and had continued from his seat in the Senate to serve as a visible champion of the space program. NASA administrators hoped that sending such a legendary figure back into space would heighten public interest in manned space flight. Criticized for spending nearly $500 million—the cost of a shuttle launch—on a publicity stunt, NASA bosses countered that the mission had a valid scientific purpose, namely to investigate the effects of space flight on aging.[28] Even if this somewhat fanciful explanation was true, it is not precisely clear why it would be useful to understand the effects of space flight on the aging process. Perhaps NASA plans to recruit a corps of senior-citizen astronauts or, alternatively, the agency may have a secret plan to expand its revenue base by constructing retirement villages on Mars.

Nothing seems too bizarre for the fertile imaginations of NASA publicists. NASA publicity has been sufficiently effective that even after another space shuttle explosion, killing seven astronauts in 2003, most Americans continued to support the space program. Asked by Gallup in 2003, in the aftermath of the *Columbia* disaster, which killed all seven crew members, whether the shuttle program should go forward, 82 percent of Americans said yes.[29] In the same survey, only 20 percent said too much money was being spent on the space program. Despite the disaster, 82 percent thought NASA was doing an excellent or at least a good job.

Fortunately, not all agencies are prone to sponsoring dangerous publicity stunts. Most use more mundane mechanisms of manipulation. Each year, federal agencies send out thousands of press releases designed to be published as news stories. For one example, an April 2005 article, sent to thousands of newspapers by the Associated Press, was headlined "Fed Unveils Financial Education Website."[30] Written by a public relations staffer pretending to be an AP reporter, the article discussed the various ways in which a new site developed by the Federal Reserve could help consumers make informed decisions. The article did not mention that it was basically a slight revision of a press release that could be found on the Fed's website. Journalists are certainly aware of the fact that the authors of press releases have their own agendas and are hardly unbiased reporters of the news. Nevertheless, the economics of publishing and broadcasting dictate that large numbers of stories will always be based upon such releases. Newspapers and television stations are businesses and, for many, the financial bottom line is more important than journalistic integrity. The use of press releases allows a newspaper or broadcast network to present more stories without requiring them to pay more staff or incur the other costs associated with investigating and writing the news. As one newspaper executive said, the public relations people who generally write news releases are our "unpaid reporters."[31]

In recent years, the simple printed press release has been joined by the "video news release," designed especially for television stations. The video release is a taped report, usually about ninety seconds long, the typical length of a television news story, designed to look and sound like any other broadcast news segment. In exchange for airing material that serves the interests of some advocate, the television station airing the video release is relieved of the considerable expense and bother of identifying and filming its own news story. The audience is usually unaware that the "news" it is watching is actually someone's canned publicity footage.

One recent example of a video news release was a pair of ninety second segments funded by the US Department of Health and Human Services (HHS) in 2004. After Congress enacted legislation adding a prescription drug benefit to the Medicare program, HHS sent a video release designed to look like a news report to local TV stations around the nation. Forty television stations aired the report without indicating that it came from the government. The segment is introduced by the local news anchor, reading from a government-suggested script. The anchor reads, "Reporter Karen Ryan helps sort through the details," of the new Medicare law. Then, against the backdrop of film showing President Bush signing the law and the reactions of apparently grateful senior citizens, an unseen narrator, speaking like a reporter, presents the new law in a positive light: "The new law, say officials, will simply offer people with Medicare more ways to make their health coverage more affordable." The segment concludes with the signoff, "In Washington, I'm Karen Ryan reporting." Viewers are not told that the entire "news" story was distributed by the government. Nor are viewers informed that Karen Ryan is not a reporter at all. She was an employee of the ad agency hired by the government to create the video release.[32] In response to criticism, an HHS spokesperson pointed out that the same sort of video news release had often been used by the Clinton administration and was commonly used by a number of firms and interest groups. "The use of video news releases is a common, routine practice in government and the private sector," he said. "Anyone who has questions about this practice needs to do some research on modern public information tools."[33]

HHS is hardly the only federal agency to distribute video news releases disguised as news stories. A frequently viewed news story about the Transportation Security Administration (TSA) and its efforts to strengthen aviation security was produced by TSA, and the "reporter" presenting the story was a public relations professional working for TSA under a false name. Similarly, a recent story about the US Department of Agriculture's efforts to open foreign markets for American farmers was actually a video news release, using an actor, produced by the Agriculture Department's office of communication.[34]

A report published in the *New York Times* indicated that at least twenty federal agencies ranging from the Department of Defense to the Census Bureau regularly have distributed hundreds of television news releases to local stations that aired them without any indication to viewers that what they were watching was government propaganda, not news. A Government Accountability Office (GAO) report, indeed, charged the HHS with violating laws prohibiting federal agencies from broadcasting propaganda aimed at Americans. HHS dismissed the report and continued its activities.[35]

From creating phony reporters to read make-believe news stories, it is but a small step to hiring real reporters to present sham accounts. This step has been taken quite frequently by some government agencies working abroad and at home. A number of cases have come to light in recent years in which the government has paid journalists to write favorable accounts of their activities and efforts. This is a common American practice when dealing with the foreign press. For example, in 2005, the US military acknowledged that contractors in its employ had regularly paid Iraqi newspapers to carry positive news about American efforts in that nation. The Washington-based Lincoln Group, a public relations firm working under contract to the federal government, says it placed more than one thousand news stories in the Iraqi and Arab press over the previous four years.[36] Iraqis reading the articles would have had no way to know that the material being presented to them was produced at the behest of the American authorities.

In a similar vein, the US military and the US Agency for International Development (USAID) operate or subsidize radio stations and newspapers in Afghanistan, staffed by local journalists who write or broadcast in local dialects. Every effort is made to maintain the impression that these media outlets are autonomous, Afghan-owned organizations with no connection to the United States. One USAID representative explained, "We want to maintain the perception that these [media] are in fact fully independent."[37] Needless to say, the US-controlled media paint a rosy picture of American efforts in Afghanistan. Apparently, there is no bad news emanating from that impoverished and war-torn country. "We have no requirements to adhere to journalistic standards of objectivity," said a US army spokesperson.[38]

The government's practice of hiring journalists, though, is not limited to operations abroad. In recent years, federal agencies have paid several journalists and commentators to report favorably on government initiatives and programs in the United States. The Department of Education, for example, paid commentator Armstrong Williams $241,000 to promote President Bush's No Child Left Behind law. Williams wrote favorably about the law in his newspaper column, commented positively about it during his cable television appearances, and urged other commentators to interview Education Secretary Roderick Paige.[39] Williams did not disclose his financial relationship with the agency whose programs he was touting. In a similar vein, the Department of Health and Human Services paid syndicated columnist Maggie Gallagher $20,000 to promote the administration's views on marriage. Gallagher wrote several columns on the topic without revealing her financial relationship with the agency.[40] In 2003, the Agriculture Department paid a writer to produce articles describing the benefits of the agency's Natural Resources Conversion Service programs. The articles appeared in a number of magazines aimed at hunting and fishing enthusiasts, with no indication that they had been produced by a government agency.[41]

Many of these federal agency activities, as the GAO has noted, were legally questionable. In 2013, however, the legal status of government propaganda was strengthened with the repeal of portions of the Smith-Mundt Act (1948) that had long prohibited government-made propaganda designed for foreign audiences from being disseminated within the United States. The new legislation applies specifically to State Department materials but is likely to be cited by other agencies as a legal basis for their own domestic propaganda efforts.

In 2014, information obtained from documents revealed by former NSA contractor Edward Snowden, suggested that government agencies were studying ways to use YouTube, Twitter, Facebook, and other social media as covert platforms for propaganda.[42] Reportedly, the British government has already taken steps in this direction and US agencies are attempting to learn the methods developed by Britain to exploit social media to disseminate ideas and viewpoints. In 2011, Britain's *Guardian* published an account alleging that the US Defense Department had contracted with a California firm to develop "sock puppet" software that would allow operators to establish a large number of false online identities to influence online conversations.[43]

The use of social media by federal agencies to "steer" public sentiment has become so commonplace that agencies hardly seek to hide their efforts. Take the Department of Health and Human Services (HHS). Numerous offices within HHS employ Facebook, Twitter, and other social media to disseminate information and opinion promoting the agency's activities. On a blog called *The Commissioner's Voice*, child support professionals and other stakeholders can learn the views of the Office of Child Support Enforcement. On YouTube, Americans can learn of the achievements of the Family and Youth Services Bureau. Via Twitter, Americans can be informed of the most recent ideas developed by the Administration for Children and Families. Via Facebook, the Centers for Disease Control attempt to influence the ways in which parents should approach their teens' driving behavior.

Today, every federal agency blogs, tweets, posts, and so forth to shape public opinion. Perhaps no single tweet is a menace to liberty. Many indeed are quite banal. But Americans are now subjected to tens of thousands of electronic nudges, resulting in more and more steering every year, much of it below the radar of the traditional media. The traditional media remain more or less on guard against efforts by the government to use them for propaganda purposes. As noted above, financial considerations led the traditional media to allow themselves to be used for propaganda via news release. Occasionally, though, the traditional media could be vigilant. Their content was filtered by reporters and editors who sometimes objected to being used as propaganda instruments. The social media, on the other hand, disseminate whatever material is uploaded to them—a perfect platform from which to steer opinion.

Regulatory Enforcement

Though pervasive, steering may not always be enough. Enforcement, particularly regulatory enforcement, has become a topic of considerable concern in Washington, with a number of officials and scholars arguing that "customer friendly" (read citizen-centered) models of government are inadequate to the problems actually faced by government agencies in dealing with citizens. One scholar, Malcolm Sparrow, writes, "The popular prescriptions for [government] reform focus on service, customers, quality, and process improvement."[44] But what is needed, according to Sparrow, is a better arsenal of "methods for securing compliance."

Why is compliance a problem? One reason is that the official view of the world is inconsistent with citizens' view of the world, leading to rules that make no sense to ordinary Americans. An example cited by journalist Philip K. Howard is, unfortunately, not unusual. In 2011, according to Howard, a tree fell into a creek during a winter storm in Franklin County,

New Jersey, causing flooding. The town was unable to do the obvious, dispatch a tractor to remove the tree, because the creek in question was a "Class C-1 creek" and, according to federal regulations, required federal permits before any natural condition could be altered. The flooding continued for twelve days, causing considerable damage to surrounding homes, before town officials were able to obtain the necessary permit.[45]

The point here is that the regulation in question was so inconsistent with the life experiences of ordinary Americans that it might as well have been formulated by officials on another planet. It is suggestive of the enormous civic distance between inside-the-Beltway officials and ordinary Americans and illustrates why compliance is an increasing problem, with a growing number of Americans paying fines and even serving prison terms for "regulatory offenses." About ten percent of those currently serving time in federal prison were convicted of regulatory offenses—twice as many as are currently incarcerated in federal penal institutions for crimes of violence.[46]

When the government's actions are divorced from the views of citizens, enforcement can become a problem. People are less likely to obey the law if they don't understand or believe in it. Federal rules and regulations have become exceedingly complex and divorced not only from the public's priorities but also from shared understandings of what constitutes good and bad behavior.

According to former US Attorney General Dick Thornburgh's testimony before Congress, in recent years federal agencies have created more than 300,000 regulatory offenses.[47] These rules are important not only for their number but also for their jurisprudential character. A number of these regulations, and sometimes even their statutory bases, differ in a very important respect from traditional American criminal statutes. In particular, many lack or have only weak *mens rea* requirements, freeing prosecutors from the obligation to prove criminal intent when they charge an individual with violating the law. *Mens rea* is, of course, one of the fundamental principles of English and American criminal law. In its most general sense, the standard of *mens rea* requires prosecutors to show that an individual charged with violating the law intentionally committed an act that a reasonable person would have known to constitute a violation of the law. The principle of *mens rea* seeks to distinguish between those who willfully commit a criminal act and those who, for example, harm another individual without malice or intent, perhaps by accident. While the latter might be sued in civil court, they would not be subject to criminal prosecution and possible imprisonment.

Unfortunately, many of the federal regulations promulgated in recent years require no showing of intent and allow individuals to be subjected to criminal prosecution and imprisonment for what most Americans would see as innocent conduct. The rationale for such laws, some of whose forebears can be found in the Progressive and New Deal Eras, is said to be to establish a regulatory scheme rather than to affix blame. Indeed, the crimes defined by these rules are sometimes called regulatory or public welfare offenses to distinguish them from more traditional criminal legislation. It is, however, probably no consolation to the individuals convicted of these offenses that the question of whether or not they are personally blameworthy is of little consequence to the government.

Take the recent and well-publicized case of Eddie Anderson, a sixty-eight-year-old former science teacher from Idaho. Anderson, who enjoyed collecting Indian arrowheads, was arrested by federal agents and charged with violating the 1979 Archaeological Resources Protection Act. Anderson and his son had been digging for arrowheads near a favorite campsite in Idaho's Salmon River Canyon, on land managed by the US Bureau of Land Management. The two men were unaware of the fact that removing arrowheads found on federal land was a felony punishable by up to two years in prison. Nevertheless, under the act and the rules written to implement it, no knowledge or intent is required for a conviction, and the Andersons were each sentenced to one year's probation and $1,500 penalties.[48]

In a similar vein, retired race car champion Bobby Unser inadvertently drove his snowmobile onto federal land when he became lost in a snowstorm in 1996.[49] When he asked authorities for help, Unser was charged with violating the Wilderness Act, which prohibits driving snowmobiles onto protected federal land. Unser was convicted of a misdemeanor and fined $75. To cite still another case, in 2007, a District of Columbia retirement home janitor, Lawrence Lewis, was sentenced to one year's probation for temporarily diverting a backed-up sewer line into an outside storm drain so it would not flood an area where sick and elderly patients were housed. Unfortunately, the drain emptied into a creek that ultimately emptied into the Potomac River. Lewis was charged with violating the Clean Water Act.[50]

Or take the notorious case of an elderly Florida man sentenced to seventeen months in federal prison for violating regulations under the Convention on International Trade of Endangered Species. What had the then-sixty-five-year-old Mr. Norris done? It seems that he was an orchid collector and sometimes ordered orchids from Latin America. These orchids often came with confusing paperwork that failed to properly identify every orchid in the container. After a federal agent posing as a fellow hobbyist ordered orchids from Norris, he was arrested and charged with being the "kingpin" of an international smuggling ring. Norris pled guilty after he could no longer afford his legal bills.[51]

These cases may seem relatively minor, but they illustrate an important point. As law professor John Baker points out, the absence of a *mens rea* requirement in regulations implementing such laws as the Wilderness Act and the Archaeological Resources Protection Act is especially troublesome because the conduct outlawed by these regulations and statutes could be classified as *malum prohibitum*, or wrong only because it is prohibited, rather than *malum in se*, acts that are wrong in themselves, such as murder or theft. For *malum prohibitum* crimes, as Baker argues, *mens rea* requirements, as well as notice, are especially important sources of protection for individuals against being prosecuted for accidental acts that they could not necessarily or even reasonably be expected to know were crimes.[52] As attorneys warn, today even those with the most innocent intentions can become ensnared in legal complexities.

Already, the erosion of *mens rea* requirements has even opened the way for individuals to be prosecuted for acts they did not actually commit. Take the case of *United States v. Hanousek*, decided by the Federal Court of Appeals for the Ninth Circuit in 1999. Edward Hanousek was employed by the Pacific & Arctic Railway and Navigation Company, a sister company of Pacific & Arctic Pipeline, Inc., as "roadmaster" of the White Pass and Yukon Railroad running from Alaska to the Yukon Territory, Canada. Among Hanousek's responsibilities was supervision of a rock-quarrying project at a site known as "6-mile," where a high-pressure oil pipeline ran parallel and adjacent to the railroad's tracks. A contractor employed by Pacific & Arctic was blasting rock at 6-mile and loading it onto rail cars for transport. On the night of October 1, 1994, at home after work, an employee of the rock-blasting contractor noticed that some rocks had fallen off a transport train and onto the railroad tracks.[53] The employee found a backhoe, drove it some fifty to one hundred yards, and began to push the rocks off the track. While so doing, he accidentally punctured the pipeline, allowing some one thousand to five thousand gallons of oil to spill into the nearby Skagway River.

After investigating the spill, the US Coast Guard, responsible for enforcing the Clean Water Act (CWA), charged Hanousek, the project supervisor, with "negligently discharging a harmful quantity of oil into a navigable water of the United States" in violation of the act.[54] Under the rules implementing the CWA, which do not include a *mens rea* provision, the government need not show criminal intent. As project supervisor, Hanousek was deemed by the government to be responsible for the accidental spill. After a short trial, he was convicted and sentenced to six months of imprisonment, six months in a halfway house, and six months of supervised release, as well as a fine of $5,000. No doubt, during his period of incarceration, Hanousek was cheered by the knowledge that his personal guilt or innocence was less important than the contribution his conviction made to maintaining the integrity of an important federal regulatory scheme.

Again, the fundamental problem is that government officials writing rules inconsistent with the life experiences and understandings of ordinary Americans find compliance a problem and resort to harsh measures. Aristotle would have understood this to be an inevitable consequence of μηδεν κοινον (*meden koinon*, lack of commonality between rulers and ruled).

We should note that in addition to steering and enforcement a third idea is gaining prominence in official Washington. This is a concept that

Harvard Law School professor and former Office of Information and Regulatory Affairs (OIRA) head Cass Sunstein has called "nudging."[55] Rather than seek to change citizens' opinions or punish them for failing to comply with official directives, Sunstein advocates what he sees as the more benign approach of arranging citizens' alternatives so that they make the officially desired choice seemingly of their own accord. An example might be a "nudge" toward organ donation by making such a donation the default option on drivers' license applications. The Obama administration briefly experimented with nudging by creating a White House Social and Behavioral Science Team to develop effective nudges. Sunstein sees nudging as an appropriate form of official paternalism. As the political philosopher Jeremy Waldron, has observed, however, nudging is an idea that envisions an elite that knows the truth and can promulgate simple rules that will secure the obedience of ordinary people.[56] Waldron rightly questions whether a nudge is morally much different from a shove.

STAFFERS, JACKSONIANS, AND MANDARINS

Among America's unelected rulers, not all have a jaundiced view of the citizenry and its role in governance. A small fraction possesses a reasonable level of knowledge about the American people and popular opinions and has some measure of respect for citizens' judgments. We find that, across all government officials, 8.7 percent correctly answered thirteen or more questions about the circumstances or opinions of Americans (out of sixteen).[57] Prominent within this group are congressional and White House staffers—these officials scored slightly higher, on average, on the combined knowledge scale (10 versus 9.7 for the civil servants and 9.6 for the members of the policy community).

The staffers, as we saw in chapter 2 are civically less distant from ordinary Americans than are the other groups in our sample, sharing a fair measure of demographic, experiential, partisan, and ideological affinity with average citizens. This lack of civic distance is reinforced by the fact that staffers have far more interaction with members of the public than do the civil servants or policy community members in our survey. Figure 3.10 shows that congressional staffers interact with the public and receive feedback from the public far more than the other two categories of officials. With respect to both interacting with the public and receiving feedback from the public, the differences between the congressional staffers and the other two categories of officials are statistically significant, meaning they are unlikely to be the results of chance.

Figure 3.10: Officials' Interaction and Feedback Loop with the Public

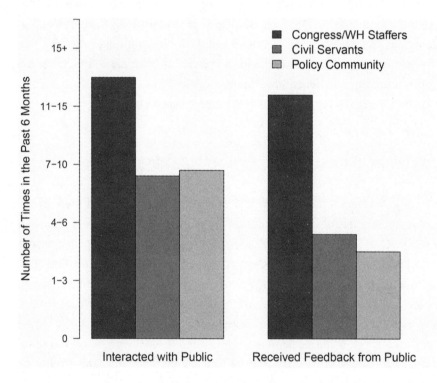

As a result of their civic closeness and interaction, staffers (as we saw in figure 3.5 above) are more likely than others to perceive themselves as the public's delegates, subject to the will of the people, rather than claim to be trustees who govern as they see fit. This perception is reinforced experientially. Staffers are, albeit indirectly, subject to the electoral process and, like the elected officials for whom they work, compelled to pay at least a modicum of attention to the citizenry. Indeed, staffers—unlike others in our sample—report that the public actually influences their decision making (see figure 3.11).

Figure 3.11: Public Influence on Officials' Decision Making

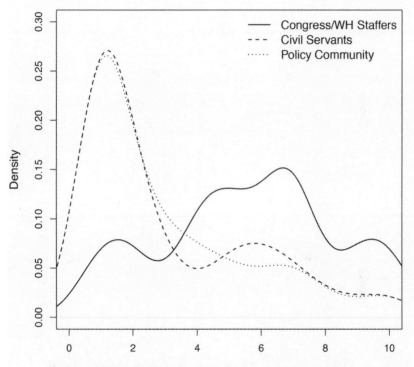

Extent to Which Public Influences Decisionmaking (1=Never, 10=A lot)

The staffers and a handful of others are, in a sense, the last remnants of Jacksonian democracy. They are appointed officials not so different from their fellow Americans, compelled regularly to interact with the public, and subject to the vicissitudes of popular politics. This Jacksonian remnant, however, appears lost in a sea of neo-mandarin officials, consultants, and contractors determined to govern as they see fit.

Chapter 4

WHAT THE GOVERNMENT DOES VERSUS WHAT THE PEOPLE WANT

The civic distance between citizens and public officials, as well as those selfsame officials' lack of civic responsibility, has important implications for governance. Can officials with, at best, a weak sense of civic responsibility govern "for the people" as democratic government requires? As we observed in chapter 1, much of "the law" at the federal level is written by administrative agencies acting outside the glare of publicity and with limited interference from Congress, the White House, or the courts. Most Americans are hardly aware of the activities of these agencies.

As we have noted, the rules and regulations promulgated by various federal bodies have an enormous impact on many aspects of American life, from food safety to air quality to the chance that a consumer will be able to obtain a mortgage. As we shall see, there seems to be little relationship between governmental and popular priorities in the United States. The executive branch seems, indeed, to march to its own drummer. But to understand the federal government's rhythms we must begin with a brief overview of the somewhat arcane processes through which federal agencies make rules.

Every high school student learns how Congress makes a law, but how many know how a law is actually implemented or that the laws enacted by Congress have little substance until federal agencies write the rules that give them effect? Take, for example, the Food Safety Modernization Act, written by Congress and signed into law by President Obama in 2010. Four years later, the act still had not been implemented because the Food and Drug Administration (FDA), charged with administering its provisions, had not yet finished writing the necessary rules and regulations that would give actual substance to the legislation conceived by Congress.

Americans are often chided by the media and by academics for their lack of knowledge of current public issues and priorities. Many of the issues considered and policies promulgated by government agencies, however, are not only unknown to the public, they are also far below the radar of media and academic scrutiny. Each year, government agencies issue thousands of rules and regulations that have the force of law, along with orders, advisories, guidelines, and policy circulars that are fully enforceable by the courts. This mass of government edicts seldom receives much attention outside the small circle of stakeholders who are in continual and close consultation with rulemaking agencies. Perhaps not surprisingly, national public opinion surveys do not even ask Americans their views on such topics as transportation or public land policy, even though the Department of Transportation and the Bureau of Land Management enact hundreds of rules and regulations each year. Instead, when querying citizens about their policy positions, surveys focus largely on social welfare issues such as healthcare, education, and poverty. While these are certainly important issues, they leave aside many critical policy realms that affect Americans' day-to-day lives.

Who outside a narrow segment of the investment community was aware of the debate surrounding a new rule adopted by the Commodity Futures Trading Commission (CFTC) in 2012 titled "Business Conduct Standards for Swap Dealers and Major Swap Participants with Counterparties?"[1] Similarly, who outside the trucking and agriculture industries was aware of the controversy over another 2012 rule, adopted by the Environmental Protection Agency (EPA), titled "Regulation of Fuels and Fuel Additives: 2013 Biomass-Based Diesel Renewable Fuel Volume?"[2]

As it happens, these two rules promise to have a large impact on the American economy. The CFTC's new rule, part of the lengthy and complex process of implementing the 2010 Dodd-Frank Act, imposes new standards for the "swaps" market, an over-the-counter market in which various financial instruments are traded by investors, usually as means of hedging risks. The new rules, many of which were not specifically required by Dodd-Frank, establish antifraud, disclosure, and other standards for swaps dealers. The estimated annual cost to investors of compliance with the rules is approximately $10 billion. The new EPA rule, for its part, sets standards for the use of biomass-based diesel fuel used mainly by trucks and by farmers. The cost to these groups of implementing the new standards is estimated at $1 billion initially and, perhaps, $288 million per year thereafter.

According to one study, 131 major (generally defined as having a likely impact of $100 million or more) rules and regulations adopted by federal agencies between 2009 and 2012 imposed $70 billion in new costs on the American public.[3] The various federal agencies writing these rules, on the other hand, assert that these costs were more than offset by the benefits derived by Americans from the rules in question.[4] Agencies are required by executive order to produce cost-benefit analyses of major new rules and, under the 2000 Right-to-Know Act, the Office of Management and Budget (OMB) is required to submit an annual report to Congress summarizing the agencies' findings. Since many benefits are nonpecuniary, such as, for example, protection of homeland security, agencies are often creative in their accounting practices, giving a dollar value to presumptive benefits to justify actual costs. Or, as OMB puts it politely, "Some rules produce benefits that cannot be adequately captured in monetary equivalents. In fulfilling their statutory mandates, agencies must sometimes act in the face of substantial uncertainty about the likely consequences."[5]

Thus, while these rules and regulations written by federal agencies usually do not capture the attention of the public or even the news media, they can have a substantial impact. They produce costs that are ultimately paid by the public in the form of higher prices and taxes, as well as benefits that may include safer products, cleaner air and water, a safer transportation system, and so forth. Occasionally, of course, a proposed rule comes to the general public's attention. In June 2014, at President Obama's behest, the EPA proposed new rules that would require coal-fired power plants to sharply reduce carbon dioxide emissions. The standards threatened to increase the costs of energy produced from coal and led to howls of protest from coal producers and from politicians in states dependent upon coal as an energy source. The federal courts entered the fray after energy producers charged that the EPA had not followed proper procedures in developing the new standards. Typically, however, debates over the costs and benefits of proposed rules take place in obscure buildings in Washington and involve small groups of bureaucrats, interest group "stakeholders," and congressional staffers, and do not come to the attention of the news media or the more general public.

In this chapter, we will examine the origins of rules and regulations, how agencies establish priorities, the formal and informal procedures that affect the promulgation of new rules, and, finally, the relationship between rulemaking and popular priorities. While agency rulemaking may seem an arcane topic, it is so central to the governance of the United States that without some appreciation of this topic it is difficult to understand how the nation is actually governed. And, without assessing the relationship between rulemaking and popular preferences, it is hard to say whether the government is actually influenced by the will of the people.

THE ELEMENTS OF FEDERAL RULEMAKING

To begin with, some rules are written directly in response to, or at the behest of, Congress. In the most obvious case, when Congress enacts a piece of legislation, one or more executive agencies must write rules and regulations to flesh out and implement the statute. Complex pieces of legislation, such as the 2010 Affordable Care Act (Obamacare), give agencies warrant to develop a large number of new rules.

Congress generally pays a great deal of attention to agency rulemaking when it comes to new legislation, sometimes giving agencies very precise directions and timetables and occasionally reviewing agency efforts. Congress has also adopted the use of *deadlines* and *hammers* embedded in legislation to compel agencies to expedite rulemaking. Political scientists Cornelius Kerwin and Scott Furlong point to the example of the Resource Conservation and Recovery Act of 1976, which contained a hammer mandating a total ban on land disposal of wastes, a disastrous outcome, if the EPA failed to develop rules that articulated an alternative policy.[6] In this way, Congress sought to force timely agency action.

The White House is also likely to become involved in the shaping of rules for new programs, especially if these are part of the president's policy agenda. Since the Clinton administration, the Office of Information and Regulatory Affairs (OIRA), an entity within OMB, has been tasked by the White House with sending the agencies regulatory directives aimed at bringing about the development of rules and regulations to promote the president's priorities. The agencies do not always fully comply with these directives and, in the case of independent commissions, view presidential directives as advisory rather than mandatory. Thus, in 2014, when President Obama asked the Federal Communications Commission (FCC) to develop a set of new rules to provide for "net neutrality" on the Internet, thus opening the Internet to all content, no matter the source, the agency chair indicated that the FCC was "moving in a different direction."[7] Only after a sharp skirmish with the White House did the agency accept most of the president's proposals.

More than 80 percent of the new rules promulgated in a typical year, however, involve existing rather than new programs.[8] Congress and the president certainly can become involved in this arena of rulemaking.[9] Major new rules are reviewed by the OMB and by the GAO. However, the rulemaking agenda for existing programs, which includes statutes that have been in place for years or even decades, is largely based upon the views and priorities of the agencies themselves.[10] Congress is only occasionally likely to become involved, and then only if some important constituency interest makes a loud complaint.[11] Political scientists Mathew McCubbins and Thomas Schwartz have referred to this congressional practice as "fire alarm" oversight.[12]

ESTABLISHING PRIORITIES

Agencies employ a variety of criteria to determine their rulemaking priorities for established programs. Large numbers of requests for interpretations and exemptions, for example, may serve as a cue to agency officials that some rule revision is needed.[13] According to political scientists William West and Connor Raso, agencies take into account such factors as economic and technological changes, changes in the business environment, and experience acquired during the implementation of existing rules.[14] A number of agencies have priority-setting systems and teams tasked with the responsibility of reviewing the effectiveness of existing agency programs and recommending new courses of action.[15] In this way, agency priorities are, in considerable measure, the result of internal perspectives and decisions.

At the same time, of course, the officials of most agencies are usually in regular contact with the groups and interests—the stakeholders—active in their own policy domains. These consultations play a significant role in shaping agency rulemaking agendas. West and Raso observe that agency officials and stakeholders, generally from the business community, are in constant touch via informal communications, conferences, and meetings of trade associations. Also important is the so-called revolving door of personnel exchange between bureaucracies and (usually corporate) stakeholders.[16] When it comes to setting the agenda for new rules and regulations affecting existing laws, bureaucrats and stakeholders are, "often impossible to separate."[17] To some extent, contacts between agencies and stakeholders are desirable if agencies are to fully understand the impact of the rules and regulations they promulgate. However, the general picture that emerges from academic and press accounts is one in which rules and regulations are developed by an inside-the-Beltway crowd of agency executives and stakeholders who regularly exchange jobs with one another.[18] This pattern is sometimes called "round up the usual suspects" rulemaking.

In 2014, for example, a *New York Times* investigation revealed that a set of carbon pollution rules put forward by the Environmental Protection Agency (EPA) had actually been drafted by an environmental group, the Natural Resources Defense Council (NRDC), working closely with agency officials. The EPA denied the accuracy of the *Times* story but was slow to respond to congressional demands for documents and transcripts of communications between agency executives and the NRDC. The NRDC, for its part, denied any impropriety and accused critics of seeking to divert attention from important environmental policy questions.[19]

Once an agency has developed a proposed rule, or even during the process of development, it is required by Executive Order 12866, issued by President Clinton, to inform OIRA of significant new proposals. In some instances, agencies are required by statute to inform the Council on Environmental Quality and the Small Business Administration. Rules made under some statutes require agencies to publish an advance notice of proposed rulemaking (ANPRM). Agencies may also consult with Congress via the Government Accountability Office (GAO). The OMB has the authority to return proposed rules to the agency if they are deemed not to comport with the president's program or if the agency has not produced an adequate cost-benefit analysis of the impact of its proposal. In some limited instances, delineated by the 1990 Negotiated Rulemaking Act, agencies are required to convene assemblies of representatives of affected interests to negotiate new rules.

After these reviews, the Administrative Procedure Act (APA) of 1946 requires agencies to post proposed rules and regulations in the *Federal Register* for public comment. So-called notice-and-comment rulemaking is the hallmark of the system created by the APA. The notice posted in the *Federal Register* generally includes the language of the proposed rule and an invitation to any interested persons to post comments on the rule within some specified period of time. During this time frame, individuals and groups may send the agency their written comments on the proposed rule. The agency is required to review and catalogue whatever comments it receives.

Despite the requirements of the APA, the GAO has found that agencies often publish final rules without prior notice.[20] Agencies can do so if they are able to affirm that a proposed rule falls into one or another category exempt from APA procedures. Some classes of rules administered by the EPA, the Department of Agriculture, the FAA, and several other agencies are exempt from APA oversight because they apply to emergency situations. Rules dealing with military and foreign affairs are exempt. Interpretive rules and general statements of policy are exempt. The purpose of the interpretive rule exemption is to "allow agencies to explain ambiguous terms in legislative enactments without having to undertake cumbersome proceedings," while the policy statement exemption is designed "to allow agencies to announce their tentative intentions for the future."[21] The reasons for these exemptions may be appropriate in principle, but in practice courts have found it difficult to distinguish between rules and policy statements, and agencies have been able to use policy statements to establish rules without notice and comment.[22]

One rather vague and large category of exemption is available if an agency finds and attaches to the final rule a statement that notice and comment was impractical, unnecessary, or contrary to the public interest. Such a "good cause" finding is unlikely to occur in the case of new and highly publicized programs. However, where agencies are revising rules for long-established laws and believe that a rule is unlikely to attract much attention outside their established communities of stakeholders, they are as likely as not to simply publish the final rule without inviting comment. Since 9-11, agencies have increasingly invoked good cause as a reason not to seek notice and comment if a rule can somehow be justified by the threat of terrorism. The federal judiciary has been reluctant to question agency assertions.[23]

Agencies also make use of a variety of other subterfuges to avoid giving prior notice of rules. The APA requires that proposed "rules" be posted for comment. The act says nothing about other forms of agency orders, such as policy circulars, technical corrections, advisories, and so forth. These forms of agency orders also have legal standing but are not subject to prior notice. The difference between a rule and an order, as defined by the APA, is essentially a question of an agency pronouncement's general applicability. A rule is a statement of general policy while an order pertains to a particular instance.

This is another difference that may seem clear in theory but is often obscure in practice. Agencies frequently employ various sorts of orders to assert general principles precisely because so doing allows them to avoid the APA. The US Supreme Court has ruled that agencies have "informed discretion" in choosing whether to announce a new policy in the form of a rule or an order.[24] And, while orders, unlike rules, do not have the full force and effect of law, the Supreme Court has ruled that orders must be given deference by courts in weighing the validity of agency actions because orders "constitute a body of experience and informed judgement to which courts and litigants may properly resort for guidance."[25]

When agencies do publish proposed rules and solicit comments, written suggestions and criticisms can have some impact.[26] Not surprisingly, the largest number of responses comes from business and trade groups.[27] Changes from rules' proposed to final form resulting from such comments are, however, generally minor. William West, for example, found that informal communications between agencies and interest groups as rules were being developed were much more important than communications received by agencies during the comment period. The latter had an only marginal impact upon the final rules promulgated by federal agencies.[28] In a very small number of statutes, such as that of the Fair Packaging and Labeling Act (1967), Congress has required that agencies hold formal public hearings prior to the promulgation of a new rule. Formal rulemaking, as it is called, is cumbersome and rarely used.

In most cases, after the conclusion of the comment period, agencies are required to publish the final form of a new rule in the *Federal Register* for a period of thirty days, to allow affected interests an opportunity to come into compliance with the revised law. Under the provisions of the 1996 Congressional Review Act (CRA), enacted as part of the Small Business Regulatory Enforcement Fairness Act, all new final rules must be submitted for review to both houses of Congress and to the GAO. If the OMB has previously determined that the rule is "major" in terms of its potential economic impact, it cannot take effect for at least sixty days, nominally giving Congress time to disallow the rule if it wishes to do so. By 2011, the GAO had reviewed 1,029 major rules, and 72 joint resolutions of disapproval were introduced relating to 49 rules.[29] In only one case was a joint resolution of disapproval actually adopted and signed by the president. This involved an OSHA ergonomics standard enacted in the final month of the Clinton administration. The newly elected Republican Congress lost no time in disallowing the rule and President Bush was only too happy to sign the resolution.[30]

What might we conclude from this brief overview of federal rulemaking? Particularly when it comes to writing or revising rules for the implementation of established statutes, agencies have a good deal of discretion. They certainly do not possess utter autonomy. Indeed, there are numerous checks in the rulemaking process designed to ensure a measure of agency accountability to Congress, the White House, and at least some constituency interests before a rule can be adopted and officially entered into the *Code of Federal Regulations*. As noted above, major rules are referred to the OMB for review of their conformity with the president's objectives and for assessment of the agencies' cost-benefit analyses. The impact of the OMB review through OIRA has varied from administration to administration but has not been negligible.

Agencies must also demonstrate compliance with a variety of statutory obligations, generally involving the analysis and public dissemination of data relevant to their regulatory efforts. For example, the 1969 National Environmental Policy Act (NEPA) requires agencies to assess whether a proposed rule is likely to have a significant impact upon the environment. If not, the agency must issue a "no significant impact finding." If yes, the agency must prepare an environmental impact statement for the OMB, describing the steps the agency will take to mitigate potential environmental damage.[31] Similarly, the 1976 Toxic Substances Control Act (TCA) requires the EPA to conduct assessments of the threats posed by various toxic substances in the environment as compared to the technical possibility and financial cost of proposed reductions of these threats. Such risk assessment must be reported in justification of proposed rules. The 1980 Regulatory Flexibility Act requires agencies to consider the impact of proposed rules on small businesses, assess potential alternatives that reduce the effects of such rules on small businesses, and make their analyses public.[32] The 1992 Unfunded Mandates Reform Act requires agencies to show that they have assessed the impact of proposed rules on state, local, and tribal entities and to prepare a regulatory impact analysis for such rules. The 2000 Data for Information Quality Act requires agencies to develop policies to ensure that the information they collect and utilize meets high standards in terms of quality and objectivity. The act allows private parties to petition agencies to correct what they believe to be errors in their information.[33] Several executive orders require agencies to assess the impact of proposed rules on the powers of the state governments.

These and the various other limits on agency actions discussed above are not insignificant, but they still leave agencies with considerable discretionary authority. First, agencies control much of their own regulatory agenda and set most of their own priorities. Second, many of the external checks on agency action apply to a small number of "major" regulations, leaving agencies more or less to their own devices on the minor rules that collectively can have a major impact. Indeed, small business groups have argued that the cumulative impact of large numbers of seemingly minor rules has been to impose a heavy regulatory burden on them. In response to such complaints, President Obama's 2011 Executive Order 13963 ordered agencies to take into account the cumulative impact of regulations, particularly insofar as small businesses were involved. It is not clear whether and how agencies have responded to this order. But it is worth noting that, in 2012, the then-administrator of OIRA, Cass Sunstein, felt it necessary to issue a memorandum to the heads of executive departments and agencies reminding them of Obama's order.[34] Finally, as noted above, many rules are published and adopted without prior notice and with little external scrutiny or presented in the form of administrative orders that receive virtually no prior scrutiny. Every rule, or order for that matter, is subject to judicial review if challenged. As we observed in chapter 1, however, courts will generally defer to agency judgments on the facts of the case and the principles the agency has applied.[35]

AGENCY AGENDAS AND PUBLIC PRIORITIES

While influenced by Congress, the president, and the courts, agencies' own priorities are important, and the extent to which these priorities are tied to the larger public's interests and priorities is a matter of some concern. Left to themselves, do the agencies pursue an agenda that comports with public concerns and priorities, or are they, perhaps in consultation with the constellation of interest groups that constitute their usual suspects, making policies and following priorities different from those of the public at large? Good government certainly means that agencies should apply their own expertise to problems, but democratic government implies that the agenda of problems to be solved should bear some resemblance to the peoples' concerns. Our findings in chapter 3 that civil servants and members of the policy community seem rather contemptuous of public opinion, Congress, and the president may certainly lead us to wonder whether agencies are inclined to govern "for the people" or according to their own lights.

A convenient source of information on the priorities defined by federal agencies is the Unified Regulatory Agenda.[36] Under the terms of the 1980 Regulatory Flexibility Act, agencies are required to publish quarterly summaries of their rulemaking agendas, including rules that have recently been completed, as well as rules currently being considered. Many agencies have been publishing these agendas since 1995. As we saw, not every agency edict is a rule, but the proposed rules reported by the Unified Regulatory Agenda offers the closest available approximation of the priorities of all federal agencies subject to the Administrative Procedure Act. Table 4.1 summarizes the 1,172 rules completed by the sixty-three federal agencies reporting such rules in 2012.[37] This year was chosen because it falls entirely within a recent congressional session, thus providing opportunities for comparative study, and because it allows us to check our tabulations against other published sources. The completed rules have been grouped into nineteen policy areas, established by the Policy Agendas Project.[38] This categorization permits a comparison of policy priorities between the bureaucracy, Congress, president, and the public.

In summary form, table 4.1 presents a snapshot of the regulatory priorities of America's administrative establishment in 2012, a fairly typical year in terms of overall regulatory volume, which, during the past decade, has averaged just over nine hundred completed rules per year.[39] Of the 1,172 regulatory proposals completed in 2012, fewer than five percent were responses to statutes enacted in 2011 or 2012 by the 112th Congress. Thus, virtually all the rules completed in 2012 were based on authority agencies purported to derive from statutes enacted by Congress in earlier years, or even previous decades.

It is evident that, in 2012, agencies varied considerably in their regulatory outputs. Nearly half the rules in question were developed by five cabinet-level departments and one agency: Treasury, Commerce, Interior, Agriculture, Transportation, and the EPA. Some agencies are responsible for a scant handful of rules. Differences in rulemaking output cannot be explained simply by agency size. Treasury, for example, is a large government department, but Commerce, Interior, and the EPA are among the smaller federal departments and agencies. Nor, as indicated above, can differences be attributed to recent statutory mandates. As statutory authority for several new rules proposed by the Department of Labor, for example, the department cited the Fair Labor Standards Act of 1938. Some agencies, to be sure, administer more statutes and some fewer than others, but, by the same token, agencies are free to make more or less use of the statutes they administer. For instance, the regulatory output of the EPA fell in 2012 even though its statutory authority had not been reduced.[40] Thus, the data reported by table 4.1 represent one way of summarizing the agencies' priorities—the national interest as seen by the federal bureaucracy—in 2012.

Table 4.1 Regulatory Priorities

Policy Area	Number of Completed Rules	Percentage of Completed Rules
Banking	314	26.79
Defense	118	10.07
Macroeconomy	95	8.11
Public Lands	83	7.08
Agriculture	78	6.66
Transportation	76	6.48
Environment	71	6.06
Health	65	5.55
Gov. Operations	63	5.38
Energy	63	5.38
International Affairs	29	2.47
Science	25	2.13
Housing	25	2.13
Crime	19	1.62
Labor	17	1.45
Social Welfare	13	1.11
Education	12	1.02
Civil Rights	3	0.26
Foreign Trade	3	0.26
Total	1172	100

Viewed through this lens, table 4.1 indicates, for example, that in 2012 federal departments and agencies sought to do a great deal more about banking, defense, and the environment; a bit more about health, international affairs, and crime; and not much about labor relations, education, and civil rights. If this idea seems at least plausible, a number of interesting analytic possibilities present themselves for comparisons of agency, public, and congressional priorities.

To begin with, we use Gallup's (open-ended) most important problem question to measure the public's policy agenda. The Policy Agendas Project categorizes answers to this survey question into the nineteen policy areas listed in table 4.1, which permits a comparison to the rulemaking agenda. Figure 4.1 displays a scatterplot of the rulemaking agenda against the public's 2012 agenda (on the left) and 2011 agenda (on the right).[41] We include the public's 2011 agenda to examine the possibility of a lagged effect. The graphs show the relationship between these two agendas. In a highly responsive political system, we would see approximately the same amount of attention devoted by each agenda to each issue (and the dots would align along a diagonal line through each square plot). In a highly *un*-responsive political system, the points would be scattered throughout the plot. This would mean the public and the bureaucracy would be paying attention to very different issues.

As is evident in the figure, the influence of the public on the rulemaking agenda is nearly nonexistent; the dots do not align on diagonal lines at all (rather, the lines summarizing the points are quite flat). We can quantify this lack of a relationship by calculating the correlation between the public's agenda and the rulemaking agenda. A positive correlation means that as one variable goes up, the other goes up as well, whereas a negative correlation suggests the opposite relationship. If the correlation between two variables is zero, we can infer that there is little to no relationship between them. In this case, the correlation is 0.09 in 2012 and 0.10 in 2011, which are quite close to zero (correlations range from -1 to 1). Although both the bureaucracy and the public prioritize the economy, the similarity ends there. Beyond the economy, the rulemaking agenda is largely focused on banking and defense. The public, in contrast, is concerned about government operations, crime, and healthcare. Whatever drives agency priorities, the views of the general public seem not to be a prominent factor.

Figure 4.1: Agency vs. Public Priorities

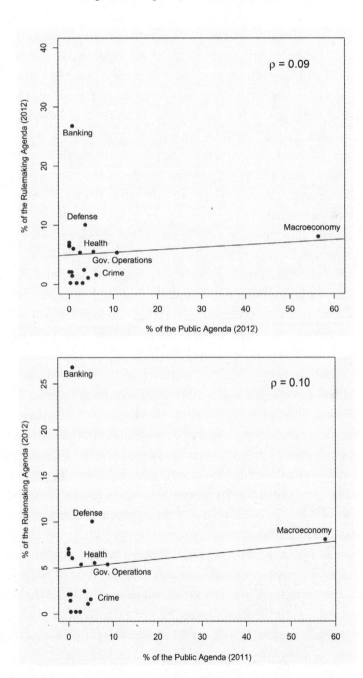

THE AGENCIES, CONGRESS, AND THE PRESIDENT

The absence of a relationship between popular priorities and agency priorities does not necessarily mean that federal agencies are indifferent to the views of ordinary Americans. There is at least one major alternative possibility. Federal agencies are at least formally accountable to the president and to Congress. It is possible that the agencies follow the priorities established by the White House and on Capitol Hill and that these institutions, not the agencies themselves, are responsible for discrepancies between rulemaking and public opinion. In other words, we may be seeing a breakdown of representative government rather than some absence of bureaucratic accountability.

To explore this possibility, we began by comparing popular priorities with congressional and presidential priorities. To measure congressional priorities, we made use of the Policy Agenda Project's count of the roll call votes in the House and Senate in 2010, 2011, and 2012 in each of the policy domains addressed above. While recent congresses have enacted relatively few laws, during every congressional session hundreds of bills are voted upon by senators and representatives in response to constituency interests and members' own priorities. Comparing roll call votes in each policy domain offers a rough indication of the overall agenda of America's legislative institution. These priorities can then be compared to the extent of citizen support in these same areas. To examine presidential priorities, we made use of the Policy Agenda's Project counts of coded statements from the State of the Union addresses for the same policy domains. The congressional and presidential agendas can then be compared to that of the American public.

Figure 4.2 displays the relationships between public priorities and those manifest in the White House and on Capitol Hill. As this figure indicates, there is a general correspondence between the concerns of the public and the actions of its elected representatives at both ends of Pennsylvania Avenue. The correlation between the president's agenda and the public's agenda is 0.71, while the correlation between the congressional agenda and the public's agenda is 0.26—both much stronger relationships than those observed in figure 4.1.

Figure 4.2: The Presidential, Congressional, and Public Agenda

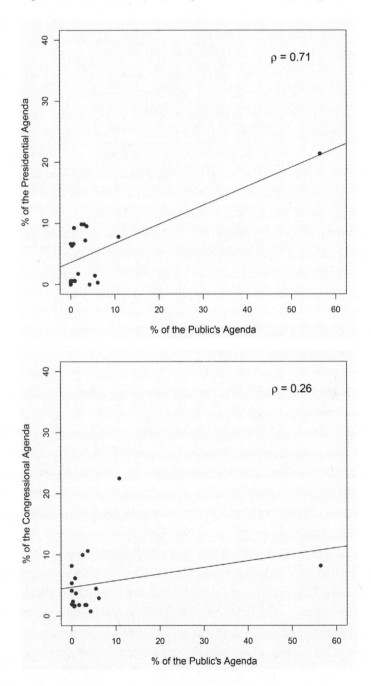

If congressional and presidential priorities are broadly consistent with public concerns, what, then, explains the apparent disjunction between agency rulemaking and public opinion? The answer seems fairly clear, if unfortunate. The priorities exhibited by the federal agencies, taken as a whole, are not in correspondence with congressional and presidential priorities. Certainly, Congress enacts the laws that the agencies implement and, as we have seen, on those occasions when the president chooses to intervene, the agencies must generally follow the bidding of the White House. However, there seems to be no general or systematic relationship between congressional and presidential priorities and those of the federal agencies. While both presidential and congressional priorities are broadly consistent with those of the general public, agency priorities do not systematically reflect those of the president or Congress. Thus, the lack of congruence between federal rules and public priorities is attributable to the actions of the agencies more than those of America's representative institutions.

RULEMAKING AND THE PRIORITIES OF OFFICIAL WASHINGTON

Agency rulemaking priorities seem unrelated to the concerns of the public, Congress, and even the White House. If, however, we look closely at the relationship between officials' opinions and agency priorities, a rather robust relationship emerges. This is the relationship between completed rules and the priorities of individual bureaucrats. In our survey, we asked public officials about their spending and action priorities. Accordingly, we can compare officials' opinions to the rules completed by federal agencies during the same time period. Here we find a close correspondence. For example, our survey results indicate that a majority of civil servants (53.25 percent) believe the government should spend more on addressing environmental issues. This preference for more government action is reflected in the rulemaking agenda—the fourth-highest percentage of regulations was made in the environmental policy area. On the other end of the spectrum, we see that only 15.02 percent of our sampled bureaucrats believe the government should spend more on civil rights, and the Unified Regulatory Agenda indicates that the lowest percentage of rules were completed in this area in 2012.

If we compare the overall rulemaking agenda to the policy priorities of sampled bureaucrats, we find a correlation of 0.21.[42] Figure 4.3 displays a comparison of the prioritization of thirteen policy areas according to officials' opinions and the rulemaking agenda. A rank of 1 means the policy area was viewed as the most important while a rank of 13 means the policy area was viewed as the least important. According to the figure, there is a high degree of correspondence between the two sets of priorities. Notice that the line summarizing the points is much steeper than the lines in figure 4.1; here, we see that the more important an issue is in government officials' estimation, the more attention is paid to that issue in the rulemaking agenda. It thus appears that the rulemaking agenda more closely reflects the preferences of America's unelected government and, perhaps, the constellation of "usual suspects" who influence rulemaking, than it mirrors the wishes of Congress, the president, or the American people. This finding hardly seems consistent with the idea of popular government.

WHAT IS TO BE DONE?

These findings suggest that it may be important for Congress and the White House to play larger roles in setting America's regulatory agenda. Statutory priorities articulated by Congress and presidential orders both seem generally consistent with popular priorities, while the federal regulatory agenda seems generally at variance with that of the general public.

As we saw above, presidents have used the OMB and fashioned instruments such as regulatory review to influence the rulemaking process. These instruments can increase presidential power, but it seems unlikely that the White House can ever develop sufficient bandwidth to systematically oversee the activities of dozens of federal agencies. Presidents can intervene occasionally but not constantly.

In principle, Congress could expand its oversight efforts and thereby have a systematic impact on the regulatory agenda. In recent years, Congress has taken small steps in this direction, enacting several pieces of legislation that require agencies to more fully report their actions and to affirm that their rulemaking efforts comport with a number of congressional priorities. As we saw above, for example, the Regulatory Flexibility Act of 1980 mandates that agencies demonstrate concrete steps to reduce the regulatory burdens imposed on small business. The National Environmental Policy Act of 1970 requires agencies to develop environmental impact statements for proposed rules. Other pieces of legislation seek to expand the scope of public involvement in rulemaking. As we noted, however, most statutory requirements apply only to major pieces of legislation and leave agencies with ample opportunity to decide which statutory provisions are not applicable to the circumstances at hand.

Figure 4.3: The Relationship between Officials' Opinions and the Rulemaking Agenda

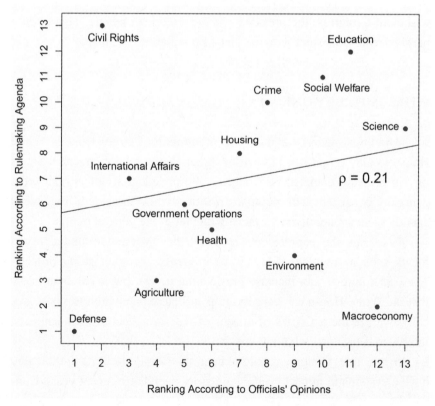

Somewhat more ambitious have been congressional efforts to develop legislative tools to control rulemaking. The most obvious of these has been some return to the idea of nondelegation. When an agency promulgates a rule, it does so with authority delegated to it by Congress. This nondelegation doctrine holds that Congress cannot re-delegate to the executive branch power delegated to it by the American people. The practical implication of the nondelegation doctrine is that statutory language spelling out the actions to be undertaken by the executive must be clear and detailed, lest broad and vague language in effect delegate too much discretionary authority to the executive. Until the early twentieth century, statutes tended to allow the executive branch little discretion during the process of implementation, and the courts zealously protected the nondelegation doctrine.

During the New Deal era of the 1930s, however, as the complexity of economic and social legislation increased and the federal bureaucracy grew in size and complexity, Congress began to delegate more and more power to executive agencies by providing them with broad statutory mandates to develop rules and regulations. This practice was challenged in a number of court cases and, initially, the Supreme Court employed the doctrine of nondelegation to strike down several major pieces of New Deal legislation. President Roosevelt's threat to "pack" the Supreme Court with pro–New Deal justices, along with personnel changes on the court, led to a majority willing to support FDR and to accept broad delegations of power to administrative agencies. While the court preserved the nondelegation doctrine as a "theoretical facade," it lost interest in interfering with the workings of the executive branch or attempting to force Congress to write precise rules into statutory language.[43]

A number of academic critics, most notably Theodore Lowi and David Schoenbrod, have argued for a return to enforcement of the nondelegation doctrine, asserting that this would enhance congressional power over rulemaking.[44] In point of fact, Congress has written specific standards into many statutes in recent years precisely in order to delimit agency discretion.[45] The problem with this approach, though, is that agencies continue to write rules years and even decades after a statute's initial enactment. Agencies quite properly assert that changing times and circumstances necessitate new rules not anticipated by the Congress of some earlier era. The federal courts will, also quite reasonably, defer to agency judgments and, for all intents and purposes, the statute will have been "captured" by the agency, however careful Congress was not to delegate too much power when the statute was enacted.

A third approach employed by Congress to maintain some semblance of control over agency rulemaking involves the use of statutory devices designed to enhance congressional control over rulemaking. One such device inserted into many statutes until it was invalidated by the Supreme Court in 1983 was the legislative veto. A statute containing legislative veto provisions required agencies to submit rules proposed under the authority of that statute to Congress for review. Though there were many variations, most of these provisions gave one or both houses of Congress an opportunity to block implementation of proposed rules by majority vote. Congress incorporated legislative veto provisions into at least two hundred statutes. The veto was seldom employed but nonetheless had some effect. Typically, the threat of a veto led to negotiations between the agency and Congress and the elimination or modification of the rule in question.[46] In 1983, of course, the Supreme Court determined, in *Immigration and Naturalization Service v. Chadha*, that the legislative veto violated the Constitution's two "presentment" clauses insofar as it was an attempt to exercise legislative power without the participation of the president as called for twice in Article I, which declares that bills passed by both houses of Congress must be presented to the president for signature and stipulates that a presidential veto can only be overridden by a two-thirds vote of both houses.[47] As Justice Byron White noted at the time, the *Chadha* decision invalidated provisions of some two hundred laws, more laws, White said, than the Court had cumulatively invalidated in its entire prior history.[48]

The *Chadha* decision also impelled Congress to consider other approaches to the question of supervision of agency rulemaking. One approach, discussed above, was embodied in the 1996 Congressional Review Act (CRA). This act requires agencies to submit proposed rules, accompanied by written reports, to the GAO. Congress then has sixty days to object to major rules. If passed by both houses, a congressional resolution of disapproval is sent to the president, who may sign or veto the joint resolution. This procedure was designed to allow Congress to review proposed agency rules while avoiding the issues raised by *Chadha*. However, the requirement that rules be disallowed by both houses of Congress and the president makes it extremely unlikely that the CRA will have any impact or even present a sufficiently credible threat to successfully force agencies to negotiate with Congress over proposed rules more than they might otherwise.[49]

Indeed, in the twenty years since the enactment of the CRA, only one rule has been disallowed and that was under rather unusual circumstances. An ergonomics standard for office furniture proposed by the Occupational Safety and Health Administration (OSHA) in the closing days of the Clinton administration was disapproved in the early days of the George W. Bush administration. The president signed the joint resolution of disapproval thus blocking the regulation. Had Clinton still been in office, the rules would now be in force.

Still another approach considered by Congress was embodied in the proposed 2011 Regulations from the Executive in Need of Scrutiny (REINS) Act that was passed by House Republicans on a party-line vote but was not taken up by the Senate. Under the terms of this proposed act, agencies would have been required to report proposed major rules to each house of Congress. Standing the CRA procedure on its head, under REINS a rule would only take effect upon the enactment of a joint congressional resolution of approval and the signature of the president.[50] Republicans strongly favored the REINS concept, but Democrats viewed the bill as an effort to curb social policy, and President Obama declared that he would veto the bill if it reached his desk.

Regardless of the partisan issues at stake here, our analysis suggests that absent congressional supervision—when agencies are left to themselvest— he rulemaking agenda is likely to be determined by the priorities of the agencies and the constellation of interests and stakeholders with whom they are closely associated in "round up the usual suspects" rulemaking. Public priorities can be inserted into this closed world through congressional action. The less Congress is involved, the more officials will produce rules unrelated to citizens' priorities.

GOVERNMENT FOR THE PEOPLE?

At the federal level, much of what Americans view as "the law" is developed and enforced by bureaucratic agencies. These agencies are nominally supervised by the president and Congress but their overall agendas seem not to bear much resemblance to the priorities expressed by these institutions or to the preferences and concerns of the general American public whom these agencies ostensibly serve.

Whose views and preferences drive the federal rulemaking agenda? It would appear that this agenda comports with the priorities of the Washington establishment—the officials, contractors, and advisers who have become America's permanent government. They, and perhaps the lobbyists who compromise the "usual suspects" involved in rulemaking, generally seem to pursue their own agenda as they develop federal rules and regulations. Does this agenda serve the public? It is unfortunately difficult to be sanguine about this possibility. This is, after all, an agenda developed by a group that, generally, has little regard for the interests of those it governs.

Chapter 5

WHAT SHOULD BE DONE TO MAKE THE GOVERNMENT LISTEN?

Amerca's unelected rulers and ordinary citizens are not, to use the vernacular, on the same political wavelength. As we observed above, in terms of their political understandings, citizens and officials live in rather divergent cognitive universes. Most Americans know little about government and many officials know little and, for that matter, care little about the citizenry. This political misalignment is corrosive to democratic governance. Citizens lack sufficient knowledge about the political world to understand, effectively articulate, or defend their interests. Officials, for their part, sometimes forget the purpose of democratic government and view ordinary Americans as objects to be manipulated in the furtherance of management goals rather than citizens toward whom they have fiduciary duties.

How can this difficult state of affairs be remedied? Let us suggest four reforms—three affecting the bureaucracy directly and one affecting American citizens. As to the bureaucracy, reform should focus on the lengths of bureaucratic careers, bureaucratic training, and bureaucratic experience. Citizens, for their part, must be taught a more realistic conception of government and politics.

The Lengths of Bureaucratic Careers

Many articles and books have been written bemoaning the lack of turnover in America's Congress. How can Congress be a representative body, critics ask, when congressional incumbents are returned election after election, thereby losing touch with the American people? It is seldom noticed, however, that the average length of service of a member of the House of Representatives is only about eight years, roughly half the average length of service of nonclerical federal executive branch officials. To put the matter simply, America's unelected governors hold their offices for many, many years—some for decades. This is one factor that separates these officials, in terms of outlook and life experience, from ordinary Americans. An official who has held office for decades, watching elected leaders come and go, can easily fancy himself or herself immune to public accountability, unauditable, as the Athenians might have said.

In the nineteenth century, of course, America made use of a system of bureaucratic staffing that its inventor, President Andrew Jackson, called "democratic rotation in office," but is better known as the spoils system. Under Jackson, between 10 and 20 percent of the government's administrative employees were removed to make room for supporters of the new administration. In later decades the numbers increased. In modern times, of course, this idea of "rotation" is seen as a rubric designed to hide the appointment of incompetent and inexperienced partisan hacks to positions of official responsibility.

Jackson liked to brush aside concerns about the competence of partisan appointees, declaring that public administration required no special capabilities: "The duties of all public officers are, or at least admit of being made, so plain and simple that men of intelligence may readily qualify themselves for their performance; and I cannot but believe that more is lost by the long continuance of men in office than is generally to be gained by their experience."[1]

Jackson's airy dismissal of the need for competence and training is misguided. We would hardly wish to see uneducated and incompetent individuals appointed to public office. However, on the question of "continuance in office," Jackson would seem to be on firmer ground. Competence and years of experience are different matters. Someone might be incompetent for many decades in office, especially since contemporary civil service rules make it nearly impossible to send packing even the most hapless or indolent bureaucrat. Jackson and his successors did not deny that experience was important. But they understood that other values were also important and that allowing public officials to serve for decades might interfere with the realization of such democratic goals as responsiveness to the public and accountability to elected officials.

Today, of America's roughly 2.5 million civil servants, only some seven or eight thousand hold their positions at the pleasure of the president and are likely to be replaced when a new administration comes into office. The remainder are shielded from the vicissitudes of politics and public opinion by civil service rules. This handful of so-called Schedule C employees are, generally, the highest-ranking civil servants. One might wonder why, if experience is so essential, the highest-ranking positions are assigned to the least experienced. The answer is that experience, though valuable, is not the only important factor. We also value consistency with democratic principles and accountability to democratically elected officials. Perhaps other layers of the federal bureaucracy might also benefit from the Schedule C process, bringing more civil servants into closer accord with shifts in public opinion and the agendas set by elected officials and voters.

In our view, relaxation of civil service protections and more frequent democratic rotation in office would increase the commonality (*koinon*) between officials and the citizens they nominally serve. Experience is a good thing but, as Andrew Jackson might have observed, bureaucratic entrenchment in office, like congressional entrenchment in office, can become too much of a good thing. We find, for example, that a government official's number of years in office is negatively correlated with the extent to which their decision making at work is influenced by the public.

Civic Training for Bureaucrats

Many scholars and journalists argue that ordinary Americans should be taught more about their government and political process, and we shall examine this idea in some detail below. America's governing elite, however, also needs civic education, focusing on the character and views of the citizenry and especially on the responsibilities of public officials in a democracy.

Currently, the training received by future public officials seems designed to inculcate in them the idea that they are to manage or lead and must, therefore, master arts of administration, manipulation, and persuasion. Note the chapter titles in typical public management textbooks: "Leadership," "Managing People," "Strategic Management," "Contracting," "Financial and Performance Management," "Marketing in Public Sector Organizations," and so forth. Similarly, management students are taught a variety of methods of ensuring citizen compliance with government edicts, methods that include persuasion, warnings, civil penalties, criminal penalties, and so forth, in what is sometimes called an "enforcement pyramid" because of the gradually increasing severity of the penalties faced by violators.[2]

These topics would all seem to exemplify useful management skills. But these texts give little if any attention to managers' fiduciary or democratic responsibilities. The same is true of the well-respected and putatively comprehensive *Oxford Handbook of Public Management*. This volume contains thirty chapters covering the various aspects of the field, from "Budgeting" through "Virtual Organizations." Only one of these chapters, though, focuses on issues of management in a democracy.[3] For the sake of comparison, consider the training received by America's military officers who *are* taught the special responsibilities of soldiers in a democracy. Soldiers, indeed, are taught that the trust of the American people is the "lifeblood" of the military.[4] Similarly, physicians-in-training spend a good deal of time learning their professional duties to the patients they serve. This idea, however, does not seem to be an important element of the professional training of public officials.

Acquainting Washington Officials with Life outside the Beltway

In addition to a curriculum oriented more toward their civic responsibilities and focused less on enforcement pyramids, the training of public officials should include and require actual public contact. Our data suggest that regular contact with the public enhances officials' sense of civic responsibility. For example, we find a significant relationship between the extent to which officials receive feedback from the public and the extent to which they indicate a preference for delegate democracy (in which policymakers act upon the preferences of constituents). For those officials who increase the feedback they receive from the public from zero times per month to seven to ten times in the past six months, the probability that they show preference for delegate democracy increases by 7 percentage points.[5] When these officials increase their contact to more than fifteen times in the past six months, their preference for delegate democracy increases by 13 percentage points.

This idea also seems consistent with the observations of a number of scholars who report that government officials assigned to field offices where they have regular contact with the public tend to exhibit increased understanding of and dedication to the interests of the citizens with whom they work.[6] The same would appear to hold true for agents of local governments who work directly with clients in such settings as public housing projects, neighborhood development corporations, and cultural and recreational services.[7] Perhaps all officials, even the most senior, might benefit from occasional rotation through field offices or other posts where they actually deal with ordinary Americans. Such a program of rustication would certainly be resented in the federal service, but public officials might, like the "street-level bureaucrats" studied by political scientist Michael Lipsky, thereby develop a greater measure of empathy and civic responsibility.

In addition, we suggest scattering government agencies or branches of agencies throughout the country. Some agencies have already undertaken such an exercise. For example, the Patent and Trademark Office (USPTO), in the last two years, has opened offices in Detroit, Silicon Valley, and elsewhere. The purpose was to bring USPTO attorneys in closer contact with today's patent and trademark issues. Contemporary technology allows employees to easily communicate with each other over vast distances. There is little need for all agencies, or parts of agencies, to be located in the same geographic area.

Consider the Department of Education (ED). Today, ED employees all send their children to Northern Virginia or suburban Maryland schools (among the nation's premier school districts), where they encounter a somewhat distorted picture of life in America's beleaguered public schools. Imagine if the ED dispersed many of its offices to, say, Oklahoma or Montana or Mississippi. The challenges facing school districts in these states are vastly different from those encountered in the affluent DC suburbs. Such a move might bring much-needed new perspectives to ED bureaucrats. Or imagine if the Environmental Protection Agency (EPA) was relocated to Texas or Kentucky. EPA employees might develop some understanding of the costs to businesses associated with EPA regulations.

In short, let us burst the Beltway bubble and scatter agencies/divisions across the country in a sensible manner. Washington always claims to be looking for new ideas. Perhaps these would be inspired by new scenery.

CITIZENSHIP TRAINING FOR THE AMERICAN PUBLIC

Civic training and rustication for public officials represents one step in the direction of reducing the cognitive distance between America's rulers and the ruled. Another component of this distance, though, is citizens' own lack of understanding of government and politics. Many Americans feel uninformed about basic political facts and have only a rudimentary conception of how the political process works. Surveys indicate that nearly 30 percent of the public believes that government is too complicated to be understood by people like themselves.[8]

As we observed in chapter 3, public officials in a democracy have a fiduciary responsibility toward the citizenry no matter how uninformed and misguided they conceive ordinary Americans to be. In a comparable fiduciary case, we generally expect physicians to work even harder to understand uninformed patients, rather than turn away from them in disgust. Nevertheless, we found that officials' feeling of obligation—their sense of civic responsibility—to the citizenry varied with the perceived distance between themselves and the general public. As Aristotle predicted, to the extent that rulers see themselves as having little in common with the ruled, a state of affairs he called μηδὲν κοινόν (meden koinon, or lack of commonality), the former are less likely to treat the latter with respect or sympathy. To put the matter simply, if Washington officialdom thought the public was more astute, it might be more reluctant to ignore its views.

Perhaps an obvious solution to this problem of civic distance would be to introduce programs in the schools and community designed to enhance Americans' understanding of the political universe. Such an undertaking is, of course, already advocated by the media, many educators, and several philanthropic foundations. Advocates of more civic education, however, often fail to give much thought to the content of the training they propose. Most seem to believe that the issue is mainly one of quantity and advocate the addition of more years of history and civics to public school curricula. Some advocate requiring all students to pass the US citizenship test, currently required for the naturalization of immigrants, as a condition for high school graduation or college admission.[9]

These ideas are well intentioned but, unfortunately, increasing the quantity of conventional history and civics lessons is not likely to do much to reduce the distance between popular and inside-the-Beltway political sensibilities. The problem is *what*, not how much, Americans are taught about political life. Contemporary programs of civic education generally present a rather unsophisticated and idealized vision of politics that seems far removed from the world of rulemakers, consultants, and advisers. Indeed, what we call civic education seems better calculated to produce rather docile subjects than politically aware citizens.

LEARNING TO BE RULED

What are citizens currently taught about government and politics? The main lessons currently promoted by the standards of citizenship education mandated by every American state consist of three broad principles.[10] The first principle is that government is necessary and America's government is particularly beneficent. Take, for example, the *Academic Standards for Civics and Government* mandated by the State of Pennsylvania.[11] Here, young students are to be taught that the "principles and ideals shaping government" are justice, truth, diversity of people and ideas, patriotism, the common good, liberty, the rules of law, leadership, and citizenship. As students move through the grade levels, these ideas are elaborated and applied to America's government. Similarly, Illinois students learn the benefits of patriotism, the principles of representative government enunciated in the Constitution, and the proper display of the American flag.[12]

The second principle taught in the nation's schools is the importance of following rules and paying taxes. Young Pennsylvania students are required to learn the benefits of obeying the rules and laws as well as the impact of violating them. They are also expected to learn why taxes are necessary. Similarly, Georgia students are taught "how thoughtful and effective participation in civic life" is characterized by obeying the law, paying taxes, serving on a jury, participating in the political process, performing public service, and registering for military duty.[13]

The third principle found in America's civics curricula is that appropriate popular political activity consists mainly of voting. Young Pennsylvanians are taught to explain what an election is, describe the voting process, and explain and evaluate the elements of the election process. New York's students were, for decades, led through the following exercise:

> To illustrate the voting process, present a situation such as: Chuck and John would both like to be captain of the kickball team. How will we decide which boy will be the captain? Help the children understand that the fairest way to choose a captain is by voting.
>
> Write the candidates' names on the chalk board. Pass out slips of paper. Explain to the children that they are to write the name of the boy they would like to have as their captain. Collect and tabulate the results on the chalk board.
>
> Parallel this election to that of the election for the presidency.[14]

These three civics lessons are certainly not ill-intentioned. They do not seem, however, calculated to encourage lively or robust forms of citizenship, or to give rise to a very sophisticated understanding of politics. Students might be better advised to watch episodes of the television program *House of Cards* to help them develop insights into the political process. And, as to the focus on electoral participation as the be all and end all of popular politics, voting can certainly be a useful form of political activity, but it is hardly the only form of political action in which citizens can engage.

An exclusive focus on voting could be seen as an effort to delimit rather than encourage popular involvement in politics.[15] But what should be taught in place of or in addition to these rather ingenuous lessons? Not surprisingly, both Plato and Aristotle had some useful thoughts on the topic.

EDUCATING CITIZENS TO RULE AND BE RULED

The Athenians thought that every person was born an ἰδιώτης (*idiote*) but, through proper education, at least some might become citizens capable of effective participation in public life. Plato, later echoed by Aristotle, thought a citizen must know both how to rule and be ruled. Of course, in the fifth and sixty centuries BCE, many Athenian citizens might literally have taken turns ruling and being ruled. But the real point of this idea is that rulers who understand what it is like to be an ordinary member of the public are more likely to treat their subjects justly and with respect. At the same time, ordinary individuals who understand the perspectives and purposes of rulers will be willing to accept just rule, but also be less vulnerable to mistreatment and manipulation. This is the essence of κοινον (*koinon*), or political commonality, between democratic citizens and democratic rulers.

Contemporary civic education for most Americans, however, is focused almost entirely on how to be ruled. Such education seems designed to train Americans to accept and obey authority but not to understand how it is wielded. Ironically, contemporary civic education could be said to undermine rather than enhance true citizenship, and doing more of the same is not likely to produce a better result.

Of course, unlike Athenian citizens, only a tiny number of Americans can expect actually to hold authority. However, teaching Americans only how to be ruled seems a recipe for the creation of a passive or even servile class. Perhaps modern Americans need not or cannot be taught actually to rule, but if Americans are not to be ἰδιῶται (*idiotes*) they need at least to understand how authority is exercised upon them—the tricks of the ruler's trade—so that they can be prepared to think and reflect, to distinguish truth from lies, to question and object, and to recognize improper uses of authority.

Teaching Americans to understand the world as seen by their rulers requires a very different sort of civic education than is common today. What should citizens know about the craft of the ruler? We offer some thoughts, certain to be controversial, to begin the discussion.

LEARNING TO THINK LIKE A RULER:
A PRIMER IN *REALPOLITIK*

To put the matter succinctly, true civic education requires ignoring conventional dogmas and approaching government and politics from a more realistict— he German term is *Realpolitik*—dare we say cynical, perspective. Indeed, while cynicism is conventionally seen as a pejorative term, it is a very appropriate political stance because politics is a realm in which bold assertions about the importance of the truth are frequently lies, while charges about the duplicity of others are often efforts to divert attention from the speaker's own misdeeds. Observers of the 2016 presidential race will not be surprised by this assertion.

Consider one of America's favorite myths. For more than two hundred years, the tale of George Washington and the cherry tree has symbolized the virtue of America's first president and, by his example, the importance of integrity as an attribute of political leadership. Unfortunately, the cherry tree story is a myth, concocted in 1806 by an enterprising preacher, Mason L. Weems, who hoped to bolster the flagging sales of his rather shallow biography of Washington.[16] While it may seem ironic that an anecdote designed to highlight the importance of truth telling is itself a fabrication, this irony is precisely the significance of the story. Parson Weems's fable helps to illustrate the duplicity and hypocrisy so often at the heart of the political process.

Critics who insist on pointing out the regular discrepancies between politicians' claims and their true purposes are inevitably accused of fostering public cynicism. The news media, in particular, are regularly charged with promoting cynicism through their negative coverage of politicians and government officials. This charge is made so often that even many journalists have come to believe it. Nearly 40 percent of the journalists responding to a recent survey agreed that journalists were too cynical.[17] Some analysts assert that public doubts about the government and politicians diminish popular participation and undermine political institutions. Harvard political scientist Joseph Nye has said that cynicism about the political process tends to reduce the "quality" of American democracy.[18] Several scholars have recently proposed that the government and private institutions should work to develop educational programs and other initiatives to promote popular political trust.[19] A number of states, as noted above, have already launched civic education campaigns designed to combat political cynicism among young people.[20] And, even as they regularly present rather unflattering accounts of the governmental and political processes, members of the national news media frequently urge Americans to eschew cynicism. "Cynicism can destroy our nation as readily as enemy bombs," wrote one columnist, who apparently loves hyperbole as much as he abhors cynicism.[21]

These condemnations of cynicism, though, seem rather misguided. Perhaps members of the nation's political class have reason to be concerned about cynicism. After all, cynical citizens hardly make enthusiastic subjects or reliable followers. Yet popular cynicism is hardly an aberration or malady to be cured through the dissemination of more effective propaganda materials. Instead, cynicism should be understood as a reasonable, if mainly intuitive, popular response to the realities of politics.[22] Millions of Americans see over and over again that politicians and government officials routinely deceive, mislead, and misinform them, offering pretexts while masking their true plans and purposes.[23]

"I have previously stated and I repeat now that the United States plans no military intervention in Cuba," said President John F. Kennedy in 1961, as he planned military action in Cuba. "As president, it is my duty to the American people to report that renewed hostile actions against United States ships on the high seas in the Gulf of Tonkin have today required me to order the military forces of the United States to take action in reply," said President Lyndon Johnson in 1964, as he fabricated an incident to justify expansion of American involvement in Vietnam. "We did not, I repeat, did not, trade weapons or anything else [to Iran] for hostages, nor will we," said President Ronald Reagan in November 1986, four months before admitting that US arms had been traded to Iran in exchange for Americans being held hostage there. "Simply stated, there is no doubt that Saddam Hussein now has weapons of mass destruction," said Vice President Dick Cheney in 2002. When it turned out that these weapons did not exist, Assistant Defense Secretary Paul Wolfowitz explained, "For bureaucratic reasons, we settled on one issue, weapons of mass destruction (as justification for invading Iraq) because it was the one reason everyone could agree on."[24] "First of all, if you've got health insurance, you like your doctor, you like your plan—you can keep your doctor, you can keep your plan. Nobody is talking about taking that away from you," said President Obama, as he prepared to launch a program that would compel many Americans to change their physicians and health plans. Need we point out that Donald Trump's proposed wall on the Mexican border could be compared to an Internet scam.

Since politicians and public officials are hypocrites, it is quite appropriate for ordinary citizens to be cynics. Ambrose Bierce defined a cynic as a "blackguard whose faulty vision sees things as they are, not as they ought to be."[25] If anything, too many Americans lack a requisite sense of cynicism. About half those responding to University of Michigan's National Election Studies surveys say the government *can be trusted* most of the time and nearly two-thirds *disagree* with the proposition that public officials don't really care what people think. These recent percentages actually represent an increase in public trust, after some decline between the 1960s and 1990s.[26] But shouldn't every American be just a bit distrustful of a class of individuals whose most prominent members, contrary to all logic and evidence, claim never to have inhaled, aver that they hardly even knew that pesky Ms. Lewinsky, or suggest they reluctantly agreed to forego the opportunity to serve in Vietnam in order to undertake the more onerous task of defending the air space over Texas. For that matter, can anyone truly believe the legions of lesser politicians who portentously declare that they are driven by an overwhelming urge to "fight" for the right of every last geezer to receive a pension check? Far from being a pathological condition, cynicism is a useful defense against such duplicity.

Yet cynicism alone is hardly an adequate guide to the reality of politics. Political cynics often see through the lies of the political class only to fall prey to even more bizarre fantasies. For example, millions of Americans who don't trust the government, also believe that federal officials are hiding evidence of extraterrestrial visitors at a secret base in New Mexico.[27] These individuals are ready to spurn official claims but, in their place, accept science fiction tales as reality. An understanding of politics requires not only a willingness to reject falsehoods but also the ability to assess objective evidence and arrive at the truth. The Chinese call this marriage of cynicism and objectivity "cynical realism," connoting an effort to substitute a true and accurate picture of political life for the lies told by the authorities.[28]

HOW MEMBERS OF THE POLITICAL CLASS REALLY THINK

Cynics are sometimes accused of being without principles. Cynical realism, however, is based upon three principles that citizens should understand if they are to think like rulers. The first of these principles is that politics mainly revolves around self-interest. In particular, actors generally compete in the political arena to increase their resources and stature. Individuals strive to enhance their own wealth, their own power, and their own status rather than for more altruistic or public-spirited purposes. Second, even if political actors actually have less selfish aims, they must almost always, nevertheless, work to acquire wealth, power, or status to achieve these other goals. As Machiavelli observed, prophets generally must arm themselves if they hope to succeed.[29] Unfortunately, though, the effort to maximize these interests often becomes an end in and of itself, even if it was not a political actor's primary initial goal. The quest for power can be as corrupting as its exercise. Third, the issues and ideas publicly espoused by political actors are more often the weapons of political struggle than its actual goals. What politicians and government officials say cannot be taken at face value but is important nonetheless.

The idea that political action is governed by selfish motives is hardly novel. Indeed, for centuries, political and social theorists have conceived self-interested conduct to be a fundamental reflection of human nature, "For it may be said of men in general," said Machiavelli, "that they are ungrateful, voluble, dissemblers, anxious to avoid danger, and covetous of gain."[30] This rather bleak view of human nature has a substantial scientific basis. Evolutionary psychologists argue that power, status, and possession of material resources have been associated with reproductive success throughout the evolution of the human species. Hence, the desire to acquire these assets is a potent driving force. Psychologist Steven Pinker writes that while humans have not evolved the rigid pecking orders characteristic of some animal species, in all human societies, "High-ranking men are deferred to, have a greater voice in group decisions . . . and always have more wives, more lovers, and more affairs with other men's wives."[31] Of course, individuals vary enormously in the extent to which they are driven by greed or the lust for power and status. Yet those drawn to political life are, by virtue of self-selection, more likely than others to desire the substance, trappings, and privileges of rank.[32]

Members of the political class are also more likely than their followers to see nationality, ethnicity, religion, and other powerful forms of social identification instrumentally, rather than in terms of their inherent validity. Of course, such forms of identification are often encouraged by politicians who see in them powerful tools for mobilizing and maintaining popular followings, even if their own piety or communal commitments may be questionable. In recent years, many Republicans have publicly courted the support of religious conservatives while privately calling them "goofy" or "the nuts."[33] So often in politics, expressed principles mainly function as vehicles for interests. And, so often in political life, leaders view associations instrumentally while followers develop strong emotional attachments to them. Leaders tend to be more cunning and calculating and are typically in a better position to know their options and act upon them.

A telling example from antiquity is that of the Athenian general Alcibiades, a man who, according to Plutarch, had an inordinate love of distinction and fame.[34] After losing a political struggle in Athens, Alcibiades took advantage of his family's ties to members of the Spartan elite and sought to make himself a leader in Sparta, Athens's mortal enemy. After his political foes came to power in Sparta, Alcibiades sought to make himself a leader among the Persians. And, after losing favor with the Persians, Alcibiades was able to take command of an Athenian army. In every instance, Alcibiades appealed to the patriotic sentiments of his followers, calling upon them to fight and die for their country, while he was himself prepared to change countries whenever it suited his interests.

Perhaps Alcibiades's modern-day equivalent is the General Motors Corporation. General Motors is well-known for ad campaigns based upon nationalistic slogans such as "Keep America Rolling" and "Our Country— Our Trucks." GM also is justifiably proud of its contribution to America's defense effort, especially during World War II, when its aircraft engines powered many of the nation's bombers and fighters. GM, however, seldom mentions the fact that, during that same war, the company also made a major contribution to Germany's military efforts. While GM built equipment for the US army, its German subsidiary, Adam Opel, built trucks, aircraft engines, and torpedoes for the Germans.[35] And, indeed, as corporate officials exhorted American workers to make an all-out effort to defeat the Germans, their colleagues in Germany urged German workers to do the same to defeat the Americans. The company profited from military contracts in both countries. Indeed, in the United States the company took a huge tax deduction for allegedly abandoning its German plants—which it reclaimed after the war—and then collected reparations from the US government for bombing its German plants during the war. Alcibiades would have been proud. In the interest of learning to think like rulers, let us consider, in turn, several of the actual driving forces of politics, beginning with money and material resources.

Money

James Madison wrote in *Federalist 10*, "The latent causes of faction are thus sown in the nature of man . . . a zeal for different opinions concerning religion, concerning government and many other points have divided mankind. . . . But the most common and durable source of faction has been the various and unequal distribution of property. Those who hold and those who are without property . . . those who are creditors and those who are debtors, a landed interest, a manufacturing interest, a mercantile interest, a moneyed interest . . ." These, according to Madison, "have ever formed distinct interests in society."[36] As Madison suggested, private pecuniary interests play a ubiquitous role in political affairs. In the United States today, local politics is often dominated by property developers and state politics by manufacturers. Even national security decisions are affected by the financial considerations of those involved in decision making. At the beginning of the Second World War, for example, Secretary of War Henry Stimson advised President Franklin Roosevelt to "hire" industrialists by providing them with lucrative military contracts. "If you are going to try to go to war, or to prepare for war, in a capitalist country, you have got to let business make money out of the process or business won't work," Stimson said.[37]

Often, competition among different groups and forces over money engages armies of lawyers and lobbyists and focuses on seemingly minor changes in statutes or administrative regulations. For example, in 2005, the multibillion-dollar life insurance industry prepared for an all-out battle to prevent President Bush from bringing about the enactment of a change in the tax code that promised to lower the tax rate on individual savings accounts. In particular, Bush had proposed the creation of tax-free Lifetime Savings Accounts that would permit individuals to save up to $5000 a year without ever being required to pay taxes on the earnings.[38]

Why would the life insurance industry be concerned about this seemingly innocuous measure? Since 1916, life insurance proceeds have been exempt from taxation to protect surviving dependents when a family's breadwinner died. Over the years, the industry managed, through assiduous lobbying, to persuade Congress to extend various forms of tax-exempt or tax-deferred status to virtually all insurance products, including annuities and other investment vehicles, which today account for hundreds of billions of dollars in income for the industry. The president's proposal threatened to create a simpler and more efficient vehicle through which individuals could obtain tax-exempt status for their savings. This, in turn, would probably divert at least some of the billions flowing into the coffers of the insurers. In response, a coalition of corporations that own insurance companies, including General

Electric and Massachusetts Mutual Life Insurance Company, as well as trade associations for independent life insurance salesmen, mobilized their forces. Leading the fight for the insurers was former Oklahoma governor and self-proclaimed "populist" Frank Keating, president of the American Council of Life Insurers, a trade association representing the industry. As a practiced politician, Keating knew better than to explain that he was fighting for the pecuniary interests of a congeries of huge and enormously profitable firms. Instead, he explained that the industry's only concerns were to make certain that Americans saved for retirement and to prevent investors from receiving unfair tax advantages at the expense of workers.[39] Surely cynicism is the only appropriate response to this rank hypocrisy.

This fight over insurance is just one example of the thousands of battles over money that are such prominent features of political life. Examples are reported in the press almost every day. In March 2014, it was revealed that a letter signed by five hundred prominent economists opposing, on economic grounds, President Obama's plan to raise the minimum wage, had been drafted and circulated by the National Restaurant Association. Restaurants employ millions of minimum-wage workers, who would be paid more under the president's proposal. The economists were unaware of the sponsorship of the proposal they signed.[40]

Approximately 25,000 associations, employing several hundred thousand representatives and lobbyists, including several hundred in our sample, are active in Washington today. More than three-fourths of these organizations represent business or professional interests, with nearly half representing business corporations. Public interest, civil rights, social welfare, and other ideologically motivated groups make up only about twenty percent of the total.[41] These representatives of business and professional groups lobby members of Congress and work to influence top government officials, including the president and vice president. Lobbyists also work tirelessly to influence the bureaucratic rulemaking process. And, in a similar vein, hundreds of corporate law firms use the courts to fight for their sponsor's interests and against laws, rules, or the actions of regulatory agencies that might prove inimical to their clients' economic interests.

One major Washington law firm, for instance, advertises that it can help clients facing government agency investigation, win disputes against other firms, and thwart any government enforcement proceedings directed against them. This firm, like many others, boasts that it employs attorneys who previously worked for the Department of Justice or the major regulatory agencies and hence will have an insider's familiarity with the tactics these agencies might employ. The cost of this expertise is astronomical. Corporate law firms bill hundreds of dollars per attorney per hour and a major case can cost a client tens of millions of dollars. That corporations are willing to pay such staggering amounts is an indication of the financial stakes of the battle. Speaking of money, corporate and professional groups also contribute hundreds of millions of dollars to political campaigns at the national, state, and local levels to help elect sympathetic politicians, or at least win the sympathies of those who are elected. A prominent former member of Congress once said that money was the "mother's milk" of politics. Who could argue?

Power

A second goal of the participants in political struggle is power. Thomas Hobbes said, "A restless desire for power is in all men . . . a perpetual and restless desire of power after power, that ceaseth only in death."[42] To be sure, individuals vary in the extent to which they are affected by Hobbes's "restless desire." Some seem content to lead quiet lives in which they command nothing more challenging than their television tuners. Others, however, appear to perpetually strive for important offices and positions that place them in charge of people, resources, and significant policy decisions. Power, of course, has many meanings. In the international arena, power usually connotes possession of personnel, weapons, and economic resources capable of intimidating or defeating potential foes. In the realm of domestic politics, though, the quest for power typically entails an effort to gain command over positions and turf. That is, individuals compete with one another to control important governmental offices, while those who control such posts vie to expand the sphere of authority or "turf" of their office vis-à-vis its rivals. Of course, some politicians seek power in order to make money. One former member of Congress, North Carolina Republican Charles Taylor, used his position in Congress to fund federal projects that aided companies he controlled.[43] Taylor was defeated in a bid for reelection in 2006.

The most visible aspect of the struggle for power in the United States is the electoral process. Every year, thousands of individuals compete for local, state, and national political office. Some seem driven to constantly strive for higher and higher office, seemingly equating the desirability of the position with the power its occupant commands. Every year, local politicians seek opportunities to run for state office. State-level politicians constantly eye national offices. And national politicians often harbor presidential ambitions. A number of well-known American politicians invested years, or even decades, seeking election to the presidency. Individuals like Henry Clay, Stephen A. Douglas, and Albert Gore Jr. devoted large fractions of their lives to unsuccessful presidential quests. Others, like Richard Nixon, Bill Clinton, and Barack Obama struggled for years and finally succeeded. But what drives such individuals to commit themselves to a life of meetings, official dinners, and deals, a life of fundraising and negotiation, a life of media scrutiny? According to presidential scholar Richard Shenkman, these aspirants for high office are "frighteningly overambitious, willing to sacrifice their health, family, loyalty and values as they sought to overcome the obstacles to power."[44] Donald Trump, Ted Cruz, Marco Rubio, and Hillary Clinton seem appropriate examples. The modern presidential selection system, which virtually requires aspirants to devote years to a single-minded quest for office, probably selects for an extraordinary level of ambition, and perhaps ruthlessness, among the major contenders for office.[45]

Turf

Closely related to political power, and especially important to Washington officialdom, is "turf." When individuals are able to secure positions of power, they often perceive an interest in expanding the power of the position they hold. In effect, the position becomes an extension of the individual, whose "restless desire for power" is expressed by enhancing the prominence of the institution at his or her command. This effort can lead to competition among rival institutions. Battles between the federal government and the states, between Congress and the White House, among bureaucratic agencies, and between the judiciary and Capitol Hill are common in the United States. Indeed, the framers of the Constitution expected such struggles when they devised America's twin systems of separation of powers and federalism. They saw such struggles as an antidote to tyranny. "Ambition must be made to counteract ambition," said Madison in *Federalist 51*.[46]

Bureaucratic turf wars are waged on an almost constant basis in Washington as rival agencies battle over jurisdiction, budgets, programs, and prestige. These struggles can last for years, and sometimes decades. For example, since the creation of the Department of Defense (DoD) and the Central Intelligence Agency (CIA) in 1947, the secretary of defense and the director of the CIA have been locked in battle over the collection and evaluation of intelligence materials. Successive secretaries of defense have sought to marginalize the CIA and to give the intelligence agencies within the DoD a monopoly in the intelligence field. This battle has been marked by skirmishes in which the CIA and DoD have refused to share information or cooperate on intelligence matters, fights in which the two agencies have sought to pin the blame for intelligence failures on one another and pitched battles in which each agency has sought to seize offices and functions from the other. Lack of cooperation among these rival agencies was one of the factors cited by the National 9-11 Commission to explain why a small group of Islamic terrorists was able to wreak so much havoc in the United States in September 2001.[47] Struggles over turf had seemingly become more important than the purposes for which all of the various intelligence agencies had nominally been created. Interestingly, in 2004, when Congress created a new cabinet-level intelligence position—the Department of Homeland Security—to oversee all US intelligence efforts, the CIA and DoD temporarily joined forces against this interloper that represented a threat to both bureaucratic empires.

The most important turf fight in Washington over the past century has been a result of the ongoing effort of successive presidents to expand the power of the White House at the expense of Congress. Over the past several decades, presidents have gained effective control over the power to make war and over federal spending, the two most important powers granted to Congress under the Constitution.[48] Presidents in recent years have also moved to circumvent Congress by relying, whenever possible, upon executive orders rather than legislation and upon executive agreements rather than treaties requiring Senate approval. Presidents have also taken more and more direct control over the administrative rulemaking process, through a practice known as regulatory review. This practice involves presidential directives to administrative agencies outlining the rules and regulations the president expects them to promulgate.[49] In these and a host of other ways, presidents have sought to satisfy their restless desire for power by expanding their turf.

Of course, international competition is the ultimate species of turf war. For millennia, the leaders of rival nations have struggled to enhance the power, position, and territorial sweep of the nation-states they controlled.[50] This struggle has involved diplomacy, economic competition, and war. In recent centuries, the leaders of rival states have often devised complex ideologies, heroic historical narratives, creative interpretations of God's will, and stirring anthems to help them rally popular support for their battles. Russia's 2014 de facto annexation of the Crimean peninsula is but the most recent example of an age-old phenomenon.

Status

Status is a third major goal for which individuals will often struggle in the political arena. Competition over status or precedence in the human pecking order is, of course, a common theme in the literature of politics. Indeed, one of the oldest literary accounts of a political assassination involved a rivalry over status: "And the Lord had respect unto Abel and to his offering; but unto Cain and to his offering He had not respect. And Cain was very wroth. . . . And it came to pass that when they were in the field, that Cain rose up against Abel his brother, and slew him."[51] Shakespeare also saw competition over status as an important force in politics. In *Julius Caesar*,

Cassius seeks to turn Brutus against Caesar, telling him, "Brutus and Caesar: What should be in that Caesar? Why should that name be sounded more? Upon what meat doth this our Caesar feed, That he has grown so great?"[52] Brutus, of course, is swayed by Cassius's appeal to his pride and joins the conspiracy to murder Caesar. Some evolutionary psychologists have argued that the desire for status or dominance over others is among the most powerful human drives. Steven Pinker, for example, writes, "People everywhere strive for a ghostly substance called authority, cachet, dignity, dominance, eminence, esteem, face, position, preeminence, prestige, rank, regard, repute, respect, standing, stature or status. People go hungry, risk their lives, and exhaust their wealth in pursuit of bits of ribbon and metal."[53]

Status, of course, takes many different forms. Wealth and power can give individuals status in their communities. However, wealth and power are not identical to status. Indeed, some individuals systematically reduce their wealth in order to increase their status. This practice is known as philanthropy. Similarly, some individuals endeavor to increase their status by relinquishing power. The Roman general Lucius Quinctius Cincinnatus, who gave up power to return to his farm, is a model of this sort of conduct. Prestigious awards and occupations can confer status. Graduation from an elite university can confer status. Membership in a famous family like the Kennedys or the Rockefellers can provide a person with considerable status. Four of the most important forms of status individuals can acquire through political activity are fame, rank, respect, and standing.

<u>Fame</u> is public renown and widespread recognition of an individual's superior endowments and accomplishments. John Adams said, "The desire for the esteem of others is as real a want of nature as hunger."[54] For many individuals in public life, the desire for fame seems, indeed, to be a potent driving force. One notable example is America's first president, George Washington. Unlike most men of his era, Washington did not fully believe in the concept of an afterlife. As a result, he was determined to become famous in this life and to live in the memory of succeeding generations.[55] Washington even saw his post-revolutionary retirement as contributing to his subsequent fame. He viewed himself as a later-day Cincinnatus, trading current power for subsequent fame.[56] John Adams was

another prominent member of America's founding generation who eagerly sought fame. Adams was jealous of the renown won by men he regarded as his inferiors, particularly George Washington and Benjamin Franklin. In one letter to his friend Benjamin Rush, Adams wrote, "The History of our Revolution will be one continued lye [sic] from one end to the other. The essence of the whole will be that Dr. Franklin's electric rod smote the earth and out sprang General Washington."[57]

Rank refers to the rung on the ladder or place in the pecking order that an individual occupies. Individuals seek political rank for its own sake as well as for the status such rank can confer in the larger society. Of course, societies vary in the extent to which even the most ambitious and talented persons are able to enhance their social and political rank. In societies, however, where mobility is a possibility, talented individuals who began life near the lower rungs of the social ladder are sometimes intensely driven to improve their rank in society through political effort. For example, as a young man, George Washington aspired, without much success, to be accepted into the elite social circles inhabited by his half-brother, Lawrence. This was another factor spurring Washington to greater and greater effort. Throughout his life, Washington seemed determined, through military success, marriage, and prodigious political effort, to achieve the rank he desperately desired. Historian Joseph Ellis writes of Washington, "Because he lacked both the presumptive superiority of a British aristocrat and the economic resources of a Tidewater grandee, Washington could only rely on the hard core of his own merit."[58] Another famous American politician whose original lack of social standing led him to strive for rank was Alexander Hamilton. Hamilton's illegitimate birth in the West Indies was often, as he wrote, "the subject of the most humiliating criticism."[59] Hamilton hoped, however, that his facility with words "would someday free him from his humble berth and place him on a par with the most powerful men of his age."[60] More recent American politicians driven to prodigious efforts to overcome humble beginnings include Richard Nixon, Bill Clinton, Ted Cruz, and Marco Rubio. And, of course, Lyndon Johnson strove for rank after the failure of his father's business interests and political career left him feeling deeply humiliated.[61]

Respect refers to the way in which an individual is viewed and treated by colleagues, coworkers, and others with whom he or she is likely to come into contact. Individuals who possess fame and rank may, as a result, be respected but, often enough, famous and important individuals are not held in very high esteem by their colleagues and intimates. For example, John Kennedy possessed about as much fame and rank as any person could hope for. In Washington, however, most members of Congress who had served with Kennedy dismissed him as a "light weight" and paid little attention to his views on policy issues.[62] Indeed, many proposals that had languished in the Senate during Kennedy's tenure were enacted after Lyndon Johnson took office. Senate barons who had been disdainful of Kennedy were ready to follow the lead of Johnson—a colleague whom they respected.

Standing. For many individuals, a goal of political involvement is simply to be involved, to have a recognized place in political affairs, to be an "insider" with standing in the community. Many individuals volunteer for partisan political activity or take part in community service efforts as much because such involvement gives them standing in political and community life as because of their commitment to the nominal cause. Many activists in the not-for-profit and public-interest sectors seem motivated by a desire for standing. One prominent public interest activist told me that he constantly sought to develop and promote new political issues because these were the vehicles through which he was able to play an active part in politics. This individual relished the role of participant and insider and sought vigorously to avoid having to sit on the political sidelines.

ALTRUISM AND INTERESTS

The desires for wealth, power, or status are extremely powerful forces in political life. Yet politics does not consist solely of self-interested conduct. Human beings are certainly capable of altruistic behavior. Take, for example, the international healthcare and advocacy group Doctors Without Borders (*Médecins Sans Frontières*, or MSF), established in France in 1971 and now operating from offices in nineteen countries, including the United

States. Each year, MSF sends about 2,500 volunteer doctors, nurses, and other medical professionals to provide medical aid in more than eighty nations. MSF volunteers often work under extremely hazardous conditions, sometimes combating deadly plagues, such as the 2005 outbreak of Marburg virus in Angola and the 2014 Ebola epidemic in West Africa, and work in the middle of revolutions and civil wars when no other healthcare is available. MSF has been willing to publicize human rights violations even when its own personnel faced threats of retribution from the perpetrators of abuses. The organization's staff members are almost all volunteers and barely 5 percent of its annual expenditures are used to pay administrative costs. On every score, MSF is a model of altruistic conduct, surely worthy of the Nobel Peace Prize it received in 1999.

The level of altruism exhibited by MSF's organizers and volunteers is, however, extraordinary in public life. Probably, for every individual or organization like MSF that eschews wealth, power, and status, there are ten seeking all three. One need only think of other nominally charitable organizations—the International Red Cross is an example—for which much of the charity ends as well as begins at home. But certainly altruistic conduct does occur. Even usually cynical evolutionary psychologists concede that "reciprocal altruism," performance of acts beneficial to others with the expectation or hope of recompense, is also part of humanity's evolutionary endowment and is necessary for any creature that engages in cooperative social behavior.[63] Perhaps this notion of reciprocal altruism helps to explain why some fundamentally self-interested individuals nevertheless make a point of being ethical, particularly when their behavior is likely to be scrutinized by others. Such individuals endeavor to pursue their interests in ways that also serve, or at least do no harm to others. Their goal is to establish mutually beneficial relationships or to profit later from their virtuous conduct. Examples of reciprocal altruism can be seen every day on committees, in business relationships, and even within families. Students who undertake unpaid public service jobs to burnish their resumes are engaging in acts of reciprocal altruism. In a sense, they are seeking to do well by doing good. Of course, many religions have long distinguished between truly altruistic conduct and beneficence undertaken in the hope of reward or recognition. For example, the Hebrew Talmud asserts that true charity must be given in secret so that neither the recipient nor anyone else will know its source.[64] One who gives charity in secret is "greater than Moses," according to the Talmud.[65]

Politicians certainly engage in reciprocally altruistic conduct and occasionally, perhaps, in truly altruistic conduct. Without a doubt, some individuals enter public life because they hope to do good, to "make a difference" to the welfare of the community. The problem, however, is that before an individual in public life can do good, with or without the expectation of later reward, they must acquire resources. In essence, and with very few exceptions, they must seek wealth, power, and status before they can achieve any other goals they might wish to pursue. And this is the problem. The effort to acquire these resources, even if undertaken for the best of reasons, can become all-consuming.

The corrupting impact of seeking power is a recurrent theme in literary treatments of politics. One of many examples is a popular 1972 film entitled *The Candidate*. In this film, an idealistic, handsome, and articulate liberal California lawyer, Bill McKay (portrayed by Robert Redford), is recruited by a cynical political consultant to run for the US Senate in an apparently hopeless race against an entrenched incumbent. McKay agrees to run, but only on the understanding that he will be free to express his political views regardless of their popularity. Initially, McKay says exactly what he thinks about every major topic, using the campaign to increase public awareness of the issues he deems important. The candidate's refreshing candor impresses the public and McKay's standing in the polls improves, turning the once hopeless contest into a tight race. As he continues to campaign, McKay more and more wants to win. He begins to accept his manager's advice and to take positions on the basis of political calculations rather than his own beliefs. Indeed, as the campaign progresses, McKay completely loses sight of his initial goals and ideals. Winning the senatorial race gradually becomes the only goal in McKay's life. Finally, when the votes are tallied and McKay finds that he has won, he turns to his manager and asks, "What do we do now?"

Another, even more famous, work of fiction that explores the corrosive impact of the quest to acquire and maintain political power is Robert Penn Warren's 1947 Pulitzer Prize–winning novel, *All the King's Men*. The central character of the novel is Willie Stark, a poor, honest, and idealistic rural Louisiana lawyer who pursues a political career in order to help his impoverished fellow citizens. After suffering a defeat in his first gubernatorial campaign, however, Willie feels a sense of anger and humiliation and vows never to lose again. He begins to surrender his ideals and puts victory ahead of all other goals. Willie eventually wins the election by making a series of deals with the very same corrupt interests against which he previously campaigned. He avers, however, that his compromises were necessary means to achieve a higher end. He says he will "make a deal with the devil," if it achieves his purposes. In the end, Willie's original honesty and idealism are lost and there is little to distinguish him from the vicious and corrupt politicians he initially set out to vanquish.

Warren's fictional Willie Stark was loosely based upon the character of Louisiana governor Huey Long, the notorious "Kingfish" who ruled the state during the Great Depression. The real Huey Long appears to have been driven mainly by intense personal ambition from the outset. At the age of twenty four he told his future wife that he planned to begin with a secondary state office, then become governor, and, in due course, win an election to the presidency of the United States.[66] Other noteworthy politicians, though, seem to have become more and more ambitious as their careers progressed. Take President Harry S. Truman, for example. Truman was rather dismayed by his initial exposure to political reality, which came when he was elected to a minor Missouri judicial post in 1928. "While it looks good from the sidelines to have control and get your name in both papers every day and pictures every other day, it's not a pleasant position," he said. "Politics should make a thief, a roué and a pessimist of anyone."[67] Yet, by 1948, Truman discovered that he "liked being in charge."[68] The greatest ambition Harry Truman had, according to his aide, Clark Clifford, "was to get elected in his own right."[69] Truman often said he wanted to take on the Republicans "in an all-out, full-scale, championship fight."[70]

Why does personal ambition seem to grow among those who become involved in political contests? The answer to this question is probably to be found in human biology or evolution. Behavior that has a powerful biological basis, such as seeking power and status, will tend to be learned and repeated if an individual undertakes it.[71] Experimental psychologist Martin Seligman employed the term "preparedness" to explain this phenomenon.[72] According to Seligman's theory, humans are prepared by evolution to learn particular things and undertake particular actions more readily than others. When stimuli fall into one of the categories for which an individual is biologically prepared, it can have an extremely potent and enduring effect.[73] Of course, individuals vary in the extent to which they are affected by any particular stimulus. Genetics and environment have made some more susceptible than others to the lure of political combat. Some individuals are able to walk away from the political battle field. When asked by the Republicans to run for president in 1884, Civil War hero General William Tecumseh Sherman famously averred that if nominated he would not accept and if elected he would not serve.

For many others, though, the experience of political competition seems to awaken a drive for power and position that easily overwhelms whatever motives and principles might have initially led them into the political arena.

INTERESTS AND PRINCIPLES

Finally, if they are to see how rulers think, citizens must understand the relationship between interests and principles in political life. While members of the political class work to promote their own political interests, they talk a good deal about political principles. During the 2012 national electoral campaign, Democrats often claimed to be deeply committed to providing healthcare for all Americans. Republicans, for their part, said they were fighting to preserve America's fiscal integrity. Both parties vowed to make certain that public officials adhered to strict rules of ethical conduct. Simply listening to politicians' claims, a credulous citizen might conclude that America's political class was an extraordinarily principled group.

Yet citizens should understand what everyone "inside the Beltway" takes as given. The principles espoused by politicians and public officials cannot simply be taken at face value. For the most part, principles must be understood as weapons of political combat rather than goals or purposes of political struggle. Politicians seldom espouse principles or advocate issues simply as matters of personal belief or from an abstract philosophical perspective. Instead, politicians generally develop and champion issues that they hope will promote their political interests. Politicians and organized political forces are seldom willing to invest time, energy, and effort on behalf of issues they do not deem likely to enhance their power, status, or financial resources. Of course, all things being equal, politicians will tend to prefer issues that make sense philosophically and seem plausible as potential policies. Some politicians, to be sure, have advanced their careers on the basis of the most ludicrous claims. Who can forget Al Sharpton and the preposterous Tawana Brawley case that brought him to national prominence?[74] For the most part though, politicians who espouse plainly foolish issues run the risk of subjecting themselves to ridicule and to exposure as frauds.

Examples of the instrumental character of political issues include some of the great principles debated during the course of American political history—the argument between Jefferson and Hamilton over the nation's future; the subsequent conflict over slavery and sectionalism that nearly destroyed the Union; and the debate over government power versus individualism conducted in the 1930s. Often these clashing principles are presented to students abstractly, as if contending forces were merely arguing competing points of political philosophy. Yet, obviously, Jefferson and Hamilton were not academic philosophers. They spoke for competing economic interests in the fledgling republic—Hamilton for New England commercial forces and Jefferson for Southern planters. Similarly, the mid-nineteenth-century struggle over slavery was more a conflict about economics and political power than a debate over moral principle. Both Northern manufacturing interests and Southern commodities producers viewed control of the western territories by forces tied to their opponents as a mortal threat to their own influence over the nation's politics and policies. Because the Republican Party was closely tied to Northern business and vehemently opposed to the expansion of the Southern plantation economy into the territories, the election of a Republican president sparked

Southern secession. It is worth noting that neither President Lincoln nor most Republicans viewed their conflict with the South as mainly involving a moral crusade against slavery. The "Great Emancipator" would never have launched a war merely for the purpose of freeing the slaves, though, of course, abolitionists within the Republican Party did see bringing an end to slavery as the main goal of the war.

In the same vein, Franklin D. Roosevelt and the New Dealers viewed the welfare institutions and entitlement programs they constructed more in terms of political power than moral principle. Welfare institutions and policies like Social Security promised to tie the administration to an enormous popular constituency and enable it to cement its influence over the nation.[75] New Dealers could reasonably hope that tens of millions of Americans would look to President Roosevelt and future Democratic administrations as the great benefactors who continued to provide them with Social Security checks, civil service jobs, and other forms of government largesse. This would guarantee Democratic domination of America's government for decades after FDR's death. For many Democrats, "Obamacare" promised to strengthen and widen the electoral ties forged by Social Security as well as to further empower bureaucracies controlled by Democrats.

A Republican example of the instrumental character of political principles is the GOP's emphasis on religious and moral appeals over the past quarter century. The Republican Party mainly represents particular segments of the American business community. So how did the party of business also come to be the party of religion? God and Mammon are not natural allies, after all. The Republican Party's concern with morality and religion began during the 1970s when GOP strategists sought issues that would attract white Southerners who were disenchanted with their traditional Democratic moorings because of the Democrats' liberal racial policies.

Issues like abortion and school prayer and, later, gay marriage turned out to be important not only to conservative Southerners, but to working-class Northerners, as well. Moral and religious appeals, in effect, allowed the GOP to transform millions of Democratic workers into Republican churchgoers—a feat of political legerdemain that helped elect several Republican presidents. The GOP's magic is all the more remarkable when we consider that not all of these presidents have been notable for their personal religious commitments. President Ronald Reagan, for example, welcomed the support of religious conservatives but almost never attended church or participated in religious services. Reagan offered a variety of excuses when asked about the incongruity of a president courting religious voters while manifesting an apparent aversion to worship. President George W. Bush appeared to be deeply religious but, as a series of secretly taped interviews with the president indicate, Bush was hardly above manipulating his religious supporters for his own political benefit.[76]

The GOP's successful emphasis on moral values and religion is even more remarkable considering how little Republican presidents and congresses have actually done to ban abortion or restore the place of religion in public life. At the risk of seeming cynical, we might suggest that GOP strategists have little interest in actually achieving the goals they espouse. If, for example, abortion was actually banned, millions of lower-middle-class religious voters might have little further reason to support Republican candidates. Moses probably made the same calculation when he kept the children of Israel wandering in the desert for forty years seeking a promised land that was just a few days away. Politicians are keenly aware of the fact that sometimes, if a promised land is reached, the citizenry can see no further reason to follow the leaders who brought them there.

Politicians, to be sure, often do believe in or, at least, do not strongly disagree with the causes they espouse. Most are, at the very least, loathe to risk being charged with gross hypocrisy by taking positions with which they are known to have disagreed in the past. Hillary Rodham Clinton's recent statements supporting faith-based approaches to social problems are amusing exceptions.[77] Clinton's religious conversion in preparation for a 2008 presidential bid probably did not persuade religious conservatives of her godliness, but certainly provided more grist for the GOP's attack mills.

If politicians believe in the principle they advocate, so much the better. Yet mere belief in a principle is seldom enough to induce political leaders to support it. It is quite unusual for politicians to back principles that run counter to their perceived political interests, even if they do happen to believe in them. For example, many members of Congress did not agree with President Bush's decision to attack Iraq in 2002. Few, however, were willing to take the politically risky step of opposing the president just because they thought he was wrong.[78]

Of course, when we do discover that a politician is espousing a cause in which he or she truly believes, we cannot assume that it was belief that led to action. In fact, belief often follows from advocacy. Most individuals will tend eventually to agree with a point of view that they repeatedly advocate, even if the advocacy was initially less than sincere. Social psychologists call this phenomenon self-persuasion.[79] Ancient biblical sages understood this concept when they argued that people did not need to believe in God before they prayed; belief, they said, would follow from prayer.[80]

BECOMING REALISTICALLY CYNICAL

We have suggested just a few of the matters with which citizens should be more fully acquainted. Of course, some might regard our political primer as promoting a view of politics that is callous or even immoral. Yet if Americans had a better understanding of the relationship between politics and self-interest and the ways in which political rhetoric was used as a weapon of political struggle, they might begin to see the sometimes cold and harsh reality of the political process as it is seen through the eyes of political elites. They might understand why Mitt Romney and other members of the Republican establishment prefer to see their party defeated than taken away from them by Donald Trump's insurgency. The real world of government and politics—*Realpolitik*—is not about George Washington and the cherry tree, not about Camelot, and not about change we can believe in, making America great again, or other myths and slogans. The real political world is a world of power, self-interest, and duplicity that needs to be addressed and explained in our national civics curriculum. The alternative to promoting clarity and realism is to continue training *idiotes* while complaining about how poorly Americans understand government. And, unfortunately, *idiotes* are entirely too vulnerable to mistreatment and manipulation by officials who, as we have seen, have little regard for them.

Some might say that if citizens became too savvy about government and politics they could not be governed, but perhaps, in truth, they would be less likely to be badly governed.

Could politically savvy citizens be so easily fooled about the realities of America's tax code or banking regulation or other elements of American policy where all is not what it seems? More than cynicism is required to understand these matters, but cynicism is a start. Cynics know never to take things at face value and to study them carefully before signing on to political ideas. With apologies to President Kennedy, when an official says "ask not," citizens should know enough to ask quite a lot.

An oft-repeated tale from antiquity concerns a meeting between Alexander the Great and Diogenes of Sinope, the original cynic. According to the tale, Alexander approached Diogenes and announced, "I am Alexander the great king." Diogenes was not inclined to be impressed by kingly affectations and, as was his custom, behaved in a rude and insolent manner. Alexander, though, was not offended and seemed to admire the old philosopher's courage. Alexander reportedly remarked, "Had I not been Alexander, I should have liked to have been Diogenes."[81] Alexander apparently saw in Diogenes an individual worthy of respect, someone who viewed the world as he did. Alexander, of course, became the Aegean world's most powerful ruler, while Diogenes spent his life as a critic of power, to say nothing of propriety. Yet the cynic, who saw the man behind the ruler's mask, had the ability to challenge the king and force the man to respect him. Americans would do well to ponder this story as they confront their own rulers. The cynical realist is ready to be a citizen. Those who believe the fairy tales taught in America's schools are likely to be *idiotes,* only prepared to be steered, compelled and nudged.

Chapter 6

WHAT IF WHAT SHOULD BE DONE ISN'T DONE?

As we have seen, public officials and members of the Washington policy community live in a different cognitive reality from most Americans. We called this difference the civic distance between the two. Official Washington, moreover, knows too little about those whom it governs, has an imprecise view of what Americans think, and seems somewhat disdainful of their views. Our data confirm what those who live in Washington know: many government officials and members of the policy community regard ordinary Americans as fools. Recently, a prominent healthcare consultant, Jonathan Gruber, one of the architects of Obamacare, spoke incautiously when referring to the stupidity of the American people, thus stating publicly what he and all his friends regard as a truism but are not supposed to say out loud.

Perhaps Americans do not know as much as they should about government and politics, but this hardly justifies the disdain exhibited by some officials for ordinary citizens. Like physicians, attorneys, accountants, and so forth, officials have a fiduciary responsibility that is not obviated by their "clients'" lack of knowledge. When the patient does not understand, the physician is expected to work harder to explain rather than to become dismissive or engage in subterfuge. Why should we expect less from civil servants? Perhaps, like physicians and attorneys, bureaucrats might be required to undertake continuing education, especially in the realm of civics, on a regular basis.

Interestingly, the inside-the-Beltway crowd overestimates the policy preferential differences between itself and the general American public. Social psychologists, as we saw, refer to this phenomenon as "false uniqueness" and observe that it is generally found when one group assumes itself to be so superior to another that it cannot imagine that areas of similarity and agreement might even exist.

Given this sense of superiority, administrators generally develop rules and regulations that conform to their own priorities and those of the policy community. Because official priorities frequently do not conform to those of the general public and are, indeed, often difficult for the public to comprehend, officials increasingly rely upon rather harsh criminal sanctions to secure compliance with the government's growing and sometimes bewildering array of rules and regulations.

If pressed, civil servants justify their unilateralism by describing themselves as "trustees" for the benighted public. In other words, they claim to serve the public's interests, which are often not equivalent to the public's preferences. This claim seems rather dubious, since it is asserted the most vigorously by officials who know the least about the public and, hence, what its interests might be.

Lincoln defined democracy as government of, by, and for the people. We are compelled to observe that the bureaucratic component of America's government, at least, falls short on all three of these dimensions. It is neither of, nor by, nor for the people!

GOVERNMENT SECRECY

If we might consider some of the broader implications of our findings, one that comes into particularly sharp focus concerns the current debate over government secrecy and citizens' privacy. Thomas Hobbes famously observed that the end or purpose of knowledge is power.[1] That is, both individuals and rulers seek knowledge about one another in order to exercise or resist the exercise of power. Popular government requires that citizens possess a good deal of knowledge about the actions of the state. Knowledge is necessary to permit citizens to evaluate rulers' claims and to hold rulers accountable for their conduct. In essence, citizens must undertake their own surveillance of the government and its officials as a precondition for exerting influence over them. This idea, as was observed above, is captured in the ancient Athenian practice of the audit (*euthyna*), in which all civil and military officials, including even priests and priestesses, were periodically required to undergo detailed public examinations of their actions.[2] The results might then be debated in the popular assembly (*ecclesia*), which was, of course, open to all male citizens who had performed the requisite period of military service. In this way, surveillance through the audit directly empowered the citizenry.

As we have seen, many of America's officials believe they should be ανυπευθυνος (anupeuthunos), or exempt from any audit by the public or even by Congress. This belief, more than national security concerns, explains the official penchant for secrecy. Tens of billions of pages of government documents currently possess one or another secret classification, and not all by security and intelligence agencies. Millions of pages of documents have been classified by such mundane bureaucracies as the Department of Agriculture, the Department of Health and Human Services, and the Department of Education, generally to prevent Americans from knowing what, or in some cases how little, these generals do.

The precise number of documents currently classified by federal agencies is not known. It is clear, however, that the number is enormous. During each of the past several decades alone, some 200,000 documents per year, totaling tens of billions of pages, have been newly classified by various federal agencies.[3] Since 2009, pursuant to an executive order issued by President Obama, a National Declassification Center (NDC) within the National Archives has hastened the declassification of several million pages of older documents.[4] During the same period, though, tens of millions of pages of new documents were classified. Thus, the rate of new classification far outpaces the rate of declassification. Critics have accused the NDC of working at a "languid pace," but of course the NDC must constantly deal with objections from agencies whose documents are being reviewed, as well as the cumbersome and time-consuming Kyl-Lott procedure for reviewing documents that may contain information pertaining to nuclear weapons.[5] Several agencies, particularly the CIA, have resisted declassification of documents and have, indeed, sought to reclassify documents that had already been declassified. In recent years, the CIA has reclassified thousands of documents, mainly related to American diplomatic history and originally belonging to the State Department or other agencies. The CIA declared that it had not been properly consulted when the declassification decisions were made.[6]

WHAT LEAKED INFORMATION HAS REVEALED

Of course, there are legitimate and proper reasons for classifying information. America's security *is* threatened by foreign foes, terrorists, and even criminal enterprises. However, much that is declared secret or even top secret seems to pose less of a threat to the nation's security than to the security of various bureaucrats. This is one of the lessons of the various leaks of information that have so troubled official Washington in recent years. The issue here is not the propriety of individuals deciding on their own what information should or should not be in the public domain. Such individual decisions can threaten the nation's security. The question at hand is, rather, what the leaks tell us about the government's classification policies. What we find is that agencies classify information that might embarrass them, whether or not it poses a risk to national security. More than anything else, the classification system seems designed to prevent members of the public from becoming fully aware of the misconduct, duplicity, and errors of those who govern them.

Take, for example, the top secret "Pentagon Papers," whose release was labeled by President Nixon's national security adviser, Gen. Alexander Haig as "a devastating security breach of the greatest magnitude."[7] Published in 1971, the documents leaked by Daniel Ellsberg represented a history of America's involvement in Vietnam from 1945 to 1967. The history and supporting documents had been developed by a Defense Department study group created by Secretary of Defense Robert McNamara and tasked with writing a detailed history of the Vietnam War. Ellsberg had briefly worked as a staffer for the study and was able to photocopy most of the information contained in the study's forty-seven volumes.

The Pentagon Papers provided a fascinating look at an important episode in American history, but all their information was historical and the only secrets they revealed concerned lies, evasions, and cover-ups by successive presidents and other government officials. Presidents Eisenhower, Truman, Kennedy, and Johnson and the various senior officials working for the White House had deceived the press, Congress, and the electorate while pursuing what turned out to be a disastrous policy in Southeast Asia. While President Kennedy was pretending to consult with South Vietnamese president Diem, he was already planning to overthrow Diem and sanctioned the coup that led to Diem's death. While President Johnson was declaring, "We want no wider war," in his 1964 reelection campaign, he had already decided to expand the war.[8] It is little wonder that the Pentagon Papers were classified top secret. An unauthorized individual reading them might have learned that America's leaders and government could not be trusted. Former solicitor general Erwin Griswold argued before the Supreme Court in 1971 that publication of the papers would cause great and irreparable harm to the nation's security. Writing in the *Washington Post* some fifteen years later, Griswold conceded that, "I have never seen any trace of a threat to the national security from the publication."[9] One might say that the threat was to the reputations of political leaders and the credibility of the government, not to the security of the nation.

For another example, take the WikiLeaks case. In 2010, a US army private, then named Bradley Manning (Manning's first name later became Chelsea after gender reassignment surgery), downloaded more than 700,000 classified documents from military servers and sent them to WikiLeaks, which shared the documents with a number of newspapers.[10] Some of the material raised genuine security concerns. The documents include videos that seemed to depict instances of misconduct by American troops in Iraq and Afghanistan and documents suggesting that American authorities had failed to investigate cases of misconduct by Iraqi police and soldiers under their indirect command. Other documents included classified cables from US embassies assessing the competence—usually incompetence—of foreign leaders. Russia's Vladimir Putin is depicted as little more than a gangster; England's Prince Andrew is shown as rude and boorish; the former president of Tunisia and his daughter are revealed to have had their favorite ice cream flown in from St. Tropez at a time when many Tunisians could barely scratch out a living. Still other documents revealed corruption on the part of US allies, including Afghanistan, the Vatican, and Pakistan.[11] Some of the leaked documents arguably deserve to be classified, if only to protect American intelligence sources. Others seem to have been classified to hide evidence of wrongdoing by the United States and its allies or to avoid embarrassing one or another governmental entity. As in the case of the Pentagon Papers, many documents were classified less to protect the nation's security than to prevent the public from glimpsing the truth behind official facades. Perhaps the American people might have benefitted from knowing some of these facts.

For their part, the 2013 NSA eavesdropping revelations paint a picture of an agency that might charitably be said to skirt the boundaries of legality. Without any evidence that this activity actually serves the national interest, the telephone and email records of tens of millions of Americans are collected and, without the necessary court orders, some unknown number of these is "inadvertently" thoroughly examined. Presumably, America's foreign foes already suspected that their electronic communications just might be monitored. Government secrecy merely prevented the American public from knowing that its calls and emails were also being watched.

Support for an unflattering view of the classification program can also be gleaned from the ongoing tug-of-war over the declassification of documents. In 2005, for example, the CIA reclassified a dozen documents that had been declassified and were publicly available in the National Archives. For the most part, these documents revealed foolish agency projects or missteps, sometimes going back a half century. One document detailed an abortive CIA effort to drop propaganda leaflets into Eastern Europe by hot air balloon. Other documents described the intelligence community's faulty analysis of the Soviet nuclear weapons program in 1949. Still another document showed that the CIA was terribly wrong in its analysis of whether or not China would intervene in the Korean War in the fall of 1950.[12] Why were these now-ancient documents reclassified? Perhaps because they caused the agency some embarrassment and this, sometimes more than national security, is deemed by the government to be an adequate reason to keep information from the public.

We can only wonder what secrets might be learned if documents classified by the Department of Agriculture or the Department of Education were exposed to the light of day. Perhaps the public might learn why some cynical Washington observers of the Department of Education say, with apologies to Churchill, that seldom in the course of human events has so little been accomplished by so many.

To combat the threat of such revelations, most domestic agencies have become enthusiastic adherents of an initiative first introduced by the Obama administration and called the "Insider Theft Program." This program was designed to prevent leaks of information and to train agency employees to recognize possible spies in their midst. Employees at the National Oceanic and Atmospheric Administration (NOAA), for example, have been encouraged to take an online tutorial from which they learn to spot potential security threats. Perhaps agency executives fear that the weather forecast will fall into the wrong hands. As government agencies attempt to prevent citizens from auditing them, the government is only too happy, as we have learned in recent years, to exercise power over its citizens through a variety of surveillance programs. Democratic government has, in this way, been turned on its head.

THE ILLUSION OF BUREAUCRATIC COMPETENCE

The framers of the American Constitution provided for representative government, and to this very day Americans regularly fill the seats of the Congress and select a president to represent them. But these elected institutions, particularly Congress, have gradually been eclipsed by a federal bureaucracy whose officials and associated policy networks cannot be said to represent anyone and yet write most of what Americans regard as the law. These officials and their associates appear to regard citizens and their elected representatives as fools to be ignored, steered, and, if need be, coerced, and they are content to govern according to their own lights.

Some readers might respond "so what?" and assert that civil servants are far more competent than Congress and considerably more able and experienced than most presidents. The federal courts seem to share this belief when they continually defer to agency interpretations of law and policy. But even those untroubled by the exchange of representative government for what they view as effective governance should consider their views. Bureaucracies seem competent but, over time, this appearance of competence can often prove to be an illusion.

To begin with, public bureaucracies almost always succumb to the temptation to micro manage. With the notable, albeit not inevitable, exception of the military in wartime, many public bureaucracies produce no discernable product whose presence or absence can be easily measured or accurately linked to the activity or inactivity of the agency. As a result, the executives of many public agencies become focused on process rather than outcomes.[13] Process is defined as carefully following hosts of rules and regulations that specify every activity in which agency employees and their unfortunate clients (the public) must engage in painstaking detail.[14]

A recent editorial in the *Economist* took America to task for having become an over-regulated nation.[15] The article noted that in the wake of Obamacare, and various other healthcare reforms such as the 1996 Kennedy-Kassebaum Act, the vast increase in the number of rules governing medical practice has meant that every hour spent treating a patient in America generates between thirty minutes and one hour of paperwork. One physician of our acquaintance reported that she recently went to visit a hospitalized patient and, to her dismay, found the patient wandering in a hospital corridor trailing tubes and somewhat disoriented. After she escorted the patient back to her bed, this physician went to find a nurse. All the nurses were hard at work in front of computer terminals, and one declared that they hadn't yet had time to see the patients because they were still completing the many forms needed to comply with various rules and regulations.

Americans are accustomed to laughing at "red tape," but on a societal level bureaucratic micromanagement is no laughing matter. Energy and effort that should be devoted to bringing about desirable outcomes are diverted to complying with rules and regulations whose annual cost to the economy is tens of billions of dollars. And, under some circumstances, red tape can actually pose an existential threat to a nation. Take the case of the rapid German victory over France in 1940. On paper, the French possessed a larger army, better equipment, and even more tanks than the Germans. The French army, however, was paralyzed by red tape. Tightly central-ized general staff control over field operations meant that units under attack were constantly awaiting orders from commanders in Paris, as the Germans, whose military doctrine of *Auftragstactic* emphasized small-unit initiative, overran French positions. No doubt, the rule-bound French army seemed very competent on the parade ground where precise obedience to regulations must have been impressive. However, rigid adherence to the rules produced an illusion of competence that contributed mightily to the collapse of the French state in 1940.[16]

The illusion of bureaucratic competence also masks a second dif-ficulty associated with bureaucratic government. This problem is the general reluctance of bureaucracies to engage in or even tolerate innova-tions that managers see as posing threats to their organizations and their own power within those organizations. Of course, agency executives are always concerned also with their agency's budget, power, and autonomy vis-à-vis other agencies. Turf battles among America's security agencies, for example, are the stuff of Washington legend. Often, the FBI, CIA, DIA, DHS, and so forth seem to regard one another with suspicion they should reserve for enemies of the United States.

Agencies are, at the same time, affected by internal political struggles. Just as organizations vie with one another, so factions within an agency compete with rival groups for money, power, and prestige. A particularly important factor in such internal and external struggles is the agency's defi-nition of its central mission and core responsibilities. For any organization, much follows from the way in which its mission is defined. Alternative definitions of the organization's mission are likely to empower different groups within the agency. Usually, one or another faction within the orga-nization bases its claim to power and preferment upon its particular ability to carry out the agency's core mission. A change in mission might threaten that power. For example, when aircraft carriers were developed, the top commanders of many navies resisted their introduction. These officers had generally built their careers on the command of battleships and other surface combatants and feared that a shift in naval missions and tactics would diminish their influence and empower a rival faction of officers, as indeed eventually took place.[17] The commitment of a bureaucracy's leaders to the mission that bolsters their own power within the organization is a major reason that bureaucracies often seem reluctant to change their practices and priorities in response to shifts in the external environment. The often-heard claim that armies are always prepared to fight the previous war expresses this idea.

Long-established bureaucratic agencies usually evolve priorities and procedures that advance both the internal and external goals of their leadership cadres. That is, agency executives will identify a mission and set of practices that justifies their own agency's budgetary claims and power vis-à-vis other institutions, while simultaneously reinforcing the established structure of power within the agency itself. Over time, this mission and associated practices can become so deeply ingrained in the minds of agency executives and staffers that adherence to it becomes a matter of habit and reflex. Students of bureaucracy refer to this set of established pattern of practices and beliefs about the organization's role and purpose as the agency's institutional "culture."[18]

Many agencies seem incredibly dedicated to missions defined long ago. The US Fish and Wildlife Service (USFWS), for example, was created in the nineteenth century to protect and conserve the nation's animal species and does so today, generally disregarding other economic and social interests. In recent years, the USFWS has worked to return wolves and grizzly bears to the Northwest, even though these animals represent an economic and even physical threat to individuals engaged in ranching and recreational pursuits in the region.[19] Often, a cataclysmic event is required to alter an agency's long-established culture or sense of mission. For example, during the early 1980s, the US Coast Guard, which viewed itself as a quasi-military force, finally accepted the idea that boating safety and environmental protection were within the scope of its mission, but only after the agency was moved from the Treasury Department to the Department of Transportation (and later to the Department of Homeland Security), provided with new leadership, given a new statutory base, and subjected to several presidential orders.[20]

All agencies, civilian as well as military, are almost certain to resist efforts to compel them to undertake activities that are foreign to their institutional cultures and, thus, seem to pose a threat to their institutional autonomy or internal balance of power. Harold Seidman avers that attempts to compel agencies to engage in such activities are usually futile. "Alien transplants," he argues, "seldom take root" and are continually "threatened with rejection."[21] For example, numerous congressional efforts to compel the Federal National Mortgage Association (Fannie Mae), a quasi-public government-sponsored enterprise, to provide loans to low-income families have failed to affect the agency's behavior. Despite its public charter, Fannie Mae conceives itself to be a commercial enterprise with a duty to operate in as profitable a manner as possible. Loans to poor borrowers who lack credit worthiness do not comport with this sense of mission and are constantly—and successfully—resisted by the agency in spite of congressional pressure.[22]

In the case of civilian agencies, top executives are, of course, appointed by the president, who may endeavor to use the appointment process to impose new priorities and even entirely new missions on established organizations. Nevertheless, presidential appointees whose ideas are inconsistent with an agency's culture and sense of purpose are almost certain to encounter stiff resistance, sometimes verging on mutiny, from their nominal subordinates. For example, Richard Nixon's efforts to appoint executives who would change the behavior of several domestic social and regulatory agencies, including the Environmental Protection Agency, sparked a series of agency revolts that included leaks to Congress and the media by senior staffers. Nixon's attempt to plug these leaks with the creation of the "plumbers squad" helped bring about the Watergate scandal and Nixon's ouster from office.[23]

Like red tape, bureaucratic resistance to change is often the subject of jokes but is also no laughing matter. Indeed, like red tape, resistance to change can have existential implications. Take the case of Imperial China. Between the sixteenth and nineteenth centuries, small European states subjugated and colonized vast stretches of the world, even though the Chinese might have appeared to be more likely candidates for this role. At the end of the fifteenth century, China possessed technology and weapons more advanced than those to be found in Europe. Ships commanded by Chinese admiral Cheng Ho cruised the Indian Ocean and certainly had the potential to cross the Pacific. The Chinese might have found and conquered the New World.[24] In early modern Europe, however, complex patterns of competition between merchants and among princes meant that new technologies were generally likely to be viewed as a potential source of profit by the former and a potential advantage in Europe's unrelenting arms race by the latter.

Competition produced a virtuous cycle of ongoing improvement in both military and civilian technologies, with each helping to advance the other. Merchants, for example, supported the construction of larger and sturdier ships, which in turn provided princes with better gun platforms for naval artillery, which in turn expanded the trade routes accessible to the merchants, and so on.

In fifteenth and sixteenth-century China, by contrast, the mandarins who effectively ruled the empire saw both commerce and technology as socially disruptive forces. They believed that both needed to be tightly regulated to preserve the peace of the empire and their own power. This perspective was exemplified by the imperial decision of 1433 to end explorations of the Indian Ocean, followed by a 1436 decree prohibiting the construction of seagoing ships.[25] Hence, China entered a period of stagnation that lasted more than five hundred years, as Portuguese. Spanish, English, Dutch, and French vessels explored the world and began an era of European supremacy.

Thus, behind the illusion of bureaucratic competence is a reality in which bureaucratic government will ultimately do much damage to a state and a society. America's officials think citizens are fools, and perhaps they are—to allow themselves to be governed by such officials.

APPENDIX A

Table A.1: Government Officials' Perspectives on Americans' Knowledge of Policy Proposals

	A Great Deal	Quite a Bit	Some	Very Little	None
Constitutional amendment to ban same-sex marriage	6.54	22.88	**41.50**	27.78	1.31
Raising income taxes on those who make more than $200K per year	2.29	17.32	**39.87**	38.56	1.96
Raising income tax on those who make less than $200K per year	1.31	15.36	38.56	**43.46**	1.31
Government coverage of prescription drugs for low-income seniors	0.33	4.26	29.51	**61.64**	4.26
Government coverage of all necessary medical care for all Americans	1.31	6.23	30.82	**57.05**	4.59
Allowing illegal immigrants to work in the United States for up to three years, after which they would have to go back to their home country	0.66	3.61	31.48	**58.36**	5.90
Citizenship for illegal immigrants	0.98	6.56	38.36	**50.49**	3.61
Holding a suspected terrorist in prison for months without bringing the person to court and charging him or her with a crime	1.91	5.91	28.52	**57.38**	6.89
The US government being required to get a court order before it can listen in on phone calls made by American citizens who are suspected of being terrorists	1.31	4.26	31.80	**56.39**	6.23

Cell entries are the percentage of respondents. Bolded entries are the largest for each row.

APPENDIX B

Using the estimates from the propensity score regression models, we can calculate first differences. These first differences allow us to quantify the expected change in the probability that an individual is a member of the government when one of the components of civic distance is changed. In other words, a first difference is the expected change in probability that results from a change in one of the independent variables. For example, we can calculate the expected change in probability that an individual is a government official by increasing that individual's income or level of news consumption. Table B.1 presents these first differences and suggests a cumulative impact of the variables on civic distance. When calculating these first differences, the treatment is defined as being a member of the government (congressional/White House staff or civil service) or the policy community.

**Table B.1: First Differences from Propensity Score Model
for the Entire Gov. Community**

	Gov. Comm. vs. American People (Government = 1)	
	$\Delta P(Y=1)$	95% CI
Household income *Below national median → Above national median*	0.13	(.103, .153)
News consumption *Read news 0 days/week → Read news 7 days/week*	0.07	(.044, 092)
Perceived complexity of political system *Strongly agrees that political system too complex to understand → strongly disagrees*	0.13	(.096, .163)
Partisan strength *Independent → Strong partisan*	-0.06	(-.091, -.033)

Cell entries display the first differences. 95 percent confidence intervals are shown in parentheses. A confidence interval is a measure of certainty about an estimate. A wider confidence interval means we are less certain about the true value of the estimate.

APPENDIX C

Our survey included ninety questions that yielded 320 variables. Many of the variables in the survey were collected in the form of matrix questions. For example, question 27 asked respondents about their consumption of nineteen different media sources, with a five-category response scale ranging from "none" to "a great deal." This question thus resulted in 19 variables.

Many of the questions in our survey were also asked of respondents to the 2012 American National Election Study and the World Values Survey (Wave 6). This was done to facilitate a comparison of political opinions and policy attitudes between government officials and the American people.

An invitation to complete the survey was emailed to 2,376 potential respondents. We identified contacts at government agencies, congressional offices, the White House, and organizations in the policy community and obtained relevant email addresses through these contacts. The response rate was 36 percent, with 16.4 percent submitting complete surveys and 19.6 percent submitting partially complete surveys. This response rate is comparable with other scholarly surveys, such as the American National Election Studies. A partially complete survey means one or more questions were unanswered.

The 856 respondents to our survey work both in and with the federal government in the Washington area. We therefore refer to them throughout the text as "inside-the-Beltway" individuals. These individuals included congressional staffers, lobbyists, those who work at think tanks, political consulting firms, government agencies, government contract firms, and other similar organizations.

The survey was conducted online using Survey Monkey from February 2013–February 2014.

SURVEY FOR WHAT THE GOVERNMENT THINKS OF PEOPLE

1. Which of the following best describes your employment status?
   __ Employed, working 1–39 hours per week
   __ Employed, working 40 or more hours per week
   __ Not employed, looking for work
   __ Not employed, NOT looking for work
   __ Retired
   __ Disabled, not able to work

2. Which of the following best describes your current place of employment?
   __ Congress
   __ White House
   __ Federal agency
   __ Non-federal government agency
   __ Federal contractor
   __ Federally funded research and development center (FFRDC)
   __ Government-sponsored enterprise (GSE)
   __ Think tank or policy institute
   __ Nonprofit organization (non-think tank)
   __ For-profit organization
   __ Other (Please specify: _____)

3. If you are a government employee, what is your GS level? _____

4. If you are in the military, what is your rank? _____

5. How long have worked in your current place of employment?
   __ Less than one year
   __ 1–2 years
   __ 3–5 years
   __ 6–7 years
   __ More than 7 years

6. What is your job title? _____

7. Please list your places of full-time employment since college:
   Employer 1: _____ Years of employment: ____ - ____
   Employer 2: _____ Years of employment: ____ - ____
   Employer 3: _____ Years of employment: ____ - ____
   Employer 4: _____ Years of employment: ____ - ____
   Employer 5: _____ Years of employment: ____ - ____

8. What is your mother's occupation? _____

9. What is your father's occupation? _____

10. What is your highest level of education?
    __ Did not graduate from high school
    __ High school graduate
    __ Some college, but no degree (yet)
    __ 2-year college degree
    __ 4-year college degree
    __ Master's degree
    __ JD
    __ MBA
    __ PhD
    __ MD
    __ Other (please specify: _____)

11. Are you registered to vote?
    __ Yes
    __ No
    __ Don't know

12. Did you vote in the 2008 presidential election?
    __ Yes
    __ No
    __ Don't know

13. Did you vote in the 2010 midterm election?
    __ Yes
    __ No
    __ Don't know

14. Did you vote in the 2012 election?
    __ Yes
    __ No
    __ Don't know

15. Are you male or female?
    __ Male
    __ Female

16. Which category below includes your age?
    __ 17 or younger
    __ 18–20
    __ 21–29
    __ 30–39
    __ 40–49
    __ 50–59
    __ 60 or older

17. Which racial or ethnic group best describes you?
    __ White
    __ Black or African-American
    __ Hispanic or Latino
    __ Asian or Asian-American
    __ Native American
    __ Mixed Race
    __ Other (please specify)
    __ Middle Eastern

18. What is your present religion, if any?
    __ Protestant
    __ Roman Catholic
    __ Mormon
    __ Eastern or Greek Orthodox
    __ Jewish
    __ Muslim
    __ Buddhist
    __ Hindu
    __ Atheist
    __ Agnostic
    __ Nothing in particular
    __ Something else

19. Thinking about politics these days, how would you describe your own
    political viewpoint?
    __ Very Liberal
    __ Liberal
    __ Moderate
    __ Conservative
    __ Very Conservative
    __ Not sure

20. Generally speaking, do you think of yourself as a . . . ?
    __ Strong Democrat
    __ Not very strong Democrat
    __ Independent-leaning Democrat
    __ Independent
    __ Independent-leaning Republican
    __ Not very strong Republican
    __ Strong Republican
    __ Not sure

21. Thinking back over the last year, what was your family's income?
    __ less than $10,000
    __ $10,000–$14,999
    __ $15,000–$19,999
    __ $20,000–$24,999
    __ $25,000–$29,999
    __ $30,000–$39,999
    __ $40,000–$49,999
    __ $50,000–$59,999
    __ $60,000–$69,999
    __ $70,000–$79,999
    __ $80,000–$99,999
    __ $100,000–$119,999
    __ $120,000–$149,999
    __ $150,000 or more
    __ Prefer not to say

22. Thinking back over the last year, what was your parents' income?
    __ less than $10,000
    __ $10,000–$14,999
    __ $15,000–$19,999
    __ $20,000–$24,999
    __ $25,000–$29,999
    __ $30,000–$39,999
    __ $40,000–$49,999
    __ $50,000–$59,999
    __ $60,000–$69,999
    __ $70,000–$79,999
    __ $80,000–$99,999
    __ $100,000–$119,999
    __ $120,000–$149,999
    __ $150,000 or more
    __ Prefer not to say

23. Do you follow what's going on in government and public affairs?
    __ Most of the time
    __ Some of the time
    __ Only now and then
    __ Hardly at all

24. How much do you enjoy keeping up with the news?
    __ A lot
    __ Some
    __ Not much
    __ Not at all

25. How do you get most your news about national and international issues? Please select up to 2 choices.
    __ Television
    __ Newspapers
    __ Radio
    __ Magazines
    __ Internet

26. How many days in the past week did you . . . ?

	0	1	2	3	4	5	6	7
Watch the national network news on TV								
Watch the local TV news shows such as *Eyewitness News* or *Action News* in the late afternoon/early evening								
Watch the local TV news shows in the late evening								
Read a daily newspaper in print								
Read a daily newspaper on the internet								
Listen to the news on the radio								

27. How much news do you get from the following sources:

	A Great Deal	Quite a Bit	Some	Very Little	None
Washington Post					
Washington Post Express					
New York Times					
Wall Street Journal					
Other national newspaper					
Washington Examiner					
The Hill (print)					
The Hill (online and emails)					
Politico (print)					
Politico (online and emails)					
Roll Call (print)					
Roll Call (online and emails)					
Government Executive					
Foreign Affairs					
Fox Cable News					
CNN					
MSNBC Cable News					
National Nightly News					
Other (please specify:)					

28. Is the percentage of Americans in poverty as reported by the government closer to . . . ?

___ 1%

___ 5%

___ 15%

___ 36%

29. Is the national unemployment rate as reported by the government closer to . . . ?

___ 5%

___ 9%

___ 15%

___ 21%

30. Is the percentage of the US population that is 65 years old or over closer to . . . ?
    __ 9%
    __ 13%
    __ 17%
    __ 22%

31. Is the percentage of the US population that is white closer to . . . ?
    __ 73%
    __ 78%
    __ 82%
    __ 88%

32. Is the percentage of the US population that is African American closer to . . . ?
    __ 9%
    __ 13%
    __ 17%
    __ 22%

33. Is per capita income in the US closer to . . . ?
    __ $18,000
    __ $22,000
    __ $27,000
    __ $33,000

34. Is the median household income in the US closer to . . . ?
    __ $41,000
    __ $47,000
    __ $52,000
    __ $57,000

35. Is the average travel time to work in the US closer to . . . ?
___ 18 minutes
___ 25 minutes
___ 30 minutes
___ 37 minutes

36. Is the percentage of individuals in the US who speak a language other than English in their homes closer to . . . ?
___ 11%
___ 16%
___ 20%
___ 25%

37. Is the home ownership rate in the US closer to . . . ?
___ 57%
___ 62%
___ 67%
___ 72%

38. Is the percentage of people in the US (aged 25+) who have a bachelor's degree or higher closer to . . . ?
___ 28%
___ 32%
___ 37%
___ 42%

39. Is the percentage of people in the US (aged 25+) who have a high school degree or higher closer to . . . ?
___ 74%
___ 80%
___ 85%
___ 91%

40. In your opinion, should federal spending on the following programs be increased, decreased or kept the same?

	Increased	Decreased	Kept the Same
Aid to poor people			
Child care			
Dealing with crime			
AIDS research			
Public Schools			
Financial Aid for college students			
Foreign aid			
Solving the problem of the homeless			
Welfare programs			
Food stamps			
Improving and protecting the environment			
Science and technology			
Social Security			
Aid to minorities			
Defense			

41. On average, do people you know through work think that federal spending on the following programs should be increased, decreased or kept the same?

	Increased	Decreased	Kept the Same
Aid to poor people			
Child care			
Dealing with crime			
AIDS research			
Public Schools			
Financial Aid for college students			
Foreign aid			
Solving the problem of the homeless			
Welfare programs			
Food stamps			
Improving and protecting the environment			
Science and technology			
Social Security			
Aid to minorities			
Defense			

42. How much does the average American know about the following programs?

	A Great Deal	Quite a Bit	Some	Very Little	None
Aid to poor people					
Child care					
Dealing with crime					
AIDS research					
Public Schools					
Financial Aid for college students					
Foreign aid					
Solving the problem of the homeless					
Welfare programs					
Food stamps					
Improving and protecting the environment					
Science and technology					
Social Security					
Aid to minorities					
Defense					

43. Does the average American think that federal spending on the following programs should be increased, decreased or kept the same?

	Increased	Decreased	Kept the Same
Aid to poor people			
Child care			
Dealing with crime			
AIDS research			
Public Schools			
Financial Aid for college students			
Foreign aid			
Solving the problem of the homeless			
Welfare programs			
Food stamps			
Improving and protecting the environment			
Science and technology			
Social Security			
Aid to minorities			
Defense			

44. With respect to the following programs, should the government follow public opinion or do what it thinks is best?

	Follow public opinion	Mostly follow public opinion	Give equal consideration to public opinion and what it thinks is best	Mostly do what it thinks is best	Mostly do what it thinks is best
Aid to poor people					
Child care					
Dealing with crime					
AIDS research					
Public Schools					
Financial Aid for college students					
Foreign aid					
Solving the problem of the homeless					
Welfare programs					
Food stamps					
Improving and protecting the environment					
Science and technology					
Social Security					
Aid to minorities					
Defense					

45. Do you favor, oppose or neither favor nor oppose . . . ?

	Favor a great deal	Favor moderately	Favor a little	Neither favor nor oppose	Oppose a little	Oppose moderately	Oppose a great deal
an amendment to the US Constitution banning marriage between two people who are the same sex?							
raising federal income taxes for people who make **more** than $200,000 per year?							
raising federal income taxes for people who make **less** than $200,000 per year?							
the US government paying for all of the cost of prescription drugs for senior citizens who are living on very little income?							
the US government paying for all necessary medical care for all Americans?							

allowing illegal immigrants to work in the United States for up to three years, after which they would have to go back to their home country?							
the US government making it possible for illegal immigrants to become US citizens?							
Imagine that the US government suspects a person in the United States of being a terrorist. Do you favor, oppose, or neither favor nor oppose the government being able to put this person in prison for months without ever bringing the person to court and charging him or her with a crime?							
the US government being required to get a court order before it can listen in on phone calls made by American citizens who are suspected of being terrorists?							

46. On average, do people you know through work favor, oppose or neither favor nor oppose . . . ?

	Favor a great deal	Favor mod- erately	Favor a little	Neither favor nor oppose	Oppose a little	Oppose mod- erately	Oppose a great deal
an amendment to the US Consti- tution banning marriage between two people who are the same sex?							
raising federal income taxes for people who make **more** than $200,000 per year?							
raising federal income taxes for people who make **less** than $200,000 per year?							
the US govern- ment paying for all of the cost of prescription drugs for senior citizens who are living on very little income?							
the US govern- ment paying for all necessary medical care for all Americans?							

allowing illegal immigrants to work in the United States for up to three years, after which they would have to go back to their home country?							
the US government making it possible for illegal immigrants to become US citizens?							
Imagine that the US government suspects a person in the United States of being a terrorist. Do you favor, oppose, or neither favor nor oppose the government being able to put this person in prison for months without ever bringing the person to court and charging him or her with a crime?							
the US government being required to get a court order before it can listen in on phone calls made by American citizens who are suspected of being terrorists?							

47. Does the average American favor, oppose or neither favor nor oppose . . . ?

	Favors a great deal	Favors moderately	Favors a little	Neither favors nor opposes	Opposes a little	Opposes moderately	Opposes a great deal
an amendment to the US Constitution banning marriage between two people who are the same sex?							
raising federal income taxes for people who make **more** than $200,000 per year?							
raising federal income taxes for people who make **less** than $200,000 per year?							
The US government paying for all of the cost of prescription drugs for senior citizens who are living on very little income?							

The US government paying for all necessary medical care for all Americans?						
allowing illegal immigrants to work in the United States for up to three years, after which they would have to go back to their home country?						
the US government making it possible for illegal immigrants to become US citizens?						

Imagine that the US government suspects a person in the United States of being a terrorist. Do you favor, oppose, or neither favor nor oppose the govern- ment being able to put this person in prison for months without ever bringing the person to court and charging him or her with a crime?							
the US govern- ment being required to get a court order before it can listen in on phone calls made by Amer- ican citizens who are suspected of being terrorists?							

48. How much do you think the average American knows about the following policy proposals:

	A Great Deal	Quite a Bit	Some	Very Little	None
an amendment to the US Constitution banning marriage between two people who are the same sex?					
raising federal income taxes for people who make **more** than $200,000 per year?					
raising federal income taxes for people who make **less** than $200,000 per year?					
The US government paying for all of the cost of prescription drugs for senior citizens who are living on very little income?					
The US government paying for all necessary medical care for all Americans?					
allowing illegal immigrants to work in the United States for up to three years, after which they would have to go back to their home country?					
the US government making it possible for illegal immigrants to become US citizens?					
the government being able to put this person in prison for months without ever bringing the person to court and charging him or her with a crime?					
the US government being required to get a court order before it can listen in on phone calls made by American citizens who are suspected of being terrorists?					

49. With respect to the following policy proposals, should the government follow public opinion or do what it thinks is best?

	Follow public opinion	Mostly follow public opinion	Give equal consideration to public opinion and what it thinks is best	Mostly do what it thinks is best	Mostly do what it thinks is best
an amendment to the US Constitution banning marriage between two people who are the same sex?					
raising federal income taxes for people who make **more** than $200,000 per year?					
raising federal income taxes for people who make **less** than $200,000 per year?					
The US government paying for all of the cost of prescription drugs for senior citizens who are living on very little income?					
The US government paying for all necessary medical care for all Americans?					
allowing illegal immigrants to work in the United States for up to three years, after which they would have to go back to their home country?					
the US government making it possible for illegal immigrants to become US citizens?					
the government being able to put this person in prison for months without ever bringing the person to court and charging him or her with a crime?					
the US government being required to get a court order before it can listen in on phone calls made by American citizens who are suspected of being terrorists?					

50. In your opinion, what is the most important problem facing the nation?
___ Jobs
___ Budget deficit
___ Social Security
___ Immigration
___ Gay marriage

51. On average, what do people you know through work think is the most important problem facing the nation?
___ Jobs
___ Budget deficit
___ Social Security
___ Immigration
___ Gay marriage

52 What does the average American think is the most important problem facing the nation?
___ Jobs
___ Budget deficit
___ Social Security
___ Immigration
___ Gay marriage

53. How much does the average American know about the most important problem facing the nation?
___ A great deal
___ Quite a bit
___ Some
___ Very little
___ None

54. When addressing the most important problem, should the government follow public opinion or do what it thinks is best?
    __ Follow public opinion
    __ Mostly follow public opinion
    __ Give equal consideration to public opinion and what it thinks is best
    __ Mostly do what it thinks is best
    __ Do what it thinks is best

55. Please read the following statements in the chart below and indicate whether you agree strongly, agree somewhat, neither agree nor disagree, disagree somewhat or disagree strongly.

	Agree strongly	Agree somewhat	Neither agree nor disagree	Disagree somewhat	Disagree strongly
People like me don't have any say about what the government does.					
Sometimes politics and government seem so complicated that a person like me can't really understand what's going on.					
Public officials don't care much what people like me think.					
Voting is the only way that people like me can have any say about how the government runs things.					

56. Please read the following statements in the chart below and indicate whether you agree strongly, agree somewhat, neither agree nor disagree, disagree somewhat or disagree strongly.

	Agree strongly	Agree somewhat	Neither agree nor disagree	Disagree somewhat	Disagree strongly
The average American doesn't have any say about what the government does.					
Sometimes politics and government seem so complicated that the average American can't really understand what's going on.					
The average American doesn't care much what people like me think.					
Voting is the only way that the average American can have any say about how the government runs things.					

57 In general, how much attention do the following government actors pay to what the American people think when they decide what to do?

	A Great Deal	Quite a Bit	Some	Very Little	None
Members of the House of Representatives					
Members of the Senate					
The President					
Bureaucrats in Executive Agencies					
Bureaucrats in Independent Agencies					
Members of the Supreme Court					
Congressional staffers					
Lobbyists					
Government contractors					
Researchers at think tanks					

58. Do elections make the following government actors pay attention to what the American people think?

	A Great Deal	Quite a Bit	Some	Very Little	None
Members of the House of Representatives					
Members of the Senate					
The President					
Bureaucrats in Executive Agencies					
Bureaucrats in Independent Agencies					
Members of the Supreme Court					
Congressional staffers					
Lobbyists					
Government contractors					
Researchers at think tanks					

59. On a scale of 1–10, rate the competence of the following actors to perform their jobs:

	1 (Not at All Competent)	2	3	4	5	6	7	8	9	10 (Highly Competent
Members of the House of Representatives										
Members of the Senate										
The President										
Bureaucrats in Executive Agencies										
Bureaucrats in Independent Agencies										
Members of the Supreme Court										
Congressional staffers										
Lobbyists										
Government contractors										
Researchers at think tanks										

60. On a scale of 1–10, how much trust do you have in the following actors?

	1 (None)	2	3	4	5	6	7	8	9	10 (A Lot)
Members of the House of Representatives										
Members of the Senate										
The President										
Bureaucrats in Executive Agencies										
Bureaucrats in Independent Agencies										
Members of the Supreme Court										
Congressional staffers										
Lobbyists										
Government contractors										
Researchers at think tanks										

61. During the past six months, approximately how many times have you interacted with members of the public?

__ 0

__ 1–3

__ 4–6

__ 7–10

__ 11–15

__ More than 15 times

62. During the past six months, approximately how many times have you received feedback from members of the general public about issues you are working on?

__ 0

__ 1–3

__ 4–6

__ 7–10

__ 11–15

__ More than 15 times

63. Please describe the ways in which you interact with the general public about your work. [open-ended]

64. Do you use the following means to communicate with members of the general public about your work?

	1 (Not at All)	2	3	4	5	6	7	8	9	10 (A Lot)
Telephone										
Email										
Website										
Fax										
In-person meeting										
Social media (please specify:)										

65. On a scale of 1-10, rate the extent to which members of the general public influence your decision-making at work.

1 (Never)	2	3	4	5	6	7	8	9	10 (Frequently)

66. Does your job require you to make decisions that affect members of the general public?
    __ Yes
    __ Sometimes
    __ No

67. Does your job require you to incorporate feedback from the general public into your decision-making?
    __ Yes
    __ Sometimes
    __ No

68. As you think about your job, where would you place yourself on a scale of delegate to trustee, where delegate represents a policy maker who acts strictly on the preferences of voters and trustee represents a policy maker who uses his or her own best judgment to decide issues?

1 (Delegate)	2	3	4	5	6	7 (Trustee)

69. Many things are desirable, but not all of them are essential characteristics of democracy. Please tell me for each of the following things how essential you think it is as a characteristic of democracy. Use this scale where 1 means "not at all an essential characteristic of democracy" and 10 means it definitely is "an essential characteristic of democracy."

	Not at all essential									Definitely essential
Governments tax the rich and subsidize the poor.	1	2	3	4	5	6	7	8	9	10
Religious authorities ultimately interpret the laws.	1	2	3	4	5	6	7	8	9	10
People choose their leaders in free elections.	1	2	3	4	5	6	7	8	9	10
People receive state aid for unemployment.	1	2	3	4	5	6	7	8	9	10
The army takes over when government is incompetent.	1	2	3	4	5	6	7	8	9	10
Civil rights protect people from state oppression.	1	2	3	4	5	6	7	8	9	10
The state makes people's incomes equal.	1	2	3	4	5	6	7	8	9	10
People obey their rulers.	1	2	3	4	5	6	7	8	9	10
Women have the same rights as men.	1	2	3	4	5	6	7	8	9	10

70. People sometimes talk about what the aims of this country should be for the next ten years. Below are listed some of the goals which different people would give top priority. Would you please say which one of these you, yourself, consider the most important and the second most important?

__ A high level of economic growth

__ Making sure this country has strong defense forces

__ Seeing that people have more say about how things are done at their jobs and in their communities

__ Trying to make our cities and countryside more beautiful

71. If you had to choose, which one of the things listed below would you say is most important and second most important?
__ Maintaining order in the nation
__ Giving people more say in important government decisions
__ Fighting rising prices
__ Protecting freedom of speech

72. If you had to choose, which one of the things listed below would you say is most important and second most important?
__ A stable economy
__ Progress toward a less impersonal and more humane society
__ Progress toward a society in which Ideas count more than money
__ The fight against crime

73. Below is a list of various changes in our way of life that might take place in the near future. Please tell me for each one, if it were to happen, whether you think it would be a good thing, a bad thing, or don't you mind?

	Good	Don't Mind	Bad
Less importance placed on work in our lives			
More emphasis on the development of technology			
Greater respect for authority			

74. – 80. Please consider your views on the various issues below. How would you place your views on this scale? 1 means you agree completely with the statement on the left; 10 means you agree completely with the statement on the right; and if your views fall somewhere in between, you can choose any number in between.

1 (Incomes should be more equal)	2	3	4	5	6	7	8	9	10 (We need larger income differences as incentives for individual effort)
1 (Private ownership of business and industry should be increased)	2	3	4	5	6	7	8	9	10 (Government ownership of business and industry should be increased)
1 (Government should take more responsibility to ensure that everyone is provided for)	2	3	4	5	6	7	8	9	10 (People should take more responsibility to provide for themselves)
1 (Competition is good. It stimulates people to work hard and develop new ideas)	2	3	4	5	6	7	8	9	10 (Competition is harmful. It brings out the worst in people)
1 (In the long run, hard work usually brings a better life)	2	3	4	5	6	7	8	9	10 (Hard work doesn't generally bring success—it's more a matter of luck and connections)
1 (People can only get rich at the expense of others)	2	3	4	5	6	7	8	9	10 (Wealth can grow so there's enough for everyone)

81. In your view, how often do the following things occur in this country's elections?

	Very Often	Fairly Often	Not Often	Not at All Often
Votes are counted fairly				
Opposition candidates are prevented from running				
TV news favors the governing party				
Voters are bribed				
Journalists provide fair coverage of elections				
Election officials are fair				
Rich people buy elections				
Voters are threatened with violence at the polls				
Voters are offered a genuine choice in the elections				

82. Do you feel that the goals and priorities of the leaders in your office are clearly communicated to the staff?
___ Very often
___ Fairly often
___ Not often
___ Not at all often

83. Do you personally have any work-related opposing views to the leaders in your office?
___ Yes
___ Somewhat
___ No

84. If you have work-related opposing views, have you expressed them to the leaders in your office?
___ Yes
___ Somewhat
___ No

85. Please describe the channels that are available to express opposing views in your office?
[open-ended]

86. Please describe your organization's relationship with Congress?
[open-ended, don't answer if work for Congress]

87. How much contact do you, personally, have with Congress as part of your job?
___ Very often
___ Fairly often
___ Not often
___ Not at all often

88. Please describe your work-related interactions with Congress.
[open-ended, don't answer if work for Congress]

89. What kind of role do you think that Congress should play in its oversight of your organization?
[open-ended, don't answer if work for Congress]

90. Are you satisfied with the job that Congress does in its oversight of your organization?
___ Extremely satisfied
___ Somewhat satisfied
___ Neither satisfied nor dissatisfied
___ Somewhat dissatisfied
___ Extremely dissatisfied

NOTES

INTRODUCTION

1. See, Cornelius Kerwin and Scott Furlong, *Rulemaking: How Federal Agencies Write Law and Make Policy*, 4th ed. (Washington, DC: CQ Press, 2011), chapter 7.

2. "State of the States Survey," Gallup, 2015, http://www.gallup.com/poll/ 189176/state-tax-burden-linked-desire-leave-state.aspx?g_source=Economy&g_medium =newsfeed&g_campaign=tiles; "Election Benchmark Survey," Gallup, 2016, http://www .gallup.com/poll/188867/half-say-better-off-eight-years-ago.aspx?g_source=ELECTION _2016&g_medium=topic&g_campaign=tiles.

3. Office of Personnel Management, Planning and Policy Analysis Data Analysis Group, *Common Characteristics of the Government* PPA-2013-05, 2005, https://www .opm.gov/policy-data-oversight/data-analysis-documentation/federal-employment -reports/common-characteristics-of-the-government/common-characteristics-of-the -government-2012.pdf.

CHAPTER 1: UNELECTED GOVERNMENT: THE FOLKS WHO REALLY RUN THINGS

1. 2012 National Election Study, http://www.electionstudies.org/studypages/ anes_timeseries_2012/anes_timeseries_2012.htm.

2. Samuel Huntington, "Congressional Responses to the Twentieth Century," in *The Congress and America's Future*, ed. David Truman (Englewood Cliffs, NJ: Prentice-Hall, 1965), pp. 5–31. See also, Brian Balogh, *A Government out of Sight: The Mystery of National Authority in Nineteenth-Century America* (New York: Cambridge University Press, 2009) and Stephen Skowronek, *Building a New American State: The Expansion of National Administrative Capacities, 1877–1920* (New York: Cambridge University Press, 1982).

3. Matthew Crenson and Benjamin Ginsberg, *Presidential Power: Unchecked and Unbalanced* (New York: W. W. Norton Publishers, 2007). Also, Andrew Rudalevige, *The New Imperial Presidency* (Ann Arbor: University of Michigan Press, 2006).

4. Crenson and Ginsberg, *Presidential Power*, pp. 359–67. See also, B. Dan Wood, *The Myth of Presidential Representation* (New York: Cambridge University Press, 2009).

5. Alan Monroe, "Consistency between Public Preferences and National Policy Decisions," *American Politics Quarterly* 7, no. 1 (January 1979): 3–18. Also, Alan D. Monroe, "Public Opinion and Public Policy, 1980–1993," *Public Opinion Quarterly* 62, no. 1 (Spring 1998): 6–18.

6. Benjamin Page and Robert Y. Shapiro, "Effects of Public Opinion on Policy," *American Political Science Review* 77, no. 1 (March 1983): 175–90. See also, Jeff Manza, Fay Cook, and Benjamin Page, eds., *Navigating Public Opinion* (New York: Oxford, 2002), part I.

7. Larry M. Bartels, *Unequal Democracy: The Political Economy of the New Gilded Age* (Princeton, NJ: Princeton University Press, 2008).

8. Clinton Rossiter, ed., *The Federalist*, No. 57 (New York: Mentor, 1961), p. 352.

9. Warren E. Miller and Donald E. Stokes, "Constituency Influence in Congress," in *Elections and the Political Order*, ed. Angus Campbell, Philip Converse, Warren Miller, and Donald Stokes (New York: Wiley, 1966), pp. 351–72.

10. Dick Morris, *Behind the Oval Office* (Los Angeles: Renaissance, 1999).

11. Some scholars have argued that bureaucracies can have a representative character. See, Kenneth J. Meier and Tabitha S. M. Morton, "Representative Bureaucracy in a Cross-National Context: Politics, Identity, Structure and Discretion," in *Politics of Representative Bureaucracy: Power, Legitimacy and Performance*, ed. B. Guy Peters, Patrick von Maravić, and Eckhard Schröter (Northampton, MA: Edward Elgar, 2015).

12. Robert Pear, "Ambiguity in Health Law Could Make Family Coverage Too Costly for Many," *New York Times*, August 12, 2012, p. 10.

13. Jerry L. Mashaw, *Greed, Chaos, and Governance: Using Public Choice to Improve Public Law* (New Haven, CT: Yale University Press, 1997), p. 106.

14. Kimberly Johnson, *Governing the American State* (Princeton: Princeton University Press, 2006). Also, Elizabeth Sanders, *Roots of Reform: Farmers, Workers, and the American State* (Chicago: University of Chicago Press, 1999); and Theda Skocpol, *Protecting Soldiers and Mothers: The Political Origins of Social Policy in the United States* (Cambridge, MA: Harvard University Press, 1995).

15. Daniel Carpenter, *The Forging of Bureaucratic Autonomy* (Princeton, NJ: Princeton University Press, 2001).

16. See, Theodore J. Lowi, *The End of Liberalism*, 2nd ed. (New York: Norton, 1979). Also, David Schoenbrod, *Power Without Responsibility: How Congress Abuses the People Through Delegation* (New Haven, CT: Yale University Press, 1993).

17. Kenneth Culp Davis, *Discretionary Justice* (Baton Rouge: Louisiana State University Press, 1969), pp. 15–21.

18. Mistretta v. U.S., 488 U.S. 361, 372 (1989).

19. Schoenbrod, *Power Without Responsibility*, chapter 2.

20. Ibid., p. 61.

21. William F. Fox, *Understanding Administrative Law*, 4th ed. (New York: Lexis Publishing, 2000), pp. 36–37.

22. Kara Scannell and Deborah Soloman, "Business Wins Its Battle to Ease a Costly Sarbanes-Oxley Rule," *Wall Street Journal*, November 10, 2006, p. 1.

23. Harold W. Stanley and Richard G. Niemi, *Vital Statistics on American Politics* (Washington, DC: Congressional Quarterly Press, 2001), p. 262.

24. John Huber and Charles Shipan, *Deliberate Discretion: The Institutional Foundations of Bureaucratic Autonomy* (New York: Cambridge University Press, 2002).

25. Andrew J. Ziaja, "Hot Oil and Hot Air: The Development of the Nondelegation Doctrine through the New Deal, a History 1813–1944," *Hastings Constitutional Law Quarterly* 35, no. 4 (May 2008): 921.

26. David M. O'Brien, *Constitutional Law and Politics: Struggles for Power and Governmental Accountability*, 4th ed. (New York: Norton, 2000), p. 368.

27. Lowi, *End of Liberalism*, pp. 94–97.

28. Jeffrey A. Wertkin, "Reintroducing Compromise to the Nondelegation Doctrine," *Georgetown Law Journal* 90 (April 2002): 1055.

29. Field v. Clark, 143 U.S. 649 (1892).

30. Wayman v. Southard, 23 U.S. 1 (1825).

31. J. W. Hampton, Jr., & Co. v. United States, 276 U.S. 394 (1928).

32. Emergency Price Control Act of 1942, 56 Stat. 23 (January 30, 1942).

33. Panama Refining Co. v. Ryan, 293 U.S. 388 (1935).

34. Schechter Poultry Corp. v. United States, 295 U.S. 495, 553 (1935).

35. Carter v. Carter Coal Co., 298 U.S. 238 (1936).

36. Yakus v. United States, 321 U.S. 414, 425 (1944).

37. Mistretta v. United States, 488 U.S. 361 (1989).

38. United States v. Booker, 125 S. Ct. 738 (2005).

39. Chevron U.S.A., Inc. v. Natural Resources Defense Council, Inc. 467 U.S. 837 (1984).

40. See, Whitman v. American Trucking Associations, Inc., 531 U.S. 457 (2001). Also, AT&T Corp. v. Iowa Utilities Board, 525 U.S. 366 (1999).

41. United States v. Mead Corp., 533 U.S. 218 (2001).

42. Eric Lipton and Coral Davenport, "Critics Hear EPA's Voice in 'Public Comments,'" *New York Times*, May 18, 2015, http://www.nytimes.com/2015/05/19/us/critics-hear-epas-voice-in-public-comments.html?_r=0.

43. City of Arlington, Tex. v. FCC, 133 S. Ct. 1863 (2013).

44. Amy Harder and Brent Kendall, "Climate Agenda on the Line: Carbon Rule's Stay Marks Unusual Blow to the President's Environmental Push," *Wall Street Journal*, February 11, 2016, p. A3.

45. Matthew D. McCubbins and Thomas Schwartz, "Congressional Oversight Overlooked: Police Patrols versus Fire Alarms," *American Journal of Political Science* 28, no. 1 (February 1984): 165–79.

46. These relationships are sometimes called "iron triangles." See, Theodore Lowi, *The End of Liberalism* (New York: Norton, 1979). Also see, Elena Kagan, "Presidential Administration," *Harvard Law Review* 114 (June 2001): 2347.

47. Henry A. Waxman, "Free Pass from Congress," *Washington Post*, July 6, 2004, p. A19.

48. Shailagh Murray, "Storms Show a System out of Balance," *Washington Post*, October 5, 2005, p. A21.

49. Family and Medical Leave Act of 1993, 29 U.S.C. 2601.

50. Caitlyn M. Campbell, "Overstepping One's Bounds: The Department of Labor and the Family and Medical Leave Act," *Boston University Law Review* 84, no. 4 (October 2004): 1077.

51. Miller v. AT&T Corp., 250 F.3d 820 (2001).

52. Campbell, "Overstepping One's Bounds," p. 1088.

53. Brian A. Reeves, "Federal Law Enforcement Officers, 2008." US Department of Justice, Bureau of Justice Statistics, Office of Justice Programs, June 2012.

54. Robert Johnson, "This Is Why NOAA Supposedly Ordered 46,000 Rounds of Ammunition," *Business Insider*, August 14, 2012, http://www.businessinsider.com/this-is-why-the-noaa-supposedly-ordered-46000-rounds-of-ammunition-2012-8.

55. Louise Radnofsky, Gary Fields, and John R. Emshwiller, "Federal Police Ranks Swell to Enforce a Widening Array of Criminal Laws," *Wall Street Journal*, December 17, 2011, p. 1.

56. John R. Emshwiller and Gary Fields, "For Feds Lying Is a Handy Charge," *Wall Street Journal*, April 10, 2012, p. 1.

57. Adam Liptak, "Justices to Weigh Finance Law as It Was Applied to Little Fish," *New York Times*, April 29, 2014, p. A14.

58. Eric Posner and Adrian Vermeule, *The Executive Unbound: After the Madisonian Republic* (New York: Oxford University Press, 2011).

59. Marissa Martino Golden, *What Motivates Bureaucrats?* (New York: Columbia University Press, 2000), pp. 6–7.

60. James F. Blumstein, "Regulatory Review by the Executive Office of the President: An Overview and Policy Analysis of Current Issues," *Duke Law Journal* 51, no. 3 (December 2001): 856.

61. Terry M. Moe, "The President and Bureaucracy," in *The Presidency and the Political System*, 4th edition, ed. Michael Nelson (Washington, DC: CQ Press, 1995), p. 432.

62. Kagan, "Presidential Administration," p. 2262.

63. Moe, "President and the Bureaucracy," pp. 430–31.

64. Joel D. Aberbach and Bert A. Rockman, *In the Web of Politics: Three Decades of the U.S. Federal Executive* (Washington, DC: Brookings, 2000), p. 169.

65. Marissa Martino Golden, *What Motivates Bureaucrats? Politics and Administration During the Reagan Years* (New York: Columbia University Press, 2000).

66. Blumstein, "Regulatory Review by the Executive Office of the President," p. 859.

67. Richard H. Pildes and Cass Sunstein, "Reinventing the Regulatory State," *University of Chicago Law Review* 62, no. 1 (Winter 1995): 1.

68. Kagan, "Presidential Administration," p. 2247.

69. Ibid., p. 2267.

70. Ibid., p. 2265.

71. Blumstein, "Regulatory Review by the Executive Office of the President," p. 860.

72. John M. Broder, "Powerful Shaper of U.S. Rules Quits, Leaving Critics in Wake," *New York Times*, August 4, 2012, p. 1.

73. Maeve P. Carey, "Counting Regulations: An Overview of Rulemaking, Types of Federal Regulations, and Pages in the Federal Register," *Congressional Research Service*, May 1, 2013, http://www.fas.org/sgp/crs/misc/R43056.pdf.

74. Alexis de Tocqueville, *Democracy in America*, vol. 2, book 4, ch. 6, ed. Phillips Bradley (New York: Vintage, 1945), p. 335.

75. Harold Seidman, *Politics, Position and Power* (New York: Oxford, 1998), p. 208.

76. Thomas Stanton, *Government Sponsored Enterprises: Mercantilist Companies in the Modern World* (Washington, DC: American Enterprise Institute, 2000).

77. Stanton, *Government Sponsored Enterprises*, p. 16.

78. Kathleen Day, "Greenspan Urges Review of Fannie, Freddie Subsidies," *Washington Post*, May 24, 2000, p. E3.

79. Stanton, *Government Sponsored Enterprises*, p. 12.

80. Ibid.

81. Ibid., p. 44.

82. Herman Schwartz, "Governmentally Appointed Directors in a Private Corporation," *Harvard Law Review* 79, no. 2 (December 1965): 350. Also, Ronald Gilson and Reinier Kraakman, "Reinventing the Outside Director: An Agenda for Institutional Investors," *Stanford Law Review* 43, no. 4 (April 1991): 863.

83. Stanton, *Government Sponsored Enterprises*, p. 37.

84. Scott Shane and Ron Nixon, "U.S. contractors Becoming a Fourth Branch of Government—Americas—International Herald Tribune," *New York Times*, February 4, 2007, http://www.nytimes.com/2007/02/04/world/americas/04iht-web.0204contract.4460796.html (accessed August 24, 2012).

85. For estimates of the "true" size of America's government, see, Paul C. Light, *The True Size of Government* (Washington, DC: Brookings Institution Press, 1999).

86. The information in the second half of this paragraph is taken from: Benjamin Ginsberg, *Presidential Government* (New Haven, CT: Yale University Press, 2016), p. 166.

87. Light, *True Size of Government*.

CHAPTER 2: THE CHASM BETWEEN US AND THEM

1. Clinton Rossiter, ed., *The Federalist Papers*, no. 52 (New York: New American Library, 1961).

2. Ibid., no. 10.

3. Some of the Constitution's framers were concerned that direct popular elections would lead to "majority tyranny" or mob rule and favored indirect elections. Others thought that direct elections might be problematic but were concerned that the Constitution might not be ratified if it did not include some provision for popular participation. The result was that members of the House of Representatives were to be chosen by direct popular vote while senators were to be chosen by the state legislatures and the president appointed by an Electoral College chosen by the state legislatures. By the 1830s, most states provided for popular selection of the presidential electors, and in 1913, of course, the Seventeenth Amendment provided for direct popular election of senators.

4. Rossiter, *Federalist Papers*, no. 57.

5. Ibid.

6. Jennifer E. Manning, "Membership of the 113th Congress: A Profile," *Congressional Research Service*, November 14, 2014, http://www.fas.org/sgp/crs/misc/R42964.pdf.

7. Herbert McClosky, Paul J. Hoffman, and Rosemary O'Hara, "Issue Conflict and Consensus among Party Leaders and Followers," *American Political Science Review* 54, no. 2 (June 1960): 406–27.

8. David Broockman and Christopher Skovron, "Politicians Think Voters Are More Conservative than They Really Are," *Democracy: A Journal of Ideas*, September 18, 2013, http://democracyjournal.org/arguments/2013/09/politicians-think-american-voters-are-more-conservative-than-they-really-are.php.html.

9. Rossiter, *Federalist Papers*, no. 57.

10. Angus Campbell, Philip E. Converse, Warren E. Miller, and David E. Stokes, *Elections and the Political Order* (New York: Wiley, 1966).

11. Martin Shefter, *Political Parties and the State* (Princeton: Princeton University Press, 1993), chapter 2.

12. James D. Richardson, ed., *Messages and Papers of the Presidents*, vol. II (Washington, DC: US Government Printing Office, 1899), p. 449.

13. Stephen Skowronek, *Building a New American State* (New York: Cambridge University Press, 1982).

14. "Partisanship in the Civil Service," *New York Times*, September 23, 1876, http://query.nytimes.com/mem/archive-free/pdf?res=F00F14F93D54107A93C1AB1782D85F428784F9.

15. Benjamin Ginsberg and Martin Shefter, *Politics by Other Means* (New York: Basic Books, 1988).

16. Andrew Cohen, "How Voter ID Laws Are Being Used to Disenfranchise Minorities

and the Poor," *Atlantic*, March 16, 2012, http://www.theatlantic.com/politics/archive/2012/03/how-voter-id-laws-are-being-used-to-disenfranchise-minorities-and-the-poor/254572/.

17. The Hatch Act was amended in 1993 to allow federal employees some political involvements, but the basic prohibitions on partisan activity remain in place.

18. Cornelius M. Kerwin and Scott R. Furlong, *Rulemaking: How Government Agencies Write Law and Make Policy*, 4th ed. (Washington, DC: CQ Press, 2011), p. 231.

19. Eric Yoder and Lisa Rein, "Federal vs. Private-Sector Pay: No Comparison Is Definitive, Auditors Say," *Washington Post*, July 23, 2012, http://www.washingtonpost.com/politics/federal-vs-private-sector-pay-no-comparison-is-definitive-auditors-say/2012/07/23/gJQAJAWM5W_story.html.

20. US Census Bureau, "American Community Survey," 2012, https://www.census.gov/acs/www/data/data-tables-and-tools/data-profiles/2012/.

21. Chris Edwards, "Reducing the Costs of Federal Worker Pay and Benefits," Cato Institute, October 1, 2015, http://www.downsizinggovernment.org/federal-worker-pay.

22. For a summary of these data, see, Edwards, "Reducing the Costs of Federal Worker Pay and Benefits."

23. Chris Edwards, "Overpaid Federal Workers," Cato Institute, August 2013, http://www.downsizinggovernment.org/overpaid-federal-workers.

24. Kenneth Meier, *Politics and the Bureaucracy: Policymaking in the Fourth Branch of Government* (North Scituate, MA: Duxbury, 1979), p. 170.

25. Gary Langer, "Vast Racial Gap on Trayvon Martin Case Marks a Challenging Conversation," ABC News, July 22, 2013, http://abcnews.go.com/blogs/politics/2013/07/vast-racial-gap-on-trayvon-martin-case-marks-a-challenging-conversation/.

26. Ronald Weitzer and Steven A. Tuch, "Race and Perceptions of Police Misconduct," *Social Problems* 51, no. 3 (2004): 305–25.

27. Angus Campbell, Philip E. Converse, Warren Miller, and Donald Stokes, *The American Voter* (New York: Wiley, 1960), chapter 17.

28. Anne Fernald, Virgina A. Marchman, and Adriana Weisleder, "SES Differences in Language Processing Skills and Vocabulary Are Evident at 18 Months," *Developmental Science* 16, no. 2 (March 2013): 234–48.

29. American National Election Study [ANES], *User's Guide and Codebook for the ANES 2012 Time Series Study* (Ann Arbor, MI / Palo Alto, CA: University of Michigan / Stanford University, 2015), http://www.electionstudies.org/studypages/anes_timeseries_2012/anes_timeseries_2012_userguidecodebook.pdf.

30. Benjamin Ginsberg, *The American Lie: Government By the People and Other Political Fables* (Boulder, CO: Paradigm, 2007), chapter 1.

31. Eduardo Porter, "Why the Health Care Law Scares the GOP," *New York Times*, October 1, 2013, http://www.nytimes.com/2013/10/02/business/economy/why-the-health-care-law-scares-the-gop.html?smid=tw-share&_r=1&.

32. "2014 Political Polarization and Typology Survey: Final Topline," Pew Research Center, Washington, DC, http://www.people-press.org/files/2014/06/APPENDIX-4 -Typology-Topline-for-Release.pdf; "Partisan Polarization Surges in Bush, Obama Years," *Trends in American Values: 1987–2012*, Pew Research Center, Washington, DC, June 4, 2012, http://www.people-press.org/files/legacy-pdf/06-04-12%20Values%20Release.pdf.

33. Robert P. Nathan, *The Plot That Failed: Nixon and the Administrative Presidency* (New York: Wiley, 1975).

34. Pamela Winston, *Welfare Policymaking in the States: The Devil in Devolution* (Washington, DC: Georgetown University Press, 2002).

35. Ginsberg and Shefter, *Politics by Other Means*, pp. 78–79.

36. Clifford Geertz, "Ideology as a Cultural System," in *Ideology and Discontent*, ed. David Apter (New York: Free Press, 1964), p. 61.

37. Ibid., p. 63.

38. Pam Fessler, "State Budget Cuts Threaten Child Welfare Programs," *National Public Radio*, March 2, 2010, http://www.npr.org/templates/story/story.php?storyId=124127356.

39. "Sen. Mike Lee Warns That the Size of Government Threatens Our Freedom," *Mr. Conservative*, May 17, 2012, http://www.mrconservative.com/2013/05/16312 -sen-mike-lee-warns-that-the-size-of-government-threatens-our-freedoms/.

40. To be sure, ideology and partisanship are not synonyms. For a discussion on their differences, see Hans Noel, *Political Ideologies and Political Parties in America* (New York: Cambridge University Press, 2014).

41. Campbell, Converse, Miller, and Stokes, *American Voter*, p. 128.

42. "Voters Skeptical that 2016 Candidates Would Make Good Presidents," Pew Research Center, Washington, DC, January 20, 2016, http://www.people-press .org/2016/01/20/voters-skeptical-that-2016-candidates-would-make-good-presidents/.

43. Judea Pearl, *Causality, Models, Reasoning and Inference* (New York: Cambridge University Press, 2009), pp. 348–52.

44. Aristotle, *Nicomachean Ethics*, book VIII, ch. 11, trans. H. Rackham (Cambridge: Harvard University Press, 1926), p. 497.

45. Membership in one of these categories of government is thus considered the "treatment group" in this analysis. When calculating propensity scores, one group is considered the treatment group. An individual's propensity score is the probability that he or she is a member of the treatment group based on the set of background characteristics included in the analysis.

46. Donald Kettl, *The Next Government of the United States* (New York: W. W. Norton, 2009), p. 31.

47. Stephen Goldsmith and William D. Eggers, *Governing By Network* (Washington, DC: Brookings Institution, 2004), p. 12.

48. Richard J. Bednar and Gary P. Quigley, "The Blended Workforce," *Govern-

ment Executive, May 9, 2007, http://www.govexec.com/excellence/management-matters/2007/05/the-blended-workforce/24375/.

49. James A. Hughes, "Blended Workforce Poses Conflict of Interest Risks," *National Defense*, November 2006, http://www.nationaldefensemagazine.org/archive/2006/November/Pages/EthicsCorner2834.aspx.

There is, of course, considerable debate about what tasks, if any, are "inherently governmental." See, Dan Guttman, "Inherently Governmental Functions and the New Millennium: The Legacy of Twentieth-Century Reform," in *Making Government Manageable: Executive Organization and Management in the Twenty-First Century*, ed. Thomas Stanton and Benjamin Ginsberg (Baltimore: Johns Hopkins University Press, 2004), pp. 40–69.

50. Matthew Crenson and Benjamin Ginsberg, *Downsizing Democracy: How America Sidelined Its Citizens and Privatized Its Public* (Baltimore: Johns Hopkins University Press, 2002).

51. Elaine C. Kamarck, *The End of Government . . . As We Know It: Making Public Policy Work* (Boulder, CO: Lynne Rienner Publishers, 2007), p. 101.

52. Cornelius Kerwin and Scott R. Furlong, *Rulemaking: How Government Agencies Write Law and Make Policy*, 4th edition (Washington, DC: CQ Press, 2003), pp. 80–81.

53. When combining the six federal spending preference variables, the numbers often cancel each other out. For example, averaging the preferences of someone who supports decreasing spending in one area (-1) and increasing spending in another area (1) yields a 0—the same mean preference as someone who supports maintain the status quo (0) in both policy areas. To preserve differences of interest as much as possible, we calculate the mean federal spending preference in those policy areas in which the government, on average, supports increasing spending and the mean preference in those policy areas in which the government, on average, supports decreasing spending.

54. Harold Seidman, *Politics, Position and Power: The Dynamics of Federal Organization*, 5th ed. (New York: Oxford University Press, 1998), chapter 8.

55. James Q. Wilson, *Bureaucracy: What Government Agencies Do and Why They Do It* (New York: Basic Books, 1989), p. 91.

56. Thomas E. Ricks, *Making the Corps* (New York: Touchstone, 1997), p. 138.

57. Seidman, *Politics, Position and Power*, chapter 8.

58. James Sterling Young, *The Washington Community, 1800–1828* (New York: Columbia University Press, 1966).

59. Ibid., p. 217.

60. Mark Leibovich, *This Town* (New York: Penguin, 2013), pp. 4–5.

61. Ibid., p. 5.

CHAPTER 3: WHAT THOSE WHO GOVERN
REALLY THINK ABOUT YOU AND ME

1. Travis J. Tritten, "$483K Rock Sculpture: VA Art Budget Comes Under Fire in Congress," *Stars and Stripes*, October 2, 2015, http://www.military.com/daily-news/2015/10/02/483k-rock-sculpture-va-art-budget-comes-under-fire-in-congress.html.

2. Walter Lippmann. *Public Opinion*. (New Brunswick, NJ: Transaction Publishers, 1946).

3. Michelle Healy, "Americans Don't Know Civics," *USA Today*, November 21, 2008, http://usatoday30.usatoday.com/news/education/2008-11-19-civics_N.htm.

4. Justin Doolittle, "The American Public's Shocking Lack of Policy Knowledge Is a Threat to Progress and Democracy," *Truthout*, October 12, 2013, http://www.truth-out.org/opinion/item/19279-the-american-publics-shocking-lack-of-policy-knowledge-is-a-threat-to-progress-and-democracy.

5. Peter Wilson, "The Affordable Care Act Is Not Incomprehensible," *American Thinker*, November 18, 2013, http://www.americanthinker.com/2013/11/the_affordable_care_act_is_not_incomprehensible.html.

6. Susan Milligan, "Iraqi WMD Turn Up in Iowa Senate Race," *US News*, May 13, 2014, http://www.usnews.com/opinion/blogs/susan-milligan/2014/05/13/jodi-ernsts-stunning-iraq-wmd-claim.

7. See, for example, Jacob S. Hacker and Paul Pierson, *Off Center: The Republican Revolution and the Erosion of American Democracy* (New Haven: Yale, 2005), p. 67.

8. Some scholars, to be sure, have argued that although many individuals may lack information or coherent policy preferences, public opinion on aggregate may still be reasonable and sensible. Benjamin I. Page and Robert Y. Shapiro, *The Rational Public* (Chicago: University of Chicago Press, 1992), for example, asserts that, "public opinion as a collective phenomenon is . . . meaningful. And indeed rational . . . it is organized in coherent patterns; it is reasonable . . . and it is adaptive to new information" (p. 14). As Scott Althaus, however, has demonstrated, this argument rests upon very shaky statistical foundations: Scott Althaus, *Collective Preferences* (New York: Cambridge University Press, 2003), chapter 2. Moreover, the notion that aggregate opinion may be reasonable despite the ignorance of individuals assumes that individuals do not communicate with or influence one another. This condition is usually violated in the case of political opinion, where the ignorant influence one another and are influenced by politicians and the media. Anyone who doubts this should listen to talk radio. See, James Surowiecki, *The Wisdom of Crowds* (New York: Doubleday, 2004).

9. Jiang Qing, *A Confucian Constitutional Order*, trans. Edmund Ryden (Princeton: Princeton University Press, 2013).

10. Peter H. Schuck, *Why Government Fails So Often* (Princeton: Princeton University Press, 2014).

11. Laurence H. Tribe, "Death by a Thousand Cuts: Constitutional Wrongs without Remedies after Wilkie v. Robbins," Cato Sup Ct. Rev. 23 (2006/2007).

12. Daniel M. Butler and David W. Nickerson, "Can Learning Constituency Opinion Affect How Legislators Vote? Results from a Field Experiment," *Quarterly Journal of Political Science* 6, no. 1 (2011): 55–83.

13. "Video: CFPB Director's Dismissive Response to Congresswoman's Question Another Sign Bureau is Unaccountable, Lacks Transparency," House Financial Services Committee, March 4, 2015, http://financialservices.house.gov/news/documentsingle.aspx ?DocumentID=398767.

14. The ranges of the response categories reflect those used in the 2011 Pew News Quiz. For example, Pew asked respondents about the unemployment rate with 5 percent, 9 percent, 15 percent, and 21 percent given as the response categories. The response categories for our questions about the circumstances of average Americans were structured in a similar manner, with the difference between response categories ranging from 4 to 6 percentage points (or 4 to 6 thousands of dollars, where appropriate).

15. "What the Public Knows—In Words and Pictures," Pew Research Center, November 7, 2011, http://www.people-press.org/files/legacy-pdf/11-7-11%20Knowledge %20Release.pdf.

16. Although our survey included twelve federal spending variables, we analyze the nine that overlap with the 2012 National Election Study to facilitate a comparison between government officials' opinions and those of the citizenry.

17. Defense is not included because the distribution of American opinion is quite evenly spread out across the three spending categories. As a result, it's impossible to identify the opinion of the "average American."

18. Ronald Ostman, "False Uniqueness," in *The International Encyclopedia of Communication*, ed. Wolfgang Donsbach (Hoboken, NJ: Wiley-Blackwell, 2008).

19. Elise Viebeck, "ObamaCare Architect: 'Stupidity' of Voters Helped Bill Pass," *The Hill*, November, 10, 2014, http://thehill.com/policy/healthcare/223578-obama care-architect-lack-of-transparency-helped-law-pass.

20. "From ISIS to Unemployment: What Do Americans Know?" Pew Research Center, Washington, DC, October 2, 2014, http://www.people-press.org/2014/10/02/ from-isis-to-unemployment-what-do-americans-know/.

21. Annenberg Public Policy Center, "Americans Know Surprisingly Little about Their Government, Survey Finds," news release, September 17, 2004, http://cdn .annenbergpublicpolicycenter.org/wp-content/uploads/Civics-survey-press-release-09-17 -2014-for-PR-Newswire.pdf.

22. The eighteen variables include the nine federal spending variables summarized in figure 3.2 and the nine policy variables summarized in table A1.

23. In chapter 2, we developed a measure of civic distance that incorporated measures of income, news consumption, perceived complexity of the political system, and strength of party identification. Based on these variables, we find that government officials are "civically distant" from the average American.

24. The coefficient on civic distance, 9.50, means that as an individual's similarity to government officials increases by a percentage point, that individual is expected to move up the scale of government nonresponsiveness 9.5 points.

25. Janet V. Denhardt and Robert B. Denhardt, *The New Public Service: Serving Not Steering* (Armonk, NY: M.E. Sharpe, 2002).

26. "Girl Saves Woodpecker, but Her Mom Fined $535," CBS News, August 4, 2011, http://www.cbsnews.com/news/girl-saves-woodpecker-but-her-mom-fined-535/.

27. Joel Achenbach, "NASA's Mission Improbable," *Washington Post*, August 17, 2013, http://www.washingtonpost.com/sf/national/2013/08/17/nasas-mission-improbable/.

28. Kathy Sawyer, "NASA Confirms Second Liftoff for First American to Orbit Earth," *Washington Post*, January 17, 1998, p. A03, http://www.washingtonpost.com/wp-srv/national/longterm/glenn/stories/confirms.htm.

29. Frank Newport, "Americans Want Space Shuttle Program to Go On," Gallup, February 3, 2003, http://www.gallup.com/poll/7708/americans-want-space-shuttle-program.aspx.

30. Brian Montopoli, "Press Release Journalism," *Columbia Journalism Review*, April 18, 2005, http://www.cjr.org/behind_the_news/press_release_journalism.php.

31. Dennis Wilcox and Glen Cameron, *Public Relations: Strategies and Tactics*, 11th ed. (New York: Pearson, 2014), p. 357.

32. Ben Fritz, Bryan Keefer, and Brendan Nyhan, *All the President's Spin* (New York: Touchstone, 2004), pp. 252–53.

33. Ibid., p. 357.

34. David Barstow and Robin Stein, "Under Bush, a New Age of Prepackaged News," *New York Times*, March 13, 2005, http://www.nytimes.com/2005/03/13/politics/13covert.html?pagewanted=print&_r=0.

35. United States Government Accountability Office, "Video News Releases: Unattributed Prepackaged News Stories Violate Publicity or Propaganda Prohibition," May 12, 2005, http://www.gao.gov/products/GAO-05-643T.

36. Jeff Gerth, "Military's Information War Is Vast and Often Secretive," *New York Times*, December 11, 2005, p. 1.

37. Ibid., p. 18.

38. Ibid.

39. Howard Kurtz, "Administration Paid Commentator," *Washington Post*, January 8, 2005, p. 1.

40. Howard Kurtz, "Writer Backing Bush Plan Had Gotten Federal Contract," *Washington Post*, January 26, 2005, p. C01, http://www.washingtonpost.com/wp-dyn/articles/A36545-2005Jan25.html.

41. Mark Memmott, "Agriculture Department Paid Journalist for Favorable Stories," *USA Today*, May 10, 2005, http://usatoday30.usatoday.com/news/washington/2005-05-10 -ag-dept-story_x.htm.

42. Micah White, *The End of Protest: A New Playbook for Revolution* (Toronto: Knopf, 2016).

43. Jeff Jarvis, "Revealed: US Spy Operations that Manipulate Social Media," *Guardian*, March 17, 2011, http://www.theguardian.com/technology/2011/mar/17/us-spy -operation-social-networks.

44. Malcolm K. Sparrow, *The Regulatory Craft: Controlling Risks, Solving Problems, and Managing Compliance* (Washington, DC: Brookings Institution, 2000), p. 2.

45. Philip K. Howard, *The Rule of Nobody* (New York: W. W. Norton, 2014), p. 1.

46. Nathan James, "The Federal Prison Population Buildup: Overview, Policy Changes, Issues, and Options," Congressional Research Service, April 15, 2014, http:// www.fas.org/sgp/crs/misc/R42937.pdf.

47. Marc A. Levin, "So-Called Crimes are Here, There, Everywhere," *Criminal Justice* 28, no. 1 (Spring 2013), http://www.americanbar.org/content/dam/aba/publications/ criminal_justice_magazine/sp13_state_level.authcheckdam.pdf.

48. Gary Fields and John R. Emshwiller, "As Criminal Laws Proliferate, More Are Ensnared," *Wall Street Journal*, July 23, 2011, http://www.wsj.com/articles/SB100014240 52748703749504576172714184601654.

49. Jack Thompson, "Bobby Unser Convicted on Wilderness Law," *Chicago Tribune*, June 13, 1997, http://articles.chicagotribune.com/1997-06-13/sports/9706130068 _1_bobby-unser-fined-federal-judge.

50. Gary Fields and John R. Emshwiller, "A Sewage Blunder Earns Engineer a Criminal Record," *Wall Street Journal*, December 12, 2011, p. 1.

51. "Rough Justice in America: Too Many Laws, Too Many Prisoners," *The Economist*, July 22, 2010, http://www.economist.com/node/16636027.

52. John S. Baker, "Revisiting the Explosive Growth of Federal Crimes," Heritage Foundation, July 16, 2008, http://www.heritage.org/research/reports/2008/06/ revisiting-the-explosive-growth-of-federal-crimes.

53. Whit Davis, "Water Criminals: Misusing Mens Rea and Public Welfare Offenses in Prosecuting Clean Water Act Violations," *Tulane Environmental Law Journal* 23, no. 2 (June 2010): 473.

54. United States v. Hanousek, 176 F.3d at 1119.

55. Cass Sunstein, *Why Nudge? The Politics of Libertarian Paternalism* (New Haven, CT: Yale University Press, 2014).

56. Jeremy Waldron, "It's All for Your Own Good," *New York Review of Books*, October 9, 2014, pp. 21–23.

57. These sixteen survey questions include the eight questions about the circumstances of average Americans summarized in figure 3.1 and eight of the nine questions

about public opinion on federal spending summarized in figure 3.2. With respect to the public opinion questions, we considered an official's guess about the average citizen's opinion to be correct if either (1) 60 percent or more of citizens fell into one category (spend more, spend the same, spend less) and the official identified that category or (2) 40 percent or more of citizens fell into two of the three categories and the official identified one of those two categories. Because citizens are fairly evenly divided on defense spending, we determined that an official could not be correct or incorrect when guessing the average American's opinion on this issue, and we therefore excluded this issue when calculating the total percent of questions correctly answered by officials.

CHAPTER 4: WHAT THE GOVERNMENT DOES
VERSUS WHAT THE PEOPLE WANT

1. Noah Melnick, Caird Forbes-Cocknell, and Stan Renas, "CFTC Adopts Final External Business Conduct Rules," *Journal on the Law of Investment & Risk Management Products: Futures & Derivatives Law Report* 32, no. 3 (March 2012).

2. Jonathan Coppess, "Three Little Words: EPA and the RFS Waiver Authority," *Choices*, Quarter 1, 2016, http://www.choicesmagazine.org/choices-magazine/submitted -articles/three-little-words--epa-and-the-rfs-waiver-authority.

3. James L. Gattuso and Diane Katz, "Red Tape Rising: Regulation in Obama's First Term," *Heritage Foundation Backgrounder* 2793, May 1, 2013, http://www.heritage.org/ research/reports/2013/05/red-tape-rising-regulation-in-obamas-first-term.

4. White House Office of Management and Budget, "2013 Draft Report to Congress on the Benefits and Costs of Federal Regulations and Agency Compliance with the Uniform Mandates Reform Act," http://www.whitehouse.gov/sites/default/files/omb/inforeg/2013 _cb/draft_2013_cost_benefit_report.pdf.

5. White House Office of Management and Budget, "2013 Draft Report," p. 4.

6. Cornelius M. Kerwin and Scott R. Furlong, *Rulemaking: How Government Agencies Write Law and Make Policy* (Washington, DC: CQ Press, 2011), p. 226.

7. Nancy Scola and Brian Fung, "FCC Chair Splits from Obama on Internet," *Washington Post*, November 12, 2014, p. 1.

8. William F. West and Connor Raso, "Who Shapes the Rulemaking Agenda?: Implications for Bureaucratic Responsiveness and Bureaucratic Control," *Journal of Public Administration Research and Theory* 23, no. 4 (October 2012): 495–519.

9. Christopher Foreman, for example, was able to identify efforts by the committees overseeing the Food and Drug Administration to induce the agency to develop new rules. Christopher Foreman, *Signals From the Hill: Congressional Oversight and the Challenge of Social Regulation* (New Haven, CT: Yale University Press, 1988).

10. West and Raso, "Who Shapes the Rulemaking Agenda?" p. 504.

11. Joel Aberbach, *Keeping a Watchful Eye: The Politics of Congressional Oversight* (Washington, DC: Brookings, 1990).

12. Mathew McCubbins and Thomas Schwartz, "Congressional Oversight Overlooked: Police Patrols versus Fire Alarms," *American Journal of Political Science* 28 (1987): 165–79.

13. Sidney A. Shapiro, "Agency Priority Setting and the Review of Existing Agency Rules," *Administrative Law Review* 48, no. 3 (Summer 1996): 370–74.

14. West and Raso, "Who Shapes the Rulemaking Agenda?" pp. 506–507.

15. Kerwin and Furlong, *Rulemaking*, p. 132.

16. William F. Fox Jr., *Understanding Administrative Law*, 4th edition (New York: Matthew Bender, 2000), p. 192.

17. West and Raso, p. 508.

18. Washington's "revolving door" is a well-known feature of life in the nation's capital. The Center for Responsive Politics offers some recent data: https://www.opensecrets.org/revolving/top.php?display=G.

19. Laura Barron-Lopez, "GOP Launches Probe of Green Groups Improper Influence on EPA," *The Hill*, September 2, 2014, http://thehill.com/policy/energy-environment/216419-gop-launches-probe-of-green-groups-improper-influence-on-epa.

20. Kerwin and Furlong, *Rulemaking*, p. 190.

21. Jeffrey S. Lubbers, *A Guide to Federal Agency Rulemaking*, 5th ed. (Chicago: American Bar Association, 2012), p. 63.

22. Lubbers, *Guide to Federal Agency Rulemaking*, p. 64.

23. Ibid., p. 95.

24. SEC v. Chenery Corp., 332 U.S. 194 (1947).

25. Skidmore v. Swift, 323 U.S. 134 (1944). See Fox, *Understanding Administrative Law*, p. 202.

26. Susan Webb Yackee, "Sweet-Talking the Fourth Branch: The Influence of Interest Group Comments on Federal Agency Rulemaking," *Journal of Public Administration Research and Theory* 16, no. 1 (January 2006): 103–24.

27. Marissa Golden, "Interest Groups in the Rule-Making Process: Who Participates? Whose Voices Get Heard?" *Journal of Public Administration Research and Theory* 8, no. 2 (April 1998): 252–53. Also, Jason Webb Yackee and Susan Webb Yackee, "A Bias Toward Business?: Assessing Interest Group Influence on the Bureaucracy," *Journal of Politics* 68, no.1 (2006): 128–39.

28. William West, "Formal Procedures, Informal Processes, Accountability, and Responsiveness in Bureaucratic Policy Making: An Institutional Policy Analysis," *Public Administration Review* 64, no. 1 (February 2004): 66–80.

29. Morton Rosenberg, "The Congressional Review Act after 15 Years: Background

and Considerations for Reform," Administrative Conference of the United States, September 16, 2011, http://www.acus.gov/sites/default/files/documents/COJR-Draft-CRA-Report-9-16-11.pdf.

30. Kerwin and Furlong, *Rulemaking*, p. 231.

31. Ibid., p. 60.

32. Small Business Administration Office of Advocacy, "A Guide for Government Agencies: How to Comply With the Regulatory Flexibility Act," June 2010, https://www.sba.gov/sites/default/files/rfaguide_0512_0.pdf.

33. Kerwin and Furlong, *Rulemaking*, p. 60.

34. Cass R. Sunstein to Heads of Executive Departments and Agencies, memorandum, "Cumulative Effects of Regulations," Executive Office of the President, Office of Management and Budget, Washington, DC, March 20, 2012, http://www.whitehouse.gov/sites/default/files/omb/assets/inforeg/cumulative-effects-guidance.pdf.

35. Lubbers, pp. 480–488.

36. "Current Unified Agenda of Regulatory and Deregulatory Actions," Office of Information and Regulatory Affairs, http://www.reginfo.gov/public/do/eAgendaMain.

37. The data were tabulated from the Unified Regulatory Agenda and then checked against the tabulation presented in Clyde Wayne Crews Jr., "Ten Thousand Commandments: An Annual Snapshot of the Federal Regulatory State," *Competitive Enterprise Institute*, 2013, http://cei.org/sites/default/files/Wayne%20Crews%20-%2010,000%20Commandments%202013.pdf.

38. Topics Codebook, Policy Agendas Project, http://www.policyagendas.org/sites/policyagendas.org/files/Topics_Codebook_2014.pdf.

39. Crews, "Ten Thousand Commandments," figure 13, p. 20.

40. Ibid., p. 21.

41. The plot includes an OLS regression line.

42. For the rulemaking agenda, we ranked policy areas according to the percentage of rules completed in those areas. For the agenda of sampled bureaucrats, we used responses to a variety of survey questions. For example, we used questions that asked whether respondents supported spending more or less in various policy areas and a question that asked respondents about the most important problem facing the nation.

43. Fox, *Understanding Administrative Law*, p. 27.

44. Theodore J. Lowi, *The End of Liberalism* (New York: W. W. Norton, 1969); David Schoenbrod, *Power Without Responsibility: How Congress Abuses the People Through Delegation* (New Haven, CT: Yale University Press, 1995).

45. Kerwin and Furlong, *Rulemaking*, p. 223.

46. Harold Bruff and Ernest Gellhorn, "Congressional Control of Administrative Regulation: A Study of Legislative Vetoes," *Harvard Law Review* 90, no. 7 (May 1977): 1369.

47. Immigration and Naturalization Service v. Chadha, 462 U.S. 919 (1983).

48. Ibid., 1002.

49. Rosenberg, "The Congressional Review Act after 15 Years," p. 13.

50. Curtis W. Copeland and Maeve P. Carey, "REINS Act," Congressional Research Service, February 24, 2011, http://www.speaker.gov/sites/speaker.house.gov/files/Uploaded Files/110830_crs_majorrules.pdf.

CHAPTER 5: WHAT SHOULD BE DONE TO MAKE THE GOVERNMENT LISTEN?

1. Andrew Jackson, *Annual Messages, Veto Messages, Protest, &c of Andrew Jackson, President of the United States* (Baltimore: Edward J. Coale, 1835).

2. Malcolm K. Sparrow, *The Regulatory Craft* (Washington, DC: Brookings, 2000), p. 40.

3. Ewan Ferlie, Laurence E. Lynn Jr., and Christopher Pollitt, *The Oxford Handbook of Public Management* (New York: Oxford University Press, 2005).

4. Don M. Snyder, Paul Oh, and Kevin Toner, "The Army's Professional Military Ethic in an Era of Persistent Conflict," *Professional Military Ethics Monograph Series*, Strategic Studies Institute, U.S. Army War College, October 2009, http://www.strategicstudiesinstitute.army.mil/pubs/display.cfm?pubID=895.

5. We estimate this effect with a logit model in which the delegate-trustee scale is recoded to be binary, feedback from the public (6-point scale) is the independent variable of interest, and political ideology and age serve as control variables.

6. Michael Lipsky, *Street-Level Bureaucracy* (New York: Russell Sage Foundation, 1980). Also, S. Maynard-Moody and S. Leland, "Stories from the Front Lines of Public Management: Street-Level Workers as Responsible Actors," in *Advancing Public Management: New Developments in Theory, Methods and Practice*, ed. J. L. Brudney, L. J. O'Toole Jr., and H. G. Rainey (Washington, DC: Georgetown University Press, 2000), pp. 109–23.

7. Richard D. Bingham, et al., *Managing Local Government: Public Administration in Practice* (New York: Sage Publications, 1991).

8. American National Election Studies [ANES], *User's Guide and Codebook for the ANES 2012 Time Series Study* (Ann Arbor, MI / Palo Alto, CA: University of Michigan / Stanford University, 2015), http://www.electionstudies.org/studypages/anes_timeseries_2012/anes_timeseries_2012_userguidecodebook.pdf.

9. Robert Pondiscio, Gilbert Sewall, and Sandra Stotsky, "Shortchanging the Future: The Crisis of History and Civics in American Schools," *Pioneer Institute*, April 2013, http://pioneerinstitute.org/download/shortchanging-the-future-the-crisis-of-history-and-civics-in-american-schools/.

10. Commission on Youth Voting and Civic Knowledge, *All Together Now: Collabo-*

ration and Innovation for Youth Engagement: The Report of the Commission on Youth Voting and Civic Knowledge (Medford, MA: Center for Information & Research on Civic Learning and Engagement, 2013), http://civicyouth.org/wp-content/uploads/2013/09/CIRCLE-youthvoting-individualPages.pdf.

11. Pennsylvania Department of Education, *Academic Standards for Civics and Government*, July 18, 2002, https://pennsylvaniasocialstudies.wikispaces.com/file/view/CIVICSANDGOVERNMENT.pdf.

12. Illinois State Board of Education, "Illinois Learning Standards: Social Science," http://www.isbe.state.il.us/ils/social_science/mandates_2.htm.

13. Georgia Department of Education, "American Government/Civics," *Georgia Performance Standards*, August 1, 2012, https://www.georgiastandards.org/standards/Georgia%20Performance%20Standards/American-Government.pdf.

14. New York State Education Department, Bureau of Elementary Curriculum Development, *Social Studies, Grade 1: A Teaching System* (Albany, NY: University of the State of New York, 1970), p. 32, https://archive.org/details/ERIC_ED048056.

15. Benjamin Ginsberg, *The Consequences of Consent* (New York: Random House, 1982).

16. Mason L. Weems, *The Life of George Washington*, ed. Marcus Cunliffe (Cambridge, MA: Belknap Press of Harvard University Press, 1962).

17. William A. Hachten, *The Troubles of Journalism: A Critical Look at What's Right and Wrong with the Press* (New York: Routledge, 2004).

18. Joseph Nye, Philip Zelikow, and David King, *Why People Don't Trust Government* (Cambridge, MA: Harvard University Press, 1997), p. 5.

19. Kevin Mattson and Richard C. Leone, *Engaging Youth*: *Combating the Apathy of Young Americans toward Politics* (New York: Century Foundation Press, 2003).

20. Ilene Grossman, "To Combat Cynicism and Voter Apathy, States Turn to Civic Education," *Firstline Midwest* 7, no. 5 (May 2000): 1.

21. Dale Turner, "Cynical Voices Can't Sing a Song of Peace," *Seattle Times*, March 29, 2003, p. B4.

22. For an excellent discussion of cynicism as a philosophical perspective, see, Suvi M. Irvine, "Don't Shoot the Messenger! Rethinking Cynicism and the Value of Political Critique" (doctoral thesis, Johns Hopkins University, 2014), https://jscholarship.library.jhu.edu/bitstream/handle/1774.2/37958/IRVINE-DISSERTATION-2015.pdf?sequence=1.

23. For recent examples, see, Frank Rich, *The Greatest Story Ever Sold* (New York: Penguin, 2006).

24. Quoted in, Alexander Cockburn and Jeffrey St. Clair, eds., "Weapons of Mass Destruction: Who Said What When," *Counterpunch*, May 29, 2003, http://www.counterpunch.org/2003/05/29/weapons-of-mass-destruction-who-said-what-when/.

25. Ambrose Bierce, *The Unabridged Devil's Dictionary* (Athens, GA: University of Georgia Press, 2001).

26. American National Election Studies [ANES], Center for Political Studies, University of Michigan, 1952–2002.

27. According to a 2002 Roper Poll, 70 percent of all Americans believe the government is hiding information about UFOs, http://www.ufoevidence.org/topics/publicopinion-polls.htm.

28. The phrase is associated with Fang Lejun, Liu Wei, and other artists working in the aftermath of the 1989 Tiananmen Square massacre.

29. Niccolo Machiavelli, *The Prince* (New York: Mentor, 1952), p. 50.

30. Ibid., p. 90.

31. Steven Pinker, *How The Mind Works* (New York: W. W. Norton, 1997), p. 495.

32. Vamik Volkan, "Narcissistic Personality Disorder and Reparative Leadership," *International Journal of Group Psychotherapy* 30, no. 2 (1980): 131–52.

33. David Kuo, *Tempting Faith* (New York: Free Press, 2006), p. 229.

34. Donald Kagan, *The Peloponnesian War* (New York, Penguin, 2003), p. 212.

35. Henry A. Turner, *General Motors and the Nazis* (New Haven, CT: Yale University Press, 2005).

36. James Madison, *The Federalist*, Number 10 (New York: Mentor, 1961), p. 79.

37. Paul Koistinen, *The Hammer and the Sword: Labor, the Military and Industrial Production, 1920–1945* (New York: Arno Press, 1979), p. 580.

38. Robert Greenstein and Joel Friedman, "President's Savings Proposals Likely to Swell Long-Term Deficits, Reduce National Saving, and Primarily Benefit Those with Substantial Wealth," Center on Budget and Policy Priorities, May 25, 2005, http://www.cbpp.org/research/presidents-savings-proposals-likely-to-swell-long-term-deficits-reduce-national-saving-and.

39. Jill Barshay, "Insurers Risk Loss of Special Status," *Congressional Quarterly Weekly*, January 24, 2005, p. 156.

40. Eric Lipton, "Industry Tied to Letter against New Wage," *New York Times*, March 16, 2014, p. 20.

41. Frank Baumgartner and Beth Leech, *Basic Interests* (Princeton: Princeton University Press, 1998).

42. Thomas Hobbes, *Leviathan* (New York: Collier, 1962), p. 80.

43. John R. Wilke, "Seat in Congress Helps Mr. Taylor Help His Business," *Wall Street Journal*, October 11, 2006.

44. Richard Shenkman, *Presidential Ambition* (New York: Harper, 1999), introduction.

45. Matthew A. Crenson and Benjamin Ginsberg, *Presidential Power: Unchecked and Unbalanced* (New York: W. W. Norton, 2007).

46. Madison, *Federalist*, Number 51, p. 322.

47. National Commission on Terrorist Attacks, *The 9/11 Commission Report: Final Report of the National Commission on Terrorist Attacks Upon the United States* (New York: W. W. Norton, 2004), chapter 11.

48. Louis Fisher, *Congressional Abdication on War and Spending* (College Station, TX: Texas A&M Press, 2000).

49. Crenson and Ginsberg, *Presidential Power*.

50. See, Hans J. Morgenthau, *Politics Among Nations*, 6th ed. (New York: Knopf, 1985). Also, John Mearsheimer, *The Tragedy of Great Power Politics* (New York: Norton, 2003).

51. J. H. Hertz, ed., *The Pentateuch and Haftorahs* (London: Soncino Press, 1992), p. 14.

52. William Shakespeare, *Julius Caesar*, act I, scene 2.

53. Pinker, *How the Mind Works*, p. 493.

54. Quoted in John O. McGinnis, "The Human Constitution and Constitutive Law," *Journal of Contemporary Legal Issues* 8 (Spring 1997): 222.

55. Joseph J. Ellis, *His Excellency, George Washington* (New York: Knopf, 2004), p. 151.

56. Ibid., p. 171.

57. Quoted in Joseph J. Ellis, *Founding Brothers* (New York: Knopf, 2000), p. 167.

58. Ellis, *His Excellency*, p. 38.

59. Ron Chernow, *Alexander Hamilton* (New York: Penguin, 2004), p. 8.

60. Ibid., p. 33.

61. Robert Caro, *The Years of Lyndon Johnson: The Path to Power* (New York: Knopf, 1982), chapter 7.

62. Christopher Matthews, *Kennedy and Nixon* (New York: Touchstone, 1996), p. 126.

63. Robert Trivers, "The Evolution of Reciprocal Altruism," *Quarterly Review of Biology* 46, no. 1 (March 1971): 35–46.

64. Babylonian Talmud, Chagigah 5a.

65. Babylonian Talmud, Bava Bathra 9b.

66. T. Harry Williams, *Huey Long* (New York: Knopf, 1969), p. 107.

67. David McCullough, *Truman* (New York: Simon and Schuster, 1992), p. 183.

68. Ibid., p. 585.

69. Ibid.

70. Ibid.

71. Eric Kandel, James Schwartz, and Thomas Jessell, *Essentials of Neural Science and Behavior* (Stamford, CT: Appleton & Lange, 1995), pp. 613–15.

72. Martin Seligman, "Phobias and Preparedness," *Behavior Therapy* 2, no. 3 (July 1971): 307–20.

73. Joseph LeDoux, *The Emotional Brain* (New York: Simon and Schuster, 1996), p. 236.

74. Michael Winerip, "Revisiting a Rape Scandal that Would Have Been Monstrous

if True," *New York Times*, June 3, 2013, http://www.nytimes.com/2013/06/03/booming/revisiting-the-tawana-brawley-rape-scandal.html?_r=0.

75. Martin Shefter, *Political Parties and the State* (Princeton: Princeton University Press, 1994), p. 82.

76. Lois Romano and Mike Allen, "Secret Tapes Not Meant to Harm, Writer Says," *Washington Post*, February 21, 2005, p. A02.

77. David Guarino, "Hill at Tufts: Use Bible to Guide Poverty Policy," *Boston Herald*, November 11, 2004, p. 23.

78. Senator Robert Byrd, *Losing America: Confronting a Reckless and Arrogant Presidency* (New York: Norton, 2004).

79. See, for example, D. Eisenstadt, M. R. Leippe, J. A. Rivers, and M. A. Stambush, "Counterattitudinal Advocacy on a Matter of Prejudice," *Journal of Applied Social Psychology* 33, no. 10 (October 1, 2003): 2123–52.

80. Philip Zimbardo and Richard Gerrig, *Psychology and Life*, 15th edition (New York: Longman, 1999), p. 753.

81. Diogenes Laertius, *The Lives of Eminent Philosophers, Vol. II*, translated Robert Drew Hicks (Cambridge: Harvard University Press, 1925). Quoted in Irvine, "Don't Shoot the Messenger," p. 36.

CHAPTER 6: WHAT IF WHAT SHOULD BE DONE ISN'T DONE?

1. Jean Hampton, *Hobbes and the Social Contract Tradition* (New York: Cambridge University Press, 1988), p. 46. Hampton indicates that this quote is "after Bacon," whom Hobbes served as a secretary.

2. Matthew Dillon and Lynda Garland, eds., *Ancient Greece: Social and Historical Documents from Archaic Times to the Death of Alexander* (New York: Routledge, 2010), p. 18.

3. "2011 Secrecy Report," OpenTheGovernment.org, Washington, DC, 2012, http://www.openthegovernment.org/sites/default/files/SRC_2011.pdf.

4. "Bi-annual Report on Operations of the National Declassification Center; Reporting period: July 1, 2012–December 31, 2012," National Archives and Records Administration, http://www.archives.gov/declassification/ndc/reports/2012-biannual-july-december.pdf.

5. Nate Jones, "Declassification-As-Usual Mindset Responsible for the National Declassification Center's Languid Pace," *The National Security Archive*, February 1, 2012, http://nsarchive.wordpress.com/2012/02/01/declassification-as-usual-mindset-responsible-for-the-national-declassifcation-centers-lanugid-pace/.

6. Matthew M. Aid, "Declassification in Reverse: The U.S. Intelligence Communi-

ty's Secret Historical Document Reclassification Program," *The National Security Archive*, February 21, 2006, http://www2.gwu.edu/~nsarchiv/NSAEBB/NSAEBB179/.

7. Gabriel Schoenfeld, *Necessary Secrets* (New York: W. W. Norton, 2011), p. 175.

8. Eric Alterman, *When Presidents Lie: A History of Official Deception and Its Consequences* (New York: Viking, 2004).

9. Schoenfeld, *Necessary Secrets*, p. 185.

10. Peter Walker, "Bradley Manning Trial: What We Know from the Leaked WikiLeaks Documents," *Guardian*, July 30, 2013, http://www.theguardian.com/world/2013/jul/30/bradley-manning-wikileaks-revelations.

11. Greg Mitchell, "A Long List of What We Know Thanks to Private Manning," *The Nation*, August 23, 2013, http://www.thenation.com/blog/175879/long-list-what-we-know-thanks-private-manning#axzz2cvltDsQm.

12. Aid, "Declassification in Reverse."

13. Ludwig von Mises, *Bureaucracy* (New Haven, CT: Yale University Press, 1945).

14. James Q. Wilson, *Bureaucracy: What Government Agencies Do and Why They Do It* (New York: Basic Books, 1989).

15. "Over-Regulated America," *The Economist*, February 18, 2012, http://www.economist.com/node/21547789.

16. Wilson, *Bureaucracy*, 16–17.

17. Stephen Peter Rosen, *Winning the Next War* (Ithaca, NY: Cornell University Press, 1991).

18. Harold Seidman, *Politics, Position, and Power: The Dynamics of Federal Organization*, 5th ed. (New York: Oxford University Press, 1998), chapter 8.

19. See, Anita Huslin, "Grizzly Proposition Aims to Return Bears to Idaho," *Washington Post*, July 3, 2000, p. A3.

20. Seidman, *Politics, Position, and Power*, p. 138.

21. Ibid., p. 118.

22. Thomas Stanton, *Government-Sponsored Enterprises: Mercantilist Companies in the Modern World* (Washington, DC: American Enterprise Institute, 2000).

23. See, Richard Posner, *An Affair of State* (Cambridge: Harvard University Press, 1999), chapter 3.

24. William H. McNeill, *The Pursuit of Power* (Chicago: University of Chicago Press, 1982), 44–45.

25. Ibid., p. 45.

INDEX

Page numbers in *italics* indicated tables, charts, and graphs.